Jill 2003

Rick Steves'
FLORENCE
2003

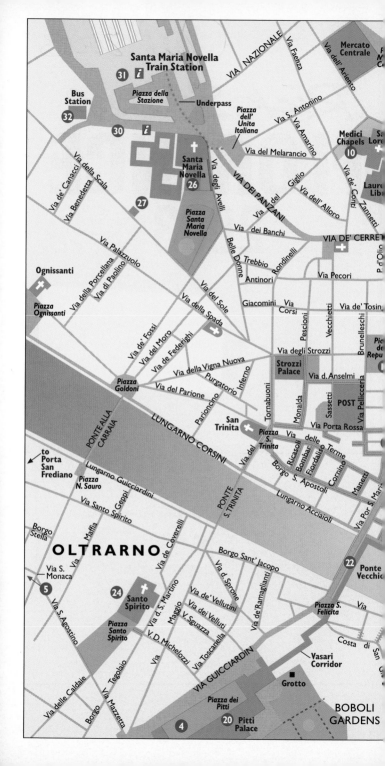

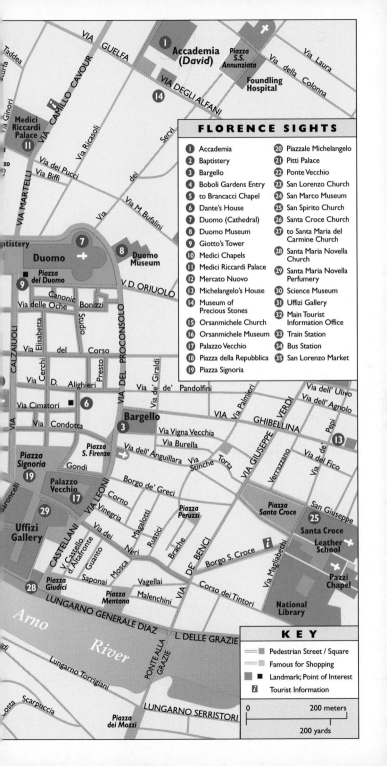

Rick Steves'
FLORENCE
2003

Santa Maria Novella · San Marco · Medici Chapels · David · Baptistery · Giotto's Tower · Duomo · Palazzo Vecchio · Ponte Vecchio · Uffizi · Bargello · Brancacci Chapel · Boboli Gardens & Pitti Palace · A R N O

by Rick Steves & Gene Openshaw

AVALON
TRAVEL

Other ATP travel guidebooks by Rick Steves

Rick Steves' Best of Europe
Rick Steves' Europe 101: History and Art for the Traveler (with Gene Openshaw)
Rick Steves' Europe Through the Back Door
Rick Steves' Mona Winks: Self-Guided Tours of Europe's Top Museums
  (with Gene Openshaw)
Rick Steves' Postcards from Europe
Rick Steves' France (with Steve Smith)
Rick Steves' Germany, Austria & Switzerland
Rick Steves' Great Britain
Rick Steves' Ireland (with Pat O'Connor)
Rick Steves' Italy
Rick Steves' Scandinavia
Rick Steves' Spain & Portugal
Rick Steves' Amsterdam, Bruges & Brussels (with Gene Openshaw)
Rick Steves' London (with Gene Openshaw)
Rick Steves' Paris (with Steve Smith and Gene Openshaw)
Rick Steves' Rome (with Gene Openshaw)
Rick Steves' Venice (with Gene Openshaw)
Rick Steves' Phrase Books: French, German, Italian, Portuguese, Spanish, and
  French/Italian/German

Avalon Travel Publishing, 1400 65th Street, Suite 250, Emeryville, CA 94608, USA

Text © 2002 by Rick Steves. All rights reserved.
Maps © 2002 Europe Through the Back Door. All rights reserved.

Photos are used by permission and are the property of the original copyright owners.

Printed in the USA by R.R. Donnelley. First printing November 2002
Distributed by Publishers Group West

Portions of this book were originally published in *Rick Steves' Mona Winks* © 2001,
1998, 1996, 1993, 1988 by Rick Steves and Gene Openshaw, and in *Rick Steves' Italy*
© 2002, 2001, 2000, 1999, 1998, 1997, 1996, 1995 by Rick Steves.

ISBN 1-56691-484-1; ISSN 1538-1609

For the latest on Rick's lectures, guidebooks, tours, and public television series,
contact Europe Through the Back Door, Box 2009, Edmonds, WA 98020, tel. 425/
771-8303, fax 425/771-0833, www.ricksteves.com, or e-mail: rick@ricksteves.com.

Europe Through the Back Door Managing Editor: Risa Laib
Europe Through the Back Door Editor: Jill Hodges
Avalon Travel Publishing Series Manager and Editor: Kate Willis
Research Assistance: Sarah Murdoch
Copy Editor: Kate McKinley
Production & Typesetting: Kathleen Sparkes, White Hart Design
Cover and Interior Design: Janine Lehmann
Maps and Graphics: David C. Hoerlein, Rhonda Pelikan, Zoey Platt
Photography: p. 23, 27 © Elizabeth Openshaw; p. 51, 68, 216 © Dominic Bonuccelli;
  all others by Rick Steves and Gene Openshaw
Front matter color photos: p. i, The Ponte Vecchio on the Arno River, Florence ©
  Terry Donnell; p. iv, view of Florence city © Randy Wells
Front cover photo: Duomo, Florence, Italy; © Trip/T. Bognar

CONTENTS

INTRODUCTION

Florence is Europe's cultural capital. As the home of the Renaissance and the birthplace of the modern world, Florence practiced the art of civilized living back when the rest of Europe was rural and crude. Democracy, science, and literature, as well as painting, sculpture, and architecture were all championed by the proud and energetic Florentines of the 1400s.

When the Florentine poet Dante saw teenaged Beatrice, her beauty so inspired him that he spent the rest of his life writing poems to her. The Renaissance opened people's eyes to the physical beauty of the world around them, inspiring them to write, paint, sculpt, and build.

Today, Florence is geographically small but culturally rich, with more artistic masterpieces per square kilometer than anyplace else. In a single day, you could look Michelangelo's *David* in the eyes, fall under the seductive sway of Botticelli's *Birth of Venus*, and climb the modern world's first dome, which still dominates the skyline.

Stroll the same pedestrian streets walked by Michelangelo, Leonardo, and Botticelli; window-shop the high-fashion boutiques; comparison-shop the gelato stands; and end the day bumping elbows with fellow diners in a crowded *osteria*.

During your visit, you'll discover that Florence—with its rough-stone beauty, art-packed museums, children licking gelato, students riding Vespas, artisans sipping Chianti, and supermodels wearing Gucci fashions—offers many of the very things you came to Italy to see.

This Information Is Accurate and Up-to-Date

This book is updated every year. Most publishers of guidebooks can afford an update only every two or three years (and even then, it's often by letter). Since this book is selective, we can personally update it annually. Even so, things change. But if you're traveling with the current edition of this book, we guarantee you're using the most up-to-date information available in print (and for the latest, visit www.ricksteves.com/update). This book will help you have an inexpensive, hassle-free trip. Your trip costs about $10 per waking hour. Your time is valuable. This guidebook saves lots of time.

Welcome to Our Florence City Guide

This book is organized this way:

Orientation includes tourist information and public transportation. The "Planning Your Time" section offers a suggested schedule with thoughts on how to best use your limited time.

Sights provides a succinct overview of Florence's most important sights, arranged by neighborhood, with ratings: ▲▲▲—Don't miss; ▲▲—Try hard to see; ▲—Worthwhile if you can make it; no rating—Worth knowing about.

The **Renaissance Walk** takes you through the core of Renaissance Florence, starting with Michelangelo's *David* and cutting through the heart of the city to the Ponte Vecchio on the Arno River.

The **Self-Guided Tours** lead you through Florence's most important sights, with tours of the Uffizi Gallery, Bargello, Museum of San Marco, Duomo Museum, Medici Chapels, Dante's House, Santa Maria Novella church, Brancacci Chapel, and the Science Museum.

Day Trips covers nearby sights: Pisa, San Gimignano, and Siena.

Sleeping is a guide to our favorite budget hotels, conveniently located in the heart of Florence and across the river in the Oltrarno neighborhood, all near the sights in this compact city.

Eating offers restaurants ranging from inexpensive eateries to splurges, with an emphasis on good value.

Florence with Children, Nightlife, and **Shopping** contain our best suggestions on these topics.

Transportation Connections covers connections by train, bus, and plane, laying the groundwork for your smooth arrival and departure.

Florence History takes you on a whirlwind tour through the ages, covering eight centuries from ancient Florence to the city today.

The **appendix** includes a climate chart for Florence, list of festivals, and Italian survival phrases.

Throughout this book, when you see a ✪ in a listing, it means that the sight is covered in much more detail in one of our

Tips for Tackling Our Self-Guided Tours

Sightseeing can be hard work. Our self-guided tours are designed to help make your visits to Italy's finest museums meaningful, fun, fast, and painless. Make reservations for the more crowded sights (see page 26). To make the most of our tours, read the tour the night before your visit, and call ahead to make sure the hours and costs have not changed.

When you arrive at the sight, use the overview map to get the lay of the land and the basic tour route. Expect a few changes—paintings can be on tour, on loan, out sick, or shifted at the whim of the curator. Even museum walls are often moved. To adapt, pick up any available free floor plans as you enter, ask an information person to glance at this book's maps to confirm they're current, or if you can't find a particular painting, just ask any museum worker. Point to the photograph in this book and ask, *"Dove?"* (pronounced DOH-vay, it means "Where?").

We cover the highlights at sights. You might want to supplement with an audioguide (dry-but-useful recorded descriptions in English, about $5), or a guided tour (usually $6 or more). Tours in English are most likely to occur during peak season. The quality of a tour depends on the guide's knowledge, fluency, and enthusiasm.

Museums have their rules; if you're aware of them in advance, they're no big deal. Keep in mind that many sights have "last entry" times 30 to 60 minutes before closing. Guards usher people out before the official closing time. Cameras are normally allowed in museums, but no flashes or tripods (without special permission). A handheld camera with ASA-400 film and an F-2 aperture will take a fine picture (or buy slides at the museum bookstore). Video cameras are usually allowed. For security reasons, you're often required to check even small bags. Many museums have a free checkroom at the entrance. They're safe. Prepare to stash anything that you can't bear to part with in a purse or pocket.

At the museum bookshop, thumb through the biggest guidebook (or scan its index) to be sure you haven't overlooked something that is of particular interest to you. If there's an on-site cafeteria, it's usually a good place to rest and have a snack or light meal. Museum WCs are free and generally clean.

self-guided tours—a page number will tell you just where to look
to find more information.

Browse through this book and choose your favorite sights.
Then have a great trip! You'll become your own guide with our
tours. You won't waste time on mediocre sights because, unlike other
guidebooks, this one covers only the best. Since your major financial
pitfall is lousy, expensive hotels, we've worked hard to assemble the
best accommodations values. Traveling like a temporary local, you'll
get the absolute most out of every mile, minute, and euro.

Trip Costs

Six components make up your trip costs: airfare, surface transportation, room and board, sightseeing/entertainment, shopping/
miscellany, and gelato.

Airfare: Don't try to sort through the mess. Find and use a
good travel agent. A basic, round-trip United States-to-Florence
(or even cheaper, Milan or Rome) flight should cost $700 to
$1,000, depending on where you fly from and when. Always
consider saving time and money in Europe by flying "open jaw"
(flying into one city and out of another).

Surface Transportation: Most of Florence's sights, clustered
in the downtown core, are within easy walking distance of each
other. If you'd rather use taxis than walk, allow about $50–70
over the course of a one-week visit (taxis can be shared by up to
4 people). The cost of round-trip transportation to day-trip destinations is affordable ($20 by train, second class, to Pisa; about $15
by bus to San Gimignano; and $25 by train, second class, to Siena).
For a one-way trip between Florence's airport and the city center,
allow $2 by bus or $15–17 by taxi (can be shared).

Room and Board: You can thrive in Florence on $80 a day
per person for room and board. This allows $10 for lunch, $20 for
dinner, and $50 for lodging (based on 2 people splitting the cost
of a $100 double room that includes breakfast). If you have more
money, we've listed great ways to spend it. Students and tightwads
can enjoy Florence for as little as $40 a day ($20 for a bed, $20 for
meals and snacks), but budget sleeping and eating require the skills
covered later in this chapter (and in greater detail in *Rick Steves'
Europe Through the Back Door*).

Sightseeing and Entertainment: Figure about $7–8 per
major sight (Michelangelo's *David*, Uffizi Gallery), $3–5 for
smaller ones (museums, climbing church towers), and $25 for
splurge experiences (e.g., walking tours and concerts). An overall average of $15 a day works for most. Don't skimp here. After
all, this category directly powers most of the experiences all the
other expenses are designed to make possible.

Shopping and Miscellany: Figure $1 per postcard, coffee, and soft drink and $2 per gelato. Shopping can vary in cost from nearly nothing to a small fortune. Good budget travelers find that this category has little to do with assembling a trip full of lifelong, wonderful memories.

Exchange Rate

We've priced things throughout this book in the euro currency, adopted by Italy and 11 other member countries of the European Union.

---

1 euro (€) = about $1.

Just like the dollar, one euro is broken down into 100 cents. Coins range from 1 cent to 2 euros, and bills from €5 to €500.

Prices, Times, and Discounts

The opening hours and telephone numbers listed in this book are accurate as of mid-2002—but once you pin Florence down, it wiggles. Especially in Florence, the opening hours of sights can change from month to month. Always get the latest listing of sights (including hours and entry fees) at a local tourist information office. Any guidebook on Italy starts to yellow even before it's printed, so prices and times in this book are approximate.

In Florence—and in this book—you'll use the 24-hour clock. It's the same through 12:00 noon, then keep going: 13:00, 14:00, and so on. For anything over 12, subtract 12 and add p.m. (14:00 is 2:00 p.m.).

Discounts for sights are not listed in this book because they are generally limited to residents of Europe and countries that offer reciprocal deals (the U.S. doesn't).

When to Go

Florence's best travel months (and busiest, most expensive months) are May, June, September, and October. Between November and April, you can usually expect pleasant weather and none of the sweat and stress of the tourist season.

The most grueling thing about travel in Florence is the summer heat in July and August, when temperatures hit the high 80s and 90s. Florence is fine in the winter, when temperatures drop to the 40s and 50s. Spring and fall can be chilly, and many hotels do not turn on their heat. Air-conditioning, when available, usually only operates from June through September. Most mid-range hotels come with air-conditioning—a worthwhile splurge in the summer. (See climate chart in the appendix.)

Red Tape, Business Hours, and Banking

You need a passport but no visa or shots to travel in Italy.

Business Hours: Traditionally, Italy uses the siesta plan. People work from about 8:00 to 13:00 and from 15:30 to 19:00, Monday through Saturday. Many businesses have adopted the government's new recommended 8:00 to 14:00 workday. In tourist areas, shops are open longer. Shoppers interested in pursuing VAT refunds (the tax refunded on large purchases made by non-European tourists) can refer to page 220.

Banking: You'll want to spend local hard cash. The fastest way to get it is by using plastic: your ATM, credit, or debit card at a cash machine (*Bancomat*). If you bring traveler's checks, use them only as a backup.

To get a cash advance from a bank machine, you'll need a four-digit PIN (numbers only, no letters) for your bank card. Before you go, verify with your bank that your card will work.

Visa and MasterCard are more commonly accepted than American Express. Bring two cards in case one is demagnetized, eaten by a machine, or rejected by a temperamental cash machine. (If your card is rejected, try again, and request a smaller amount; some cash machines won't let you take out more than about €150—don't take it personally.) Just like at home, credit or debit cards work easily at larger hotels, restaurants, and shops, but smaller businesses prefer payment in hard cash.

Regular banks have the best rates for cashing traveler's checks. For a large exchange, it pays to compare rates and fees. Bank of Sicily consistently has good rates. Banking hours are generally 8:30 to 13:30 and 15:30 to 16:30 Monday through Friday, but can vary wildly. Banks are slow; simple transactions can take 15–30 minutes. Post offices and train stations usually change money if you can't get to a bank. Skip the modern-looking change offices that advertise great rates but charge exorbitant 9 percent fees.

Use a money belt. Thieves target tourists. A money belt (order online at www.ricksteves.com or call 425/771-8303 for our free newsletter/catalog) provides peace of mind and allows you to carry lots of cash safely.

Don't be petty about changing money. The greatest avoidable money-changing expense is wasting time every few days to return to a bank. Change a week's worth of money, get big bills, stuff them in your money belt, and travel!

Travel Smart

Many people travel through Italy thinking it's a chaotic mess. They feel any attempt at efficient travel is futile. This is dead wrong—and expensive. Italy, which seems as orderly as spilled spaghetti, actually functions well. Only those who understand this and travel smart can enjoy Italy on a budget.

Buy a phone card and use it for reservations and double-checking hours of sights. (We've included phone numbers for this purpose.) Enjoy the friendliness of the local people. Ask questions. Most locals are eager to point you in their idea of the right direction. Pack along a pocket-size notebook to organize your thoughts. Those who expect to travel smart, do.

Sundays have the same pros and cons as they do for travelers in the United States: Sightseeing attractions are generally open; shops and banks are closed. City traffic is light. Rowdy evenings are rare on Sundays. Saturdays are virtually weekdays with earlier closing hours.

Museums and sights, especially the biggies, usually stop admitting people 30 to 60 minutes before closing time.

Hotels are often booked up on Easter (April 20 in 2003), April 25, May 1, June 24 (in Florence), in August, and on Fridays and Saturdays. Religious holidays and train strikes can catch you by surprise anywhere in Italy.

Really, this book can save you lots of time and money. But to have an A trip, you need to be an A student. Read it all before your trip; note the days when museums are closed and whether reservations are mandatory. For instance, you can wait two hours in line to get into the Uffizi, or make a quick phone call to get a reservation in advance and walk right in. Saving Michelangelo's *David* for your Florentine finale is risky, and on Monday, impossible. If you cut your Siena day trip short, you'll miss the city's medieval magic at twilight. A smart trip is a puzzle—a fun, doable, and worthwhile challenge.

Tourist Information

Florence has several tourist information offices (abbreviated TI in this book); for a listing, see page 20.

Before your trip, contact the nearest Italian TI in the United States and briefly describe your trip and request information. You'll get the general packet and, if you ask for specifics (city map, calendar of festivals, etc.), an impressive amount of help. If you have a specific problem, they're a good source of sympathy.

Contact the office nearest you:

In **New York:** 630 5th Ave. #1565, New York, NY 10111, brochure hotline tel. 212/245-4822, tel. 212/245-5618, fax 212/586-9249, e-mail: enitny@italiantourism.com.

In **Illinois:** 500 N. Michigan Ave. #2240, Chicago, IL 60611, brochure hotline tel. 312/644-0990, tel. 312/644-0996, fax 312/644-3019, e-mail: enitch@italiantourism.com.

In **California:** 12400 Wilshire Blvd. #550, Los Angeles,

CA 90025, brochure hotline tel. 310/820-0098, tel. 310/820-1898, fax 310/820-6357, e-mail: enitla@earthlink.net.

Web sites: www.firenze.turismo.toscana.it (Florence tourist information), www.italiantourism.com (Italian Tourist Board in the United States), www.museionline.it (museums in Italy, in English), and www.fs-on-line.com (train info and schedules).

Recommended Guidebooks

For most travelers, this book is all you need. The well-researched Access guide (which combines Florence and Venice) and the colorful Eyewitness guide (on Florence and Tuscany) are popular with travelers. Eyewitness is fun for its great, easy-to-grasp graphics and photos, and it's just right for people who want only factoids. But the Eyewitness books are relatively skimpy on content and they weigh a ton. You can buy them in Florence (no more expensive than in the U.S.) or simply borrow them for a minute from other travelers at certain sights to make sure you're aware of that place's highlights. If you'll be traveling elsewhere in Italy, consider *Rick Steves' Italy 2003*.

In Florence, local guidebooks are cheap and give you a map and a decent commentary on the sights (sold at kiosks). For brand-name guidebooks, try **Feltrinelli International** (Mon–Sat 9:00–19:30, closed Sun, Via Cavour 20 red, a few blocks north of the Duomo and across the street from the TI on Via Cavour, tel. 055-219-524), **Edison Bookstore** (daily 9:00–24:00, sells CDs, novels on Renaissance, facing Piazza della Repubblica, tel. 055-213-110), or **Paperback Exchange** (cheaper but smaller selection, Mon–Fri 9:00–19:30, Sat 10:00–13:00 & 15:30–19:30, closed Sun, shorter hours in Aug, Via Fiesolana 31 red, at corner of Via Fiesolana and Via dei Pilastri, 6 blocks east of Duomo, tel. 055-247-8154).

Rick Steves' Books and Videos

Rick Steves' Europe Through the Back Door 2003 gives you budget-travel tips on minimizing jet lag, packing light, planning your itinerary, traveling by car or train, finding beds without reservations, changing money, avoiding rip-offs, outsmarting thieves, hurdling the language barrier, staying healthy, taking great photographs, using your bidet, and much more. The book also includes chapters on 35 of Rick's favorite "back doors," six of which are in Italy.

Rick Steves' Country Guides are a series of eight guidebooks that cover Italy; Great Britain; Ireland; Spain and Portugal; France; Germany, Austria, and Switzerland; Scandinavia; and the Best of Europe. These are updated annually; most are available in bookstores in December, the rest in January.

Rick Steves' City Guides include this book, Rome, Venice, Paris, London, and—new for 2003—*Rick Steves' Amsterdam, Bruges & Brussels.* These handy, easy-to-pack guidebooks offer thorough coverage of Europe's greatest cities, complete with extensive self-guided tours through the greatest museums. They're updated annually and come out in December and January.

Rick Steves' Europe 101: History and Art for the Traveler (with Gene Openshaw, 2000), which gives you the story of Europe's people, history, and art, is heavy on Italy's ancient, Renaissance, and modern histories. Written for smart people who were sleeping in their history and art classes before they knew they were going to Europe, *101* helps resurrect the rubble.

Rick Steves' Mona Winks: Self-Guided Tours of Europe's Top Museums (with Gene Openshaw, 2001) gives you fun, easy-to-follow self-guided tours of Europe's 25 most exhausting, important museums and cultural sites. All of the *Mona Winks* chapters on Florence are included in this Florence guidebook. But if you'd like similar coverage for the great museums in Venice (St. Mark's Cathedral, Doge's Palace, and the Accademia), Rome (Forum, Colosseum, National Museum of Rome, St. Peter's Basilica, Vatican Museum, and the Borghese Gallery), Madrid, Paris, London, and Amsterdam, *Mona*'s for you.

In Italy, a phrase book is as fun as it is necessary. *Rick Steves' Italian Phrase Book* (1999) will help you meet the people and stretch your budget. It's written by a monoglot who, for 25 years, has fumbled through Italy struggling with all the other phrase books. Use this fun and practical communication aid to make accurate hotel reservations over the telephone, have the man in the deli make you a sandwich, and ask for a free taste of cantaloupe-flavored gelato at the *gelateria.*

Rick's public-television series, *Rick Steves' Europe,* airs a new season of 14 shows—with five on Italy—in the fall of 2002. Including the earlier *Travels in Europe* series, this brings the total of half-hour shows on Italy Rick has written and hosted to 15 (and more than 80 shows total). These air throughout the United States on public television stations. Each episode is also available on an information-packed home video (order online at www.ricksteves.com or call 425/771-8303 for our free newsletter/catalog).

Rick Steves' Postcards from Europe (1999), an autobiographical book, packs 25 years of travel anecdotes and insights into the ultimate 2,000-mile European adventure. Through his guidebooks, Rick shares his favorite European discoveries with you. In *Postcards,* he introduces you to his favorite European friends. Half of the book is set in Italy: Florence, Venice, Rome, and the Cinque Terre.

All of Rick Steves' books are published by Avalon Travel Publishing (www.travelmatters.com).

Maps

The maps in this book, designed and drawn by Dave Hoerlein, are concise and simple. Dave is well-traveled in Florence and Italy and has designed the maps to help you orient quickly and get to where you want to go painlessly. In Florence, any TI or your hotel will have helpful free maps. We like the €2.60 "new map" of Florence that lists the sights (sold at newsstands). For a longer Italy trip, consider our Rick Steves' Italy Planning Map, which includes a map of Florence. With sightseeing destinations listed prominently, it's designed for the traveler (see www.ricksteves.com or call 425/771-8303 for catalog).

Tours of Florence and Italy

Travel agents will tell you about normal tours of Italy, but they won't tell you about ours. At Europe Through the Back Door, we offer one-week getaways to **Florence,** to **Venice,** and to **Rome** (departures Feb–Dec, 20 people max).

Our longer Italy tours come with two great guides and a big, roomy bus. The 20-day **Best of Italy** tour features all of the biggies and a few of our favorite "back doors" (April–Oct, 24 people). The 15-day **Village Italy** adventure laces together intimate towns (April, Sept, and Oct, 20 people). For more information, call 425/771-8303 or visit www.ricksteves.com.

Transportation

The downtown core of Florence is walkable, though it involves dodging Vespas (the noisy little motor scooters). If you'd rather take buses or taxis, you'll find these covered in the Orientation chapter. If you have a car, stow it. You don't want to drive in Florence. Transportation to day-trip destinations is covered in the Day Trips chapter. For specifics on transportation throughout Italy by train or car, see *Rick Steves' Italy 2003.*

In Florence, get train tickets, reservations, and supplements at travel agencies rather than at the congested train station. The cost is either the same or there's a minimal charge. Ask your hotel for the nearest travel agency, or try American Express.

American Express offers all the normal services, but is most helpful as an easy place to get your train tickets, reservations, supplements (all the same price as at the station), or even just information on train schedules (Mon–Fri 9:00–17:30, Sat money exchange only 9:00–12:30, CC, 3 short blocks north of Palazzo Vecchio on Via Dante Alighieri 22 red, tel. 055-50981).

Telephones, Mail, and E-mail

Smart travelers use the telephone every day, to check opening hours, confirm hotel reservations, and phone home.

Phone Cards: There are two kinds of phone cards—official Italian phone cards that you insert into the phone instead of coins and long-distance scratch-off PIN cards that can be used from virtually any phone (you dial a toll-free number and enter your PIN).

Insertable Italian phone cards are sold in varying denominations at tobacco shops, post offices, and machines near phone booths (many phone booths indicate where the nearest phone-card sales outlet is). Rip off the perforated corner to "activate" the card before you insert it into the phone.

PIN cards, sold at small newsstand kiosks and hole-in-the-wall long-distance phone shops, are usually the least expensive way to call back to the United States (about 10 min/$1). Since you don't insert these cards into a phone, you can use them from most phones, including the one in your hotel room (if it's set on pulse, switch it to tone). Because there are so many brand names, ask for an international telephone card (*carta telefonica prepagate internazionali;* pron. KAR-tah teh-leh-FOHN-ee-kah pray-pah-GAH-tay in-ter-naht-zee-oh-NAH-lee); specify that you want a card for making calls to America or Canada to avoid getting the PIN cards that are only good within particular regions in Italy. After you buy a card, scratch off and reveal your Personal Identification Number, dial the toll-free access number, punch in your PIN, and talk. If the PIN doesn't work on one phone, try another phone. Get a low denomination in case the card is a dud. If you have difficulty using PIN cards to make local calls, use the insertable phone cards, coins, or hotel-room phones for local calls, and save the PIN card for international calls.

The orange SIP public telephones are everywhere and take cards or coins. About a quarter of the phones are broken (which could explain why so many Italians carry cell phones). The rest of the phones work reluctantly. Dial slowly and deliberately, as if the phone doesn't understand numbers very well. Often a recorded message in Italian will break in, brusquely informing you that the phone number does not exist (*non-esistente*), even if you're dialing your own home phone number. Dial again with an increasing show of confidence, in an attempt to convince the phone of your number's existence. If you fail, try a different phone. Repeat as needed.

When spelling out your name on the phone, you'll find *a* (pronounced "ah" in Italian), *i* (pronounced "ee"), and *e* (pronounced "ay") are confusing to Americans. Say "*a,* Acqua," "*e,* Empoli," and "*i,* Italia" to clear up that problem. If you plan to access your voice mail from Italy, be advised that you can't always dial extensions or secret codes once you connect (you're on vacation—relax).

Dialing within Italy: Italy has a direct-dial phone system (no area codes). To call anywhere within Italy, just dial the number. For example, the number of one of our recommended Florence hotels is 055-293-451. To call it from the Florence train station, dial 055-293-451. If you call it from Venice, it's the same: 055-293-451.

Italian phone numbers vary in length; a hotel can have, say, a 10-digit phone number and an 11-digit fax number.

Italy's toll-free numbers start with 800 (like U.S. 800 numbers, though in Italy you don't dial a "1" first). In Italy, you can dial these 800 numbers—called *freephone* or *numero verde* (green number)—free from any phone without using a phone card or coins.

Dialing International Calls: When calling internationally, dial the international access code (00 if you're calling from Europe, 011 from the U.S. or Canada), the country code of the country you're calling (39 for Italy; see appendix for list of other countries), and the local number. To call the Florence hotel (mentioned above) from the United States, dial 011 (the U.S. international access code), 39 (Italy's country code), then 055-293-451. To call the ETBD office from Italy, we dial 00 (Europe's international access code), 1 (the U.S. country code), 425 (Edmonds' area code), and 771-8303. European time is six/nine hours ahead of the East/West coasts of the United States.

Hotel-room phones are reasonable for calls within Italy (the faint beeps stand for €0.10 phone units) but a terrible rip-off for calls to the United States (unless you use a PIN card or your hotel allows toll-free access to your calling card service—see below).

Calling Card Services: While still convenient, these services—AT&T, MCI, and Sprint—are no longer a good value. It's much cheaper to call the United States using a PIN card or Italian phone card, but some people prefer to use their easier, pricier calling cards. Each card company has a toll-free number in each European country (for Italy: AT&T tel. 172-1011, MCI tel. 172-1022, Sprint tel. 172-1877), which puts you in touch with an English-speaking operator. The operator takes your card number and the number you want to call, puts you through, and bills your home phone number for the call. Oddly, you need to use a small-value coin or Italian phone card to dial the toll-free number. MCI, the cheapest of the lot, charges about $2.50 per minute with no surcharges. Sprint and AT&T charge about the same per minute, but tack on hefty surcharges and fees (if you get an answering machine, it'll cost you $7–8 to say, "Hi, sorry I missed you."). For less than 25 cents, call first with a coin or Italian phone card to see if the answering machine is off or if the right person's at home.

It's outrageously expensive to use your calling card to phone from one European country to another (it costs more than phoning the U.S.). When you're in Europe—calling internationally to anywhere—it's cheaper to simply dial direct using a phone card you bought in Europe (sold per country at newsstands).

Cell Phones: Affluent travelers like to buy cell phones (about $70 on up) in Europe to use for making local and international calls. The cheaper phones generally work only if you're making calls from the country where you purchased it (e.g., a phone bought in Italy won't work in France). Pricier phones allow you to call from any country, but it'll cost you about $40 per country to outfit the phone with the necessary chip and prepaid phone time. If you're interested, stop by any European shop that sells cell phones (you'll see an array of phones prominently displayed in the store window). Depending on your trip and budget, ask for a phone that works only in that country or one that can be used throughout Europe. And if you're really on a budget, skip cell phones and use PIN cards instead.

Mail: Mail service is miserable throughout Italy. Postcards get last priority. If you must have mail stops, consider a few pre-reserved hotels along your route or use American Express offices. Most American Express offices in Italy will hold mail for one month. This service is free to anyone using an AmEx card (and available for a small fee to others). Allow 14 days for U.S.-to-Italy mail delivery, but don't count on it. Federal Express makes pricey two-day deliveries. Phoning is so easy that we've completely dispensed with mail stops. If possible, mail nothing precious from Italy.

E-mail: E-mail use among Italian hoteliers is increasing. We've listed e-mail addresses when possible. Drab little cybercafés are popular throughout Florence; ask your hotelier for the one nearest your hotel.

Tipping

Tipping in Italy isn't as automatic and generous as it is in the U.S., but for special service, tips are appreciated, if not expected. As in the United States, the proper amount depends on your resources, tipping philosophy, and the circumstance, but some general guidelines apply.

Restaurants: Check the menu to see if the service is included (*servizio incluso*—generally 15 percent); if the *servizio* is *non incluso*, a tip of 5–10 percent is typical (for details, see page 205).

Taxis: To tip the cabbie, round up. For a typical ride, round up to the next euro on the fare (to pay a €13 fare, give €14); for a long ride, to the nearest €10 (for a €75 fare, give €80). If the cabbie hauls your bags and zips you to the airport to help you catch your flight, you might want to toss in a little more. But if you feel like you're being driven in circles or otherwise ripped off, skip the tip.

Special Services: It's thoughtful to tip a couple of euros to someone who shows you a special sight and who is paid in no other way (such as the man who shows you an Etruscan tomb in his back-yard). Tour guides at public sites sometimes hold out their hands for tips after they give their spiel; if I've already paid for the tour, I don't tip extra, though some tourists give a euro or two, particularly for a job well done. I don't tip at hotels, but if you do, give the porter a euro for carrying bags and leave a couple of euros in your room at the end of your stay for the maid if the room was kept clean. In general, if someone in the service industry does a super job for you, a tip of a couple of euros is appropriate . . . but not required.

When in doubt, ask. If you're not sure whether (or how much) to tip for a service, ask your hotelier or the TI; they'll fill you in on how it's done on their turf.

Culture Shock—Accepting Italy as a Package Deal

We travel all the way to Italy to enjoy differences—to become temporary locals. You'll experience frustrations. Certain truths that we find "God-given" or "self-evident," such as cold beer, ice in drinks, bottomless cups of coffee, hot showers, and bigger being better, are suddenly not so true. One of the benefits of travel is the eye-opening realization that there are logical, civil, and even better alternatives. A willingness to go local ensures that you'll enjoy a full dose of Italian hospitality.

If there is a negative aspect to the image Italians have of Americans, it is that we are big, loud, aggressive, impolite, rich, and a bit naive. While Italians, flabbergasted by our Yankee excesses, say in disbelief, "*Mi sono cadute le braccia!*" ("I throw my arms down!"), they nearly always afford us individual travelers all the warmth we deserve.

Send Us a Postcard, Drop Us a Line

If you enjoy a successful trip with the help of this book and would like to share your discoveries, please fill out the survey at the end of this book and send it to us at Europe Through the Back Door, Box 2009, Edmonds, WA 98020. We personally read and value all feedback. Thanks in advance—it helps a lot.

For our latest travel information on Italy, tap into our Web site at www.ricksteves.com. To check on any updates for this book, visit www.ricksteves.com/update. Rick's e-mail address is rick @ricksteves.com. You can request a free issue of our "Back Door" quarterly newsletter online (or call 425/771-8303).

Judging from all the happy postcards we receive from readers, it's safe to assume you'll enjoy a great, affordable vacation—with the finesse of an independent, experienced traveler.

From this point on, "we" (your coauthors) will shed our respective egos and become "I."

BACK DOOR TRAVEL PHILOSOPHY
From *Rick Steves' Europe Through the Back Door*

Travel is intensified living—maximum thrills per minute and one of the last great sources of legal adventure. Travel is freedom. It's recess, and we need it.

Experiencing the real Europe requires catching it by surprise, going casual . . . "Through the Back Door."

Affording travel is a matter of priorities. (Make do with the old car.) You can travel—simply, safely, and comfortably—anywhere in Europe for $80 a day plus transportation costs. In many ways, spending more money only builds a thicker wall between you and what you came to see. Europe is a cultural carnival and, time after time, you'll find that its best acts are free and the best seats are the cheap ones.

A tight budget forces you to travel close to the ground, meeting and communicating with the people, not relying on service with a purchased smile. Never sacrifice sleep, nutrition, safety, or cleanliness in the name of budget. Simply enjoy the local-style alternatives to expensive hotels and restaurants.

Extroverts have more fun. If your trip is low on magic moments, kick yourself and make things happen. If you don't enjoy a place, maybe you don't know enough about it. Seek the truth. Recognize tourist traps. Give a culture the benefit of your open mind. See things as different but not better or worse. Any culture has much to share.

Of course, travel, like the world, is a series of hills and valleys. Be fanatically positive and militantly optimistic. If something's not to your liking, change your liking. Travel is addictive. It can make you a happier American, as well as a citizen of the world. Our Earth is home to six billion equally important people. It's humbling to travel and find that people don't envy Americans. They like us, but, with all due respect, they wouldn't trade passports.

Globetrotting destroys ethnocentricity. It helps you understand and appreciate different cultures. Travel changes people. It broadens perspectives and teaches new ways to measure quality of life. Many travelers toss aside their hometown blinders. Their prized souvenirs are the strands of different cultures they decide to knit into their own character. The world is a cultural yarn shop. And Back Door Travelers are weaving the ultimate tapestry. Come on, join in!

ORIENTATION

The best of Florence lies mostly on the north bank of the Arno River. The main historical sights cluster around the red-brick dome of the cathedral (Duomo). Everything is within a 20-minute walk of the train station, cathedral, or Ponte Vecchio (Old Bridge). The less impressive but more characteristic Oltrarno (south bank) area is just over the bridge. Though small, Florence is intense. Prepare for scorching summer heat, kamikaze Vespas, slick pickpockets, few WCs, and erratic museum hours.

Planning Your Time

Plan your sightseeing carefully. The major sights—the Uffizi Gallery and the Accademia (*David*)—close on Monday. While many spend several hours a day in lines (at the Uffizi and Accademia), thoughtful travelers avoid this by making reservations (see page 52). Do our recommended Renaissance Walk in the morning or late afternoon to avoid heat and crowds. Stop often for gelato.

Florence in One Day

  8:30   Accademia (*David*); reserve in advance.
10:00   Renaissance Walk through town center,
            climb Giotto's Tower.
12:00   Shop around San Lorenzo and
            have lunch.
15:00   Bargello Museum (best statues).
17:00   Uffizi Gallery (best paintings);
            reserve in advance.
19:00   Oltrarno Walk (best local color).
20:00   Dinner in Oltrarno or on
            Piazza della Signoria.

Florence Overview

Florence in Two Days
Day 1
8:30   Accademia (*David*); reserve in advance.
10:00   Museum of San Marco (Fra Angelico).
12:00   Medici Chapels (Michelangelo).
14:00   Lunch, market, wander, shop.
15:00   Duomo Museum (fine statues, Donatello, Michelangelo).
16:30   Baptistery.
17:00   Climb Giotto's Tower.
18:00   Renaissance Walk through heart of old town.
20:00   Dinner on or near Piazza della Signoria.

Day 2
9:00   Bargello (best statues).
11:00   Dante's House and/or Science Museum.
13:00   Lunch, free to wander and shop.
15:00   Santa Maria Novella (Masaccio), old perfumery.
17:00   Uffizi Gallery (best paintings); reserve in advance.
19:00   Oltrarno Walk.
20:00   Dinner in Oltrarno.

Florence in Three (or Four) Days
Day 1
8:30   Accademia (*David*); reserve in advance.
10:00   Museum of San Marco (Fra Angelico).

12:00 Markets, shop, wander.
13:00 Lunch.
14:00 Medici Chapels (Michelangelo).
15:00 Santa Maria Novella and old perfumery.
16:30 Baptistery.
17:00 Giotto's Tower.
18:00 Renaissance Walk through heart of old town.
20:00 Dinner on or near Piazza della Signoria.

Day 2
 9:00 Bargello (best statues).
11:00 Science Museum.
13:00 Lunch, free to wander and shop.
16:30 Uffizi Gallery (best paintings); reserve in advance.
19:00 Sunset at Piazzale Michelangelo.

Day 3
10:00 Duomo Museum.
12:00 Dante's House and Santa Croce Church.
14:00 Lunch.
15:00 Pitti Palace, Boboli Gardens.
18:00 Oltrarno Walk.
20:00 Dinner in Oltrarno.

Day 4
Side-trip to Siena (sights open daily; 1.25–2 hrs by bus).

Daily Reminder

Sunday: Today the Duomo's dome, the Science Museum, and the Museum of Precious Stones are closed. These sights close early: the Duomo Museum (at 13:40), the Baptistery's interior (at 14:00), and Dante's House (also at 14:00). A few sights are open only in the afternoon: Santa Croce Church (15:00–17:30) and the Brancacci Chapel and Santa Maria Novella (both 13:00–17:00).

The Museum of San Marco, which is open on the second and fourth Sunday of the month until 19:00, closes entirely—as does the Bargello—on the first, third, and fifth Sunday. The Medici Chapels and Modern Art Gallery (in the Pitti Palace) close on the second and fourth Sunday. (Need a calendar? Look in the appendix.)

Monday: The biggies are closed—Accademia (*David*) and Uffizi Gallery—as well as the Vasari Corridor and the Palatine Gallery/Royal Apartments (in the Pitti Palace).

The Medici Chapels and Modern Art Gallery (in the Pitti Palace) close on the first, third, and fifth Monday of the month. The Museum of San Marco and the Bargello close on the second and fourth Monday. The Orsanmichele Church and Boboli Gardens close on the first and last Monday.

Good bets: Duomo Museum, Giotto's Tower, Brancacci Chapel, Michelangelo's House, Dante's House, Science Museum, Palazzo Vecchio, and churches.

Tuesday: All sights are open except for Dante's House, Michelangelo's House, and the Brancacci Chapel. The Science Museum closes early (13:00).

Wednesday: All sights are open except for the Medici Riccardi Palace.

Thursday: All sights are open. The Museum of Precious Stones stays open late (19:00) while these sights close early: Duomo (15:30) and Palazzo Vecchio (14:00).

Friday: All sights are open. The Church of Santa Maria Novella opens late (13:00–17:00) and Palazzo Vecchio closes late (maybe until 23:00 in summer).

Saturday: All sights are open, but the Science Museum closes early (13:00). These sights close early on the first Saturday of the month: Duomo (15:30) and the Duomo's dome (15:20). The Museum of San Marco stays open until 19:00. The Accademia, Uffizi, and Palatine Gallery/Royal Apartments may stay open until 22:00 in summer.

Arrival in Florence

For a rundown on Florence's train station, bus station, and airport, see Transportation Connections, page 224.

Tourist Information

There are three TIs in Florence: across from the train station, near Santa Croce, and on Via Cavour.

The TI across the square from the train station is most crowded—expect long lines (Mon–Sat 8:30–19:00, Sun 8:30–13:00; off-season Mon–Sat 8:30–17:30, Sun 8:30–13:00; with your back to tracks, exit the station—it's across the square in wall near corner of church, Piazza Stazione, tel. 055-212-245, www.firenze.turismo.toscana.it). Note: In the station, avoid the Hotel Reservations "Tourist Information" window (marked *Informazioni Turistiche Alberghiere*) near the McDonald's; it's not a real TI but a hotel reservation business.

The TI near Santa Croce Church is pleasant, helpful, and uncrowded (Mon–Sat 9:00–19:00, Sun 9:00–14:00, shorter hours off-season, Borgo Santa Croce 29 red, tel. 055-234-0444).

Another winner is the TI three blocks north of the Duomo (Mon–Sat 8:15–19:15, Sun 8:30–13:30, closed Sun in winter, Via Cavour 1 red, tel. 055-290-832 or 055-290-833; international bookstore across street).

At any TI, pick up a map, a current museum-hours listing (extremely important, since no guidebook—including this one—has ever been able to predict the hours of Florence's sights), and any information on entertainment. The free monthly *Florence Concierge Information* magazine lists museums, plus lots that I don't: concerts and events, markets, sporting events, church services, shopping ideas, bus and train connections, and an entire similar section on Siena. Get yours at the TI or from any expensive hotel (pick one up, as if you're staying there).

Helpful Hints

Theft Alert: Florence has particularly hardworking thief gangs. They specialize in tourists and hang out where you do: near the train station, the station's underpass (especially where the tunnel surfaces), and major sights. Also be on guard at two squares frequented by drug pushers (Santa Maria Novella and Santo Spirito). American tourists—especially older ones—are considered easy targets.

Medical Help: To track down a doctor who speaks English, call 055-475-411 (reasonable hotel calls, cheaper if you go to the clinic at Via L. Magnifico 59) or get a list of English-speaking doctors from the TI. A 24-hour pharmacy is at the train station.

Addresses: Street addresses list businesses in red and

residences in black or blue (color-coded on the actual street number and indicated by a letter following the number in printed addresses: n = black, r = red). *Pensioni* are usually black but can be either. The red and black numbers each appear in roughly consecutive order on streets but bear no apparent connection with each other. I'm lazy and don't concern myself with the distinction (if one number's wrong, I look for the other) and find my way around fine.

Laundrettes: The Wash & Dry Lavarapido chain offers long hours and efficient, self-service Laundrettes at several locations (about €6.20 for wash and dry, daily 8:00–22:00, tel. 055-580-480). Close to recommended hotels: Via dei Servi 105 (and a rival Laundrette at Via Guelfa 22 red, off Via Cavour; both near *David*); Via del Sole 29 red and Via della Scala 52 red (between train station and river); and Via dei Serragli 87 red (across the river in Oltrarno neighborhood).

Getting Around Florence

I organize my sightseeing geographically and do it all on foot. A €1 ticket gives you one hour on the buses, €1.80 gives you three hours, and €4 gets you 24 hours (tickets not sold on bus— buy in *tabacchi* shops or newsstands before 21:00, validate on bus; after 21:00 buy tickets on bus).

The minimum cost for a taxi ride is €4, or, after 22:00, €5 (rides in the center of town should be charged as tariff #1). A taxi ride from the train station to Ponte Vecchio costs about €8. Taxi fares and supplements are clearly explained on signs in each cab.

Tours and Talks

Walking Tours of Florence—This company offers a variety of tours (up to 4 a day Mon–Sat) featuring downtown Florence, Uffizi highlights, or Tuscany (countryside, Siena, San Gimignano, or Pisa), presented by informative, entertaining, native English–speaking guides. The "Original Florence" walk hits the main sights but gets offbeat to weave a picture of Florentine life in medieval and Renaissance times. You can expect lots of talking, which is great if you like history. Tours, offered year-round regardless of weather, start at their office and are limited to a maximum of 22; extra guides are available if more people show up (€24 for 3-hr Original Florence walk, office open Mon–Sat 8:30–18:00, closed for lunch off-season, Piazza Santo Stefano 2 black, a short block north of Ponte Vecchio; go east on tiny Vicolo San Stefano, in Piazza Santo Stefano at #2; booking necessary for Uffizi tour, private tours available, tel. 055-264-5033, cellular 0329-613-2730, www.artviva.com). The owner of the company, Rosanne Magers, also offers private tours (tel. 055-264-5033, e-mail: walkingtours@artviva.com).

Florentia—These top-notch, historical walking tours of Florence and Tuscany are led by local scholars. The tours, ranging from introductory city walks to in-depth visits of museums and lesser-known destinations, are geared for thoughtful and well-heeled travelers (semi-private tours start at $45 per person, max 8 per group; private tours start at $180 for half-day tour, reserve in advance, tel. 055-225-535, U.S. tel. 510-549-1707, www .florentia.org, e-mail: info@florentia.org).

Florence Art Lectures—These 90-minute talks on the Florentine Renaissance, designed for English-speaking tourists, are held in a classy 13th-century *palazzo* near the Santa Croce Church (€20, offered May–Sept only, Mon–Sat at 14:30, includes glass of wine, espresso, or cold drink, Piazza Santa Croce 21, tel. 055-245-354, www.florenceart.org). They also offer art lectures combined with a lunch or dinner, as well as museum tours and city walking tours at sunset.

Local Guide—**Paola Migilorini** offers museum tours, city walking tours, and Tuscan excursions by van ($100 for 2-hr walking tour or Uffizi tour, Via S. Gallo 120, tel. 055-472-448, cellular 347-657-2611, www.florencetour.com, e-mail: info@florencetour.com).

SIGHTS

In this chapter, Florence's most important sights have the shortest listings and are marked with a ⚫ (and page number). These sights are covered in much more detail in one of the tours included in this book.

A number of these sights—from Michelangelo's *David* to the Ponte Vecchio over the Arno River—are connected by the Renaissance Walk (see page 36).

Sights: North of the Duomo (Cathedral)

▲▲▲**Accademia (Galleria dell' Accademia)**—This museum houses Michelangelo's *David* and powerful (unfinished) *Prisoners*. Beyond the magic marble are two floors of mildly interesting pre-Renaissance and Renaissance paintings, including a couple of lighter-than-air Botticellis.

Cost, Hours, Location: €6.50 (plus €1.55 reservation fee). Open Tue–Sun 8:15–18:50, until 22:00 on holidays and maybe on summer Sat, closed Mon (last entry 30 min before closing, Via Ricasoli 60, tel. 055-238-8609). ⚫ See page 39 of the Renaissance Walk.

Nearby: Piazza Santissima Annunziata, behind the Accademia, displays lovely Renaissance harmony. Facing the square are two fine buildings: the 15th-century Santissima Annunziata church (worth a peek) and Brunelleschi's Hospital of the Innocents (*Spedale degli Innocenti*, not worth going inside), with terra-cotta medallions by Luca della Robbia. Built in the 1420s, the hospital is considered the first Renaissance building.

Florence Sights

★ PIAZZA
SIGNORIA   ⚡ VIEW   G = GELATERIA

400 METERS
400 YARDS

▲▲**Museum of San Marco (Museo di San Marco)**—
One block north of the Accademia on Piazza San Marco, this
museum houses the greatest collection anywhere of frescoes and
paintings by the early Renaissance master Fra Angelico. Don't
miss the cell of Savonarola, the charismatic monk who rode in
from the Christian right, threw out the Medicis, turned Florence
into a theocracy, sponsored "bonfires of the vanities" (burning

books, paintings, and so on), and was finally burned himself when Florence decided to change channels (€4, daily 8:15–13:50, Sat–Sun until 19:00, but closed first, third, and fifth Sun and second and fourth Mon of each month, tel. 055-238-8608). The ticket office can sell tickets (often with immediate reservation) to Uffizi and Accademia. ● See Museum of San Marco Tour on page 83.

Museum of Precious Stones (Museo dell' Opificio delle Pietre Dure)—This unusual gem of a museum features mosaics of inlaid marble and semiprecious stones. You'll see remnants of the Medici workshop from 1588, including 500 different semiprecious stones, the tools used to cut and inlay them, and room after room of the sumptuous finished product. The fine loaner booklet describes it all in English (€2, Mon–Sat 8:15–14:00, Thu until 19:00, closed Sun, Via degli Alfani 78, around corner from Accademia). This ticket booth can also sell tickets with reservations (perhaps same day) to the Uffizi and Accademia.

▲▲Medici Chapels (Cappelli dei Medici)—The highlight is a chapel with interior decoration by Michelangelo, including the brooding Night, Day, Dawn, and Dusk statues (€6, daily 8:15–17:00 but closed the second and fourth Sun and the first, third, and fifth Mon of each month, tel. 055-238-8602). ● See Medici Chapels Tour on page 114.

Nearby: Behind the chapels on Piazza Madonna is a lively market scene that I find just as interesting. Take a stroll through the huge double-decker Mercato Centrale (central market) one block north.

Medici Riccardi Palace (Palazzo Medici Riccardi)—Lorenzo the Magnificent's home is worth a look for its art. The tiny Chapel of the Magi contains colorful Renaissance gems—the *Procession of the Magi* frescoes by Benozzo Gozzoli. Another room has a High Baroque ceiling fresco by Luca Giordano, a prolific artist from Naples known as Fast Luke (*Luca fa presto*) for his ambidextrous painting abilities (€4, Thu–Tue 9:00–19:00, closed Wed, Via Cavour 3, kitty-corner from San Lorenzo Church, 1 long block north of Baptistery).

Sights: Duomo and Nearby

▲▲Duomo—Florence's Gothic Santa Maria dei Fiori cathedral has the third-longest nave in Christendom (free, Mon–Wed and Fri–Sat 10:00–17:00 except first Sat of month 10:00–15:30,

Tips on Sightseeing in Florence

Make Reservations to Avoid Lines:
Florence has a great reservation system for its top five sights—Uffizi,
Accademia, Bargello, Medici Chapels,
and the Pitti Palace. Two of these
sights nearly always have long lines:
the Accademia (Michelangelo's *David*)
and the Uffizi (Renaissance art). You
can easily avoid long waits—up to
two hours at the Uffizi on busy days—
by making a reservation by phone.
Frankly, it's stupid not to.

While you can generally make a reservation a day in
advance (upon arrival in Florence), you'll have a wider selection of entry times by calling a few days ahead. You dial 055-
294-883 (Mon–Fri 8:30–18:30, Sat 8:30–12:00, closed Sun),
an English-speaking operator walks you through the process,
and two minutes later you say *grazie*, with appointments (15-
minute entry window) and six-digit confirmation numbers for
each of the top museums and galleries.

If you haven't called ahead, you can make reservations for
the top sights at the minor, less-crowded sights (such as the
Museum of San Marco or Museum of Precious Stones). Clerks
at the ticket booths at these sleepy sights can reserve and sell
tickets to the major sights—often for admission the same day—
allowing you to skip right past the dreary mob scene.

Hours of Sights Can Change Suddenly: Because of
labor demands, hours of sights change without warning. Pick
up the latest listing of museum hours at a TI, or you'll miss
out on something you came to see. Don't put off seeing a
must-see sight such as *David*; you never know when a place
will unexpectedly close for a holiday, strike, or restoration.

Churches: Many churches now operate like museums,
charging an admission fee to see their art treasures. Modest
dress is required in some churches, and recommended for all
of them—that means no short shorts (or short skirts) and no
bare shoulders. Be respectful of worshippers; don't use a flash.
Churches usually close from 12:30 to 15:00 or 16:00.

Chill Out: Schedule into your sightseeing several cool
breaks where you can sit, pause, and refresh yourself with a
sandwich, gelato, or coffee.

Thu 10:00–15:30, Sun 13:30–16:45, tel. 055-230-2885). The church's noisy neo-Gothic facade from the 1870s is covered with pink, green, and white Tuscan marble. Since nearly all of its great art is stored in the Duomo Museum (behind the church), the best thing about the interior is the shade. The inside of the dome is decorated by one of the largest paintings of the Renaissance, a huge (and newly restored) *Last Judgment* by Vasari and Zuccari.

The cathedral's claim to artistic fame is Brunelleschi's magnificent dome—the first Renaissance dome and the model for domes to follow. ✪ See page 42 of the Renaissance Walk.

▲**Climbing the Cathedral's Dome**—For a grand view into the cathedral from the base of the dome, a peek at some of the tools used in the dome's construction, a chance to see Brunelleschi's "dome-within-a-dome" construction, a glorious Florence view from the top, and the equivalent of 463 plunges on a Stairmaster, climb the dome (€6, Mon–Sat 8:30–19:00 except first Sat of month 8:30–15:20, closed Sun, enter from outside church on south or river side, expect a long, dreadfully slow-moving line if you don't arrive by 8:30, tel. 055-230-2885).

▲**Giotto's Tower (Campanile)**—If you're not interested in experiencing dome-within-a-dome architecture, you'll likely feel that climbing Giotto's 82-meter-tall (270-foot) bell tower beats scaling the neighboring Duomo's dome because it's 50 fewer steps, faster, and offers the same view plus the dome (€6, daily 8:30–19:30, last entry 40 min before closing). ✪ See page 43 of the Renaissance Walk.

▲**Baptistery**—Michelangelo said its bronze doors were fit to be the gates of Paradise. Check out the gleaming copies of Ghiberti's bronze doors facing the Duomo. Making a breakthrough in perspective, Ghiberti used mathematical laws to create the illusion of receding distance on a basically flat surface. The earlier, famous competition doors are around to the right (north); Ghiberti, who beat Brunelleschi, got the job of designing these doors.

A local document from A.D. 860 already refers to Florence's oldest building (the original Baptistery, located on this same site) as "ancient." Inside, sit and savor the medieval mosaic ceiling where it's Judgment Day, and Jesus is giving the ultimate thumbs up and thumbs down (€3 interior open Mon–Sat 12:00–19:00,

Sun 8:30–14:00, bronze doors are on the outside, so always "open"; original panels are in the Duomo Museum). See page 44 of the Renaissance Walk.

▲▲**Duomo Museum (Museo dell' Opera del Duomo)**— The underrated cathedral museum, behind the church at #9, is great if you like sculpture. Look for Donatello's anorexic *Mary Magdalene* and playful choir loft, a late Michelangelo *Pietà*, Brunelleschi's models for his dome, and the original restored panels of Ghiberti's doors to the Baptistery (€6, Mon–Sat 9:00–19:30, Sun 9:00–13:40, closed on holidays, tel. 055-230-2885). ✪ See Duomo Museum Tour on page 98.

Sights: Between the Duomo and Piazza della Signoria

▲▲▲**Bargello (Museo Nazionale)**—This under-appreciated sculpture museum is in a former prison that looks like a mini–Palazzo Vecchio. It has Donatello's painfully beautiful *David* (the very influential first male nude to be sculpted in a thousand years), works by Michelangelo, and rooms of Medici treasures cruelly explained in Italian only—mention that English descriptions would be wonderful (€4, daily 8:15–13:50 but closed first, third, and fifth Sun and second and fourth Mon of each month, last entry 30 min before closing, Via del Proconsolo 4, tel. 055-238-8606). ✪ See Bargello Tour on page 74.

▲**Dante's House (Casa di Dante)**—Dante's house consists of five rooms in an old building with lots of documents and photos relating to his life and work. Well-described in English, it's interesting to literary buffs (€3, Mon and Wed–Sat 10:00–17:00, Sun 10:00–14:00, closed Tue, across the street and around the corner from Bargello, at Via S. Margherita 1). ✪ See Dante's House Tour on page 124.

▲**Orsanmichele Church**—In the ninth-century, this loggia (a covered courtyard) was a market used for selling grain (stored upstairs). Later, it was closed in to make a church. Notice the grain spouts on the pillars inside. The glorious tabernacle (1359) by Orcagna takes you back (free, daily 9:00–12:00 & 16:00–18:00, closed first and last Mon of month, on Via Calzaiuoli, enter through the back door, may be closed due to staffing problems). The iron bars spanning the vaults were the Italian Gothic answer to the French Gothic external buttresses. ✪ See page 46 of the Renaissance Walk.

Across the street is the...

▲**Orsanmichele Museum (Museo Orsanmichele)**—For some peaceful time alone with the original statues that filled the niches of Orsanmichele, climb to the top of the church (entry behind church, across street). Be there at 9:00, 10:00, or 11:00, when the door opens daily and art-lovers in the know climb four flights of stairs to this little-known museum, containing statues by Ghiberti, Donatello, and others (info in Italian, but picture guides on wall help you match art with artists). Upstairs is a tower room with city views (free).

A block away, you'll find the...

▲**Mercato Nuovo**—This market loggia is how Orsanmichele looked before it became a church. Originally a silk and straw market, Mercato Nuovo still functions as a rustic market today (at intersection of Via Calimala and Via Porta Rossa). Prices are soft. Notice the circled *X* in the center, marking the spot where people hit after being hoisted up to the top and dropped as punishment for bankruptcy. You'll also find *Porcellino* (a statue of a wild boar nicknamed "little pig"), which people rub and give coins to in order to ensure their return to Florence. Nearby is a wagon selling tripe (cow innards) sandwiches.

▲**Piazza della Repubblica**—This large square, the belly-button of Florence, sits on the site of Florence's original Roman Forum. The lone column is the only remaining bit of Roman Florence except for the grid street plan. Look at the map to see the ghost of Rome: a rectangular fort with this square marking the intersection of the two main roads (Via Corso and Via Roma).

Today's piazza, framed by a triumphal arch, is really a nationalistic statement celebrating the unification of Italy. Florence, the capital of the country (1865–1870) until Rome was liberated, lacked a square worthy of this grand new country. So the neighborhood here was razed to open up a grand modern forum surrounded by grand circa-1890 buildings.

Medieval writers described Florence as so densely built up that when it rained, pedestrians didn't get wet. Torches were used to light the lanes in midday. The city was prickly with noble family towers (like San Gimignano) and had Romeo-and-Juliet-type family feuds. But with the rise of the Medicis (c. 1300), no noble family was allowed to have an architectural ego trip taller then theirs, and nearly all other towers were taken down.

Sights: On and Near Piazza della Signoria

▲▲▲**Uffizi Gallery**—This is the greatest collection of Italian paintings anywhere, featuring works by Giotto, Leonardo, Raphael, Caravaggio, Rubens, Titian, and Michelangelo and a roomful of Botticellis, including his *Birth of Venus.* Because only 780 visitors are allowed inside the building at any one time, during the day there's generally a very long wait. The good news: no Louvre-style mob scenes. The museum is nowhere near as

Floods in Florence

Summer visitors to Florence gaze at the lazy green creek called the Arno River and have a tough time imagining it being a destructive giant. But rare, powerful flooding is a part of life in Florence. The Arno River washed away the Ponte Vecchio in 1177 and 1333. And on November 4, 1966, a huge rain turned the Arno into a wall of water inundating the city with mud stacked as much as six meters (20 feet) high. Fourteen thousand families were left homeless, and a huge amount of art was destroyed or damaged.

Almost as impressive as the flood was the huge outpouring of support, as the art-loving world came to the city's rescue. While money poured in from far and wide, volunteers nicknamed "mud angels" mopped things up. After the flood, scientists made great gains in restoration techniques as they cleaned and repaired masterpieces from medieval and Renaissance times.

Today, you'll see plaques around town showing the high-water marks (about 2 meters, or 6 feet, around the Duomo). But now that a new dam has tamed the Arno, kayakers glide peacefully on the river, sightseers enjoy the great art with no thought of a flood, and locals...still get nervous after every heavy rain.

big as it is great. Few tourists spend more than two hours inside. The paintings are displayed on one comfortable floor in chronological order from the 13th through 17th centuries.

Cost, Hours, Reservations: €8, plus €1.55 for recommended reservation, Tue–Sun 8:15–18:50, until 22:00 on holidays and maybe on summer Sat, closed Mon (last entry 45 min before closing; after entering take elevator or climb 4 long flights of stairs). To avoid the long lines, it's smart to call ahead to reserve an entry time. ⊗ For details on making reservations and for a self-guided tour, see Uffizi Gallery Tour on page 52.

Enjoy the Uffizi square, full of artists and souvenir stalls. The surrounding statues honor the earthshaking artists (Michelangelo), philosophers (Machiavelli), scientists (Galileo), writers (Dante), and explorers (Amerigo Vespucci), and the great patron of so much Renaissance thinking, Lorenzo "the Magnificent" de Medici. ⊗ For more, see page 49 of the Renaissance Walk.

▲**Palazzo Vecchio**—With its distinctive castle turret, this fortified palace, once the home of the Medici family, is a Florentine landmark. But if you're visiting only one palace interior in town, the Pitti Palace is better. The Palazzo Vecchio interior is wall-papered with mediocre magnificence, worthwhile only if you're a real Florentine art and history fan. The museum's most famous statues are Michelangelo's *Genius of Victory*, Donatello's static *Judith and Holerfernes*, and Verrocchio's *Winged Cherub* (a copy tops the fountain in the free courtyard at entrance, original inside).

Scattered throughout the museum are a dozen computer terminals with information in English on the Medici family, Palazzo Vecchio, and the building's architecture and art, including an animated clip showing how Michelangelo's *David* was moved from the square to the Accademia (€5.70, Fri–Wed 9:00–19:00, Thu 9:00–14:00, in summer maybe open until 23:00 on Mon and Fri, ticket office closes 1 hour earlier, WC in second courtyard can be accessed without paying palace admission, tel. 055-276-8465). ✪ See page 47 of the Renaissance Walk.

Even if you don't go to the museum, do step into the free courtyard (behind the fake *David*) just to feel the essence of the Medicis. Until 1873, Michelangelo's *David* stood at the entrance, where the copy is today. While the huge statues in the square are important only as the whipping boys of art critics and rest stops for pigeons, the nearby Loggia dei Lanzi has several important statues. Look for Cellini's bronze statue of Perseus holding the head of Medusa. The plaque on the pavement in front of the fountain marks the spot where the monk Savonarola was burned in MCDXCVIII (for more on the monk, see Museum of San Marco Tour on page 83).

▲▲**Science Museum (Museo di Storia della Scienza)**—This is a fascinating collection of Renaissance and later clocks, telescopes, maps, and ingenious gadgets. One of the most talked-about bottles in Florence is the one here containing Galileo's finger. Loaner English guidebooklets are available. It's friendly, comfortably cool, never crowded, and just a block east of the Uffizi on the Arno River (€6.50, Mon and Wed–Fri 9:30–17:00, Tue and Sat 9:30–13:00, closed Sun, Piazza dei Giudici 1, tel. 055-239-8876). ✪ See Science Museum Tour on page 151.

▲**Ponte Vecchio**—Florence's most famous bridge is lined with shops that have traditionally sold gold and silver. A statue of Cellini, the master goldsmith of the Renaissance, stands in the center, ignored by the flood of tacky tourism. ✪ See page 50 of Renaissance Walk.

Notice the "prince's passageway" above the bridge. In less secure times, the city leaders had a fortified passageway connecting the Vecchio Palace and Uffizi with the mighty Pitti Palace, to which they could flee in times of attack. This passageway, called the **Vasari Corridor,** is open to the persistent by request only (€8, Tue–Sat at 9:30, closed Mon, tel. 055-265-4321).

Sights: Santa Croce Church and Nearby

▲▲**Santa Croce Church**—This 14th-century Franciscan church, decorated with centuries of precious art, holds the tombs of great Florentines (€3, Mon–Sat 9:30–17:30, Sun 15:00–17:30, in winter Mon–Sat 9:30–12:30 & 15:00–17:30, Sun 15:00–17:30, modest dress code enforced, tel. 055-244-619). The loud 19th-century Victorian Gothic facade faces a huge square ringed with tempting shops and littered with tired tourists. Escape into the church.

Working counterclockwise from the entrance, you'll find the tomb of Michelangelo (with the allegorical figures of painting, architecture, and sculpture), a memorial to Dante (no body… he was banished by his hometown because of political differences), the tomb of Machiavelli (who wrote the book on hardball politics), a relief by Donatello of the Annunciation, and the tomb of the composer of the *William Tell* Overture (a.k.a. the *Lone Ranger* theme), Rossini. To the right of the altar, step into the sacristy where you'll find a bit of St. Francis' cowl and old sheets of music. In the bookshop, notice the photos of the devastating flood of 1966 high on the wall. Beyond that is a touristy—but mildly interesting—"leather school." The chapels lining the front of the church are richly frescoed. The chapel to the right of the main altar is a masterpiece by Giotto featuring scenes from the life of St. Francis. On your way out, you'll pass the tomb of Galileo (allowed in by the Church long after his death).

The neighboring **Santa Croce Museum** includes Brunelleschi's **Pazzi Chapel,** considered one of the finest pieces of Florentine Renaissance architecture (covered by €3 Santa Croce church admission fee, Thu–Tue 10:00–18:00, closed Wed, entrance outside church; facing facade it's the door to the right).

▲**Michelangelo's House (Casa Buonarroti)**—Fans enjoy a house owned by Michelangelo, which has some of his early, much-less-monumental statues and sketches (€6.50, Wed–Mon 9:30–14:00, closed Tue, English descriptions, Via Ghibellina 70).

Sights: Near the Train Station

▲▲**Church of Santa Maria Novella**—This 13th-century Dominican church is rich in art. Along with crucifixes by Giotto and Brunelleschi, there's every textbook's example of the early Renaissance mastery of perspective: *The Holy Trinity* by Masaccio; it's opposite the side entrance (€2.60, Mon–Thu and Sat 9:30–17:00, Fri and Sun 13:00–17:00). ✪ See Santa Maria Novella Tour on page 133.

Nearby: A palatial **perfumery** is around the corner 100 meters down Via della Scala at #16 (free but shopping encouraged, Mon–Sat 9:30–19:30, closed Sun). Thick with the lingering aroma of centuries of spritzes, it started as the herb garden of the Santa Maria Novella monks. Well-known even today for its top-quality products, it is extremely Florentine. Pick up the history sheet at the desk and wander deep into the shop. From the back room, you can peek at Santa Maria Novella's cloister with its dreamy frescoes and imagine a time before Vespas and tourists.

Sights: South of the Arno River

▲▲**Pitti Palace**—From the Uffizi, follow the course of the elevated passageway (closed to non-Medicis) across the Ponte Vecchio to the gargantuan Pitti Palace, which has several separate museums.

The **Palatine Gallery/Royal Apartments (Galleria Palatina)** is the biggie, featuring palatial room after chandeliered room, its walls sagging with masterpieces by minor artists and minor pieces by masters. Its Raphael collection is the biggest anywhere (first floor, €6.50, Tue–Sun 8:30–18:50, perhaps summer Sat until 22:00, closed Mon, buy tickets on right-hand side of courtyard).

The **Modern Art Gallery** features Romanticism, neoclassicism, and Impressionism by 19th- and 20th-century Tuscan painters (second floor, €5, daily 8:30–13:50 but closed second and fourth Sun and first, third, and fifth Mon).

The **Grand Ducal Treasures (Museo degli Argenti)** is the Medici treasure chest, with jeweled crucifixes, exotic porcelain, gilded ostrich eggs, and so on to entertain fans of applied arts (ground floor, €7.75, virtually the same hours as Modern Art Gallery).

Behind the palace, the huge landscaped **Boboli Gardens** offer a shady refuge from the city heat (€2, daily 9:00–18:30, until 19:30 June–Aug, until 16:30 in winter, but closed first and last Mon of month).

▲▲**Brancacci Chapel**—For the best look at Masaccio's works (he's the early Renaissance master invented perspective), see his restored frescoes here. Since only a few tourists are let in at a time, seeing the chapel often involves a wait (€3.10, Mon and Wed–Sat 10:00–17:00, Sun 13:00–17:00,

closed Tue, cross Ponte Vecchio and turn right a few blocks to Piazza del Carmine). ✪ See Brancacci Chapel Tour on page 142.

The neighborhoods around the church are considered the last surviving bits of old Florence.

Santo Spirito Church—This has a classic Brunelleschi interior and a very early Michelangelo crucifix, painted on carved wood, given by the sculptor to the monastery in appreciation for the opportunity they gave him to dissect and learn about bodies. Pop in here for a delightful Renaissance space and a chance to marvel at a Michelangelo all alone (free, Thu–Tue 9:00–12:00 & 16:00–17:30, Wed 9:00–12:00, Piazza Santo Spirito).

▲**Piazzale Michelangelo**—Overlooking the city (look for the huge statue of David), this square is worth the 30-minute hike, drive, or bus ride (either #12 or #13 from the train station) for the view of Florence and the stunning dome of the Duomo. After dark, it's packed with local schoolkids feeding their dates slices of watermelon. Just beyond it is the stark and beautiful, crowd-free, Romanesque San Miniato Church.

Oltrarno Walk—If you never leave the touristy center, you won't really see Florence. There's more to the city than tourism. Ninety percent of its people live and work—mostly in small shops—where tourists rarely venture. This self-guided tour follows a perfectly straight line (you can't get lost). Cross the Ponte Vecchio and walk west on the road toward Pisa—it changes names, from Borgo San Jacopo and Via di Santo Spirito to Borgo Frediano—until you reach the city wall at Porta San Frediano. Along this route, you can check out several of my favorite restaurants (see Eating, page 204). As you walk, consider these points:

After one block, at the fancy **Hotel Lungarno,** step up to the Arno River viewpoint for a great look at the Ponte Vecchio. Recall the story of Kesserling, the Nazi commander-in-chief of Italy who happened to be an art-lover. As the Nazis retreated in 1944, he was commanded to blow up all the bridges. Rather than destroy the venerable Ponte Vecchio, he disabled it by blowing up the surrounding neighborhood. Turn around and cross the street to see the ivy-covered nub of a medieval tower—ruined August 6, 1944.

Along this walk, you'll see plenty of artisans at work and lots of inviting little **shops.** You're welcome to drop in, but remember, it's polite to say *"Buon giorno"* and *"Ciao."* "Can I take a look?" is *"Posso guardare?"* (pron. POH-soh gwahr-DAH-ray).

The streets are busy with *motorini* (Vespas and other motor bikes). While these are allowed in the city, nonresident cars are not (unless they are electric). Notice that parked cars have a *residente* permit on their dash. You'll see a police officer (likely a woman) later on the walk, keeping traffic out.

Look for little architectural details. Tiny shrines protect the corners of many blocks. Once upon a time, the iron spikes on the walls impaled huge candles, which provided a little light. Electricity changed all that, but notice there are no electric wires visible. They're under the streets.

This street is lined with apartment buildings punctuated by the occasional *palazzo*. The skyline and architecture are typical of the 13th to 16th centuries. Huge *palazzi* (recognized by their immense doors, lush courtyards, and grand stonework) were for big-shot merchants. Many have small wooden doors designed to look like stones (like at 3b on Borgo San Frediano). While originally for one family, these buildings are now subdivided, as evidenced by the huge banks of doorbells at the door.

The **Church of Santa Maria del Carmine,** with its famous Brancacci Chapel and Masaccio frescoes, is a short detour off Borgo San Frediano (see Brancacci Chapel Tour on page 142).

A couple of blocks before Porta San Frediano (and its tower), look left up Piazza dei Nerli. The bold yellow schoolhouse was built during Mussolini's rule—grandly proclaiming the resurrection of the Italian empire.

Porta San Frediano, built about 1300, is part of Florence's medieval wall, which stretches impressively from here to the river. The tower was originally twice as high, built when gravity ruled warfare. During the Renaissance, when gunpowder dominated warfare, the tower—now just an easy target—was lopped. In medieval times, a kilometer-wide strip outside the wall was cleared to deny attackers any cover. Notice the original doors—immense and studded with fat iron nails to withstand battering rams. Got a horse? Lash it to a ring.

Tour over. You passed several fun eateries, and the colorful Trattoria Sabatino is just outside the wall (all described in Eating, page 204). *Ciao.*

Side Trip to Fiesole

For a candid peek at the Florentine suburb Fiesole, ride bus #7 for about 25 minutes through neighborhood gardens, vineyards, orchards, and large villas to the last stop—Fiesole (3/hr, departs Florence from Piazza Adua at the northeast side of the train station and also from Piazza San Marco). Fiesole is a popular excursion because of its intimate eateries and its sublime views of Florence. Catch the sunset from the terrace just below La Reggia Ristorante; from the Fiesole bus stop, face the bell tower and take the very steep Via San Francisco on your left. You'll find the view terrace near the top of the hill.

RENAISSANCE
WALK

After centuries of labor, Florence gave birth to the Renaissance. We'll start with the Renaissance poster boy, Michelangelo's *David*. A short walk away are the Baptistery doors that "started" the Renaissance and the dome that captured its soaring spirit. Finally, we'll reach Florence's political center, dotted with monuments of that proud time. Great and rich as this city is, it's easily covered on foot. Our walk through the top sights is one kilometer long (about a half mile), running from the Accademia (home of Michelangelo's *David*), past the Duomo to the Arno River.

Orientation

Accademia (Michelangelo's *David*): €6.50 (plus €1.55 reservation fee), Tue–Sun 8:15–18:50, until 22:00 on holidays and maybe on summer Sat, closed Mon (last entry 30 min before closing, Via Ricasoli 60, tel. 055-238-8609). No photos or videos are allowed. The museum is most crowded on Sun, Tue, and the first thing in the morning. It's easy to reserve ahead; see page 23 for details.

The Duomo (cathedral): Free, Mon–Wed and Fri–Sat 10:00–17:00 (except first Sat of month 10:00–15:30), Thu 10:00–15:30, Sun 13:30–16:45. Tel. 055-230-2885.

Climbing the **dome** costs €6 (Mon–Sat 8:30–19:00 except first Sat of month 8:30–15:20, closed Sun; enter from outside church on south or river side, arrive by 8:30 to avoid a long wait in line).

Giotto's Tower: €6, daily 8:30–19:30, last entry 40 min before closing.

Baptistery: €3, interior open Mon–Sat 12:00–19:00, Sun 8:30–14:00. The famous bronze doors are on the outside so they're always "open" (viewable) and free. The original panels are in the Duomo Museum.

Getting There: The Accademia is a 15-minute walk from the train station or a 10-minute walk from the cathedral (head northeast on Via Ricasoli). Taxis are reasonable.

Information: The nearest TI is on Via Cavour, two blocks from the Accademia (pick up update of current museum hours). Two fine bookshops are across the street from the Accademia. WCs are in the Accademia, in cafés along the walk, and in the Palazzo Vecchio (second courtyard).

Length of Our Tour: Three hours.

Photography: Photos are prohibited in the Accademia. In churches and other museums, photos without a flash are generally OK.

Cuisine Art: You'll find cafés, self-service cafeterias, bars, and gelato shops along the route.

Starring: Michelangelo, Brunelleschi, and Ghiberti.

The Tour Begins

The Duomo, the cathedral with the distinctive red dome, is the center of Florence and the orientation point for this walk. If you ever get lost, home's the dome.

We'll start at the Accademia (2.5 long blocks north of the Duomo), though you could easily start at the Duomo and visit the Accademia later.

• *Head to the Accademia. If there's a line, as you shuffle your way along, notice the perspective tricks on the walls of the ticket room.*

THE FLORENTINE RENAISSANCE (1400–1550)

In the 13th and 14th centuries, Florence was a powerful center of banking, trading, and textile manufacturing. The resulting wealth fertilized the cultural soil. Then came the Black Plague in 1348. A third of the population died, but the infrastructure remained strong, and the city rebuilt stronger than ever. Led by Florence's chief family, the art-crazy Medicis, and with the natural aggressive and creative spirit of the Florentines, it's no wonder the long-awaited Renaissance finally took root here.

The Renaissance—the "rebirth" of Greek and Roman culture that swept across Europe—started around 1400 and lasted about 150 years. In politics, the Renaissance meant democracy. In science, a renewed interest in exploring nature. The general mood was optimistic and "humanistic," with a confidence in the power of the individual.

In medieval times, poverty and ignorance had made life "nasty, brutish, and short" (for lack of a better cliché). The church was the people's opiate, and their lives were only a preparation for a happier time in heaven after leaving this miserable vale of tears.

Medieval art was the church's servant. The most noble art

Renaissance Walk Overview

form was architecture—churches themselves—and other arts were considered most worthwhile if they embellished the house of God. Painting and sculpture were narrative and symbolic, to tell Bible stories to the devout and illiterate masses.

As prosperity rose in Florence, so did people's confidence in life and themselves. Middle-class craftsmen, merchants, and bankers felt they could control their own destinies, rather than being at the whim of nature. They found much in common with the ancient Greeks and Romans, who valued logic and reason above superstition and blind faith.

Renaissance art was a return to the realism and balance of Greek and Roman sculpture and architecture. Domes and round arches replaced Gothic spires and pointed arches. In painting and sculpture, Renaissance artists strove for realism. Merging art and science, they used mathematics, the laws of perspective, and direct observation of nature to paint the world on canvas.

This was not an anti-Christian movement, though it was a logical and scientific age. Artists saw themselves as an extension of God's creative powers. At times, the church even supported the Renaissance and commissioned many of its greatest works. Raphael frescoed Plato and Aristotle on the walls of the Vatican. But for the first time in Europe since Roman times, we also find rich laymen who wanted art simply for art's sake.

After 1,000 years of waiting, the smoldering fires of Europe's classical heritage burst into flame in Florence.

The Accademia—Michelangelo's *David*

Start with the ultimate. When you look into the eyes of Michelangelo's *David*, you're looking into the eyes of Renaissance Man. This 4.5-meter (14-foot) symbol of divine victory over evil represents a new century and a whole new Renaissance outlook. This is the age of Columbus and classicism, Galileo and Gutenberg, Luther and Leonardo—of Florence and the Renaissance.

In 1501, Michelangelo Buonarotti, age 26, a Florentine, was commissioned to carve a large-scale work for the Duomo. He was given a block of marble that other sculptors had rejected as too

tall, shallow, and flawed to be of any value. But Michelangelo picked up his hammer and chisel, knocked a knot off what became David's heart, and started to work.

The figure comes from a Bible story. The Israelites, God's chosen people, are surrounded by barbarian warriors led by a brutish giant named Goliath, who challenges the Israelites to send out someone to fight him. Everyone is afraid except one young shepherd boy—David. Armed only with a sling, which he throws over his shoulder, David cradles some stones in his other hand and heads out to face Goliath.

The statue captures David as he's sizing up his enemy. He stands relaxed but alert, leaning on one leg in a classical pose. In his powerful right hand, he fondles the stones he'll fling at the

More Michelangelo

If you're a fan of Earth's greatest sculptor, you won't leave
Florence until there's a check next to each of these:
• Bargello Museum: several Michelangelo sculptures
  (✪ see Bargello Tour on page 74).
• Duomo Museum: another moving *Pietà* (✪ see Duomo
  Museum Tour on page 98).
• Medici Chapels: The *Night* and *Day* statues, plus others
  done for the Medici tomb (located at Church of San
  Lorenzo; ✪ see Medici Chapels Tour on page 114).
• Laurentian Library: Michelangelo designed the entrance
  staircase (located at Church of San Lorenzo).
• Uffizi: a rare Michelangelo painting (✪ see Uffizi
  Gallery Tour on page 52).
• Michelangelo's House, Casa Buonarotti: a house
  Michelangelo once owned, at Via Ghibellina 70,
  with some early works.
• Church of Santa Croce: Michelangelo's tomb.

giant. His gaze is steady—searching with intense concentration,
but also with extreme confidence. Michelangelo has caught the
precise moment when David is saying to himself, "I can take
this guy."

David is a symbol of Renaissance optimism. He's no brute
but a civilized, thinking individual who can grapple with and overcome problems. He needs no armor, only his God-given body and
wits. Look at his right hand, with the raised veins and strong,
relaxed fingers. Many complained that it was too big and overde-
veloped. But this is the hand of a man with the strength of God.
No mere boy could slay the giant. But David, powered by God,
could...and did.

Originally, the statue was commissioned to go on top of the
church, but the people loved it so much they put it next to the
Palazzo Vecchio on the main square, where a copy stands today.
(If the relationship between the head and body seems a bit out
of proportion, it's because Michelangelo designed it to be seen
"correctly" from far below the rooftop of a church.) Note the
crack in David's left arm where it was broken off during a riot
near the Palazzo Vecchio.

Florentines could identify with David. Like David, they
considered themselves God-blessed underdogs fighting their city-
state rivals. In a deeper sense, they were civilized Renaissance

people slaying the ugly giant of medieval superstition, pessimism, and oppression.

• *Hang around awhile. Eavesdrop on tour guides.* David *stands under a wonderful Renaissance-style dome. Lining the hall leading up to* David *are other statues by Michelangelo—his* Prisoners (Prigioni), St. Matthew, *and a* Pietà.

Prisoners

These unfinished figures seem to be fighting to free themselves from the stone.
Michelangelo believed the sculptor was
a tool of God, not creating but simply
revealing the powerful and beautiful figures He put in the marble. Michelangelo's
job was to chip away the excess, to reveal.
He needed to be in tune with God's will,
and whenever the spirit came upon him,
Michelangelo worked in a frenzy, often
for days on end without sleep.

The *Prisoners* give us a glimpse of this
fitful process, showing the restless energy
of someone possessed, struggling against
the rock that binds him. Michelangelo was
known to shout at his figures in frustration: "Speak!" You can still
see the grooves from the chisel, and you can picture Michelangelo
hacking away in a cloud of dust. Unlike most sculptors, who built
a model and then marked up their block of marble to know where to
chip, Michelangelo always worked freehand, starting from the front
and working back. These figures emerge from the stone (as his colleague Vasari put it) "as though surfacing from a pool of water."

The *Prisoners* were designed for the never-completed tomb of
Pope Julius II (who also commissioned the Sistine Chapel ceiling).
Michelangelo may have abandoned them simply because the project itself petered out, but he may have deliberately left them unfinished. Having satisfied himself that he'd accomplished what he set
out to do, and seeing no point in polishing them into their shiny,
finished state, he went on to a new project.

As you study the *Prisoners*, notice Michelangelo's love and
understanding of the human body. His greatest days were spent
sketching the muscular, tanned, and sweating bodies of the workers
in the Carrara marble quarries. Here, the prisoners' heads and
faces are the least-developed part—they "speak" with their poses.
Comparing these restless, claustrophobic *Prisoners* with the serene
and confident *David* gives an idea of the sheer emotional range in
Michelangelo's work.

Pietà (by Michelangelo or, more likely, by his followers)

In the unfinished *Pietà* (the threesome closest to *David*), they struggle to hold up the sagging body of Christ. Michelangelo emphasizes the heaviness of Jesus' dead body, driving home the point that this divine being suffered a very human death. Christ's massive arm is almost the size of his bent and broken legs. By stretching his body—if he stood up he'd be over two meters (7 feet) tall—its weight is exaggerated.

• *Leaving the Accademia (possibly after a look at its paintings, including 2 Botticellis), turn left and walk 5–10 minutes to the Duomo down Via Ricasoli. The dome of the Duomo is best viewed just to the right of the facade on the corner of the pedestrian-only street (see map on page 43).*

The Duomo—Florence's Cathedral

The dome of Florence's cathedral helped kick off the Florentine Renaissance by inspiring other artists to great things. The big but unremarkable church itself (nicknamed the Duomo) is Gothic, built in the Middle Ages by architects who left it unfinished.

Think of the confidence of the age: The Duomo was built with a big hole in its roof awaiting a dome. This was before the technology to span it with a dome was available. No matter. They knew that someone soon could handle the challenge. In the 1400s, the architect Brunelleschi was called on to finish the job. Brunel-

leschi capped the church Roman-style—with a tall, self-supporting dome as grand as the ancient Pantheon, which he had studied intensely.

He used a dome within a dome. First, he built the grand white skeletal ribs, which you can see, then he filled them in with interlocking bricks in a herring-bone pattern. The dome grew upward igloo-style, supporting itself as it proceeded from the base. When they reached the top, Brunelleschi arched the ribs in and "nailed" them in place with the lantern. His dome, built in only 14 years, was the largest since Rome's Pantheon.

Brunelleschi's dome was the wonder of the age, the model for many domes to follow, from St. Peter's to the U.S. Capitol. People gave it the ultimate compliment, saying "not even the ancients could have done it." Michelangelo, setting out to construct the dome of St. Peter's, drew inspiration from the dome of Florence. He said, "I'll make its sister...bigger, but not more beautiful."

The Duomo

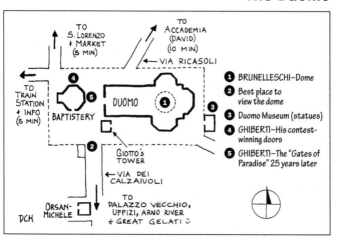

The church's facade looks old, but is actually only from 1870. Its "retro" look captures the feel of the original medieval facade— green, white, and pink marble sheets that cover the brick construction; Gothic (pointed) arches; and three horizontal stories decorated with mosaics and statues. Still, the facade is generally ridiculed. (While one of this book's authors thinks it's the most beautiful church facade this side of heaven, the other one naively agrees with those who call it "the cathedral in pajamas.") The inside of the church is worth a walk only for its coolness and a look at how bare the terrible flood of 1966 left it.

Bell Tower ("Giotto's Tower")

You can climb the dome, but the bell tower (to the right of the facade) is easier and rewards you with a view of the dome. Giotto, like any good Renaissance genius, wore several artistic hats. Considered the father of modern painting, he designed this 82-meter (270-foot) tall bell tower for the Duomo two centuries before the age of Michelangelo. In his day, Giotto was called the ugliest man to ever walk the streets of Florence, but he left the city what, in our day, many call the most beautiful bell tower in all of Europe.

The bell tower served as a sculpture

gallery for Renaissance artists—notice Donatello's four prophets on the side that faces out (west side). These are copies, but the originals are at the wonderful Duomo Museum, just behind the church (✪ see Duomo Museum Tour on page 98). In it you'll also get a close-up look at Brunelleschi's wooden model of his dome, Ghiberti's doors (described below), and a late *Pietà* by Michelangelo.

• *The Baptistery is the small octagonal building in front of the church.*

Baptistery, Dome, and Ghiberti's Bronze Doors

Florence's Baptistery is dear to the soul of the city. The locals, eager to link themselves to the classical past, believed (wrongly) that this was a Roman building. It *is* Florence's oldest building (11th century). Most festivals and parades either started or ended here. Go inside (for a modest €3 fee) for a fine example of pre-Renaissance mosaic art (1200s–1300s) in the Byzantine style.

The Last Judgment on the ceiling gives us a glimpse of the medieval worldview. Life was a preparation for the afterlife, when

you would be judged good or bad, black or white, with no in-between. Christ, peaceful and reassuring, would bless you with heaven (on His right hand) or send you to hell (below Christ's double-jointed left hand, at the base of the ceiling) to be tortured by demons and gnashed between the teeth of monsters. This hellish scene looks like something right out of the *Inferno* by Dante... who was dipped into the baptismal waters right here.

The Baptistery's bronze doors bring us out of the Middle Ages and into the Renaissance. Florence had great civic spirit, with different guilds and merchant groups embellishing their city with great art. For the Baptistery's north doors (on the right side as you face the Baptistery with the Duomo at your back), the city staged a competition in 1401 for the commission. All the greats entered, and 25-year-old Lorenzo Ghiberti won easily, beating out heavyweights such as Donatello and Brunelleschi (who, having lost the Baptistery gig, was free to go to Rome, study the Pantheon, and later design the Duomo's dome). The original

entries of Brunelleschi and Ghiberti are in the Bargello, where you can judge them for yourself.

Later, in 1425, Ghiberti was given another commission, for the east doors (facing the church), and this time there was literally no contest. The bronze panels of these doors (the ones with the crowd of tourists looking on) added a whole new dimension to art—depth. Michelangelo said these doors were fit to be the gates of Paradise. (These panels are copies. The originals are in the nearby Duomo Museum.) Here we see how the Renaissance was a merging of art and science. Realism was in, and Renaissance artists used math, illusion, and dissection to get it.

In the "Jacob and Esau" panel (just above eye level on the left), receding arches, floor tiles, and banisters create a background for

a realistic scene. The figures in the foreground stand and move like real people, telling the Bible story with human details. Amazingly, this spacious, three-dimensional scene is made from bronze only a few centimeters deep.

Ghiberti spent 27 years (1425–1452) working on these panels. That's him in the center of the door frame, atop the second row of panels—the head on the left with the shiny male-pattern baldness.

• *Facing the Duomo, turn right onto the pedestrian-only street that runs south from here towards the Arno River.*

Via dei Calzaiuoli

The pedestrian-only Via dei Calzaiuoli was a major street of the ancient Roman grid plan that became Florence. Throughout the city's history, this street has connected the religious center (where we are now) with the political center (where we're heading), a five-minute walk away. In the last decade, traffic jams have been replaced by potted plants, and this is a pleasant place to stroll, people-watch, window-shop, catch the drips on your gelato cone, and wonder why American cities can't become pedestrian-friendly.

Two blocks down, look right on Via degli Speziali to see a triumphal arch celebrating the unification of Italy. In ancient

Roman times, the Piazza della Repubblica where the arch stands was the city center. If you're in the mood for some of the world's best edible art, you're in the right place. Drop by one of several nearby ice cream parlors for a cup of gelato. *Perche non?* (Why not?) *Gelati* tips: *Nostra Produzione* and *Produzione Propia* mean gelato is made on the premises. Also, gelato displayed in metal tins, rather than the normal white plastic, indicates it's likely to be homemade. A simple cone or cup will do; avoid fancy, rip-off €10 "tourist specials." Look at the price list, which usually shows pictures of scoops (one, two, or three) followed by the pertinent price.

Orsanmichele Church—Florence's Medieval Roots

The Orsanmichele Church (at the intersection with Via dei Tavolini) provides an interesting look at Florentine values. It's a combo church/granary. Originally this was an open loggia (covered porch) with a huge warehouse upstairs to store grain to feed the city during sieges. The arches of the loggia were artfully filled in and the building gained a new purpose—as a church.

Circle the church. Each niche was filled with an important statue. In Gothic times, statues were set deeply in the niches, simply embellishing the house of God. Here we see statues (as restless as man on the verge of the Renaissance) stepping out from the protection of the church. Donatello's *St. Mark* (along Via del Calzaiuoli, at northeast corner of church), done in the new Renaissance style, has a classical *contraposto* (weight on one foot) stance. And even though he's fully clothed, you know his anatomy is fully there.

Donatello's great *St. George* (at northwest corner of church) is alert, stepping out, announcing the new age with its new outlook. (The original statue is in the Bargello.) Compare

this Renaissance-style *St. George* with Nanni's smaller-scale, deeply set, and less sophisticated *Four Saints* statue to its left.

Below some of the niches, you'll find the symbols of the various guilds and groups that paid for the art, such as the carpenters and masons guild below the *Four Saints*. At the back of the church is the headquarters of the wool merchants' guild—another rich old

Orsanmichele Church

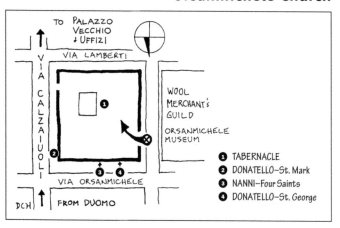

TO PALAZZO VECCHIO & UFFIZI

VIA LAMBERTI

VIA CALZAIUOLI

WOOL MERCHANT'S GUILD

ORSANMICHELE MUSEUM

VIA ORSANMICHELE

DCH ↑ FROM DUOMO

❶ TABERNACLE
❷ DONATELLO—St. Mark
❸ NANNI—Four Saints
❹ DONATELLO—St. George

building rotting in the shadow of the Florentine superstars (contains the Orsanmichele Museum, see page 28, opposite entrance to Orsanmichele Church).

The entrance to the church is around back, one short block off Via del Calzaiuoli. Step inside and find the pillars with spouts in them (over half a meter—two feet—off the ground) for delivering grain from the storage rooms upstairs. Stand before the Gothic tabernacle. Notice its medieval elegance, color, and disinterest in depth and realism. This is a wonderfully medieval scene—Florence in 1350. Remember the candlelit medieval atmosphere that surrounds this altarpiece as you view similar altarpieces out of context in the Uffizi Gallery.

• *Dante's House (Casa di Dante, see page 124) and Florence's best collection of sculpture, the Bargello (see page 74), are a few blocks east down Via del Tavolini. But let's continue down the mall 50 more meters, to the huge and historic square.*

Palazzo Vecchio—Florence's Political Center

The main civic center of Florence is dominated by the Palazzo Vecchio, the Uffizi Gallery, and the marble greatness of old Florence littering the cobbles. This square still vibrates with the echoes of Florence's past—executions, riots, and great celebrations. Today, it's a tourist's world with pigeons, postcards, horse buggies, and tired hubbies.

Before you towers the Palazzo Vecchio, the Medicis' palatial city hall—a fortress designed to contain riches and survive the many riots that went with local politics. The windows are just beyond the

Palazzo Vecchio

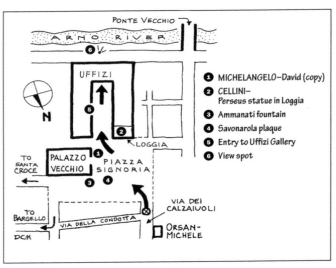

MICHELANGELO–David (copy)
CELLINI–
Perseus statue in Loggia
Ammanati fountain
Savonarola plaque
Entry to Uffizi Gallery
View spot

reach of angry stones, the tower was a handy lookout post, and justice was doled out sternly on this square. Michelangelo's *David* once stood (until 1873) where the replica stands today. The original *David*, damaged in a riot (when a bench thrown out of a palace window knocked its left arm off), was moved indoors for its protection.

To the right is the loggia, once a forum for public debate, perfect for a city that prided itself on its democratic traditions. But later, when the Medicis figured good art was more desirable than free speech, it was turned into an outdoor sculpture gallery. Notice the squirming Florentine themes—conquest, dominance, rapes, and severed heads. Benvenuto Cellini's *Perseus*, the Loggia's most noteworthy piece, shows the Greek hero who decapitated the snake-headed Medusa. They say Medusa was so ugly she turned humans who looked at her to stone—though one of this book's authors thinks she's kinda cute.

• *Step past the replica* David *through the front door into the Palazzo Vecchio's courtyard.*

This palace replaced the Bargello as Florence's civic center. You're surrounded by art for art's sake—a statue frivolously marking the courtyard's center, and ornate walls and columns. Such luxury was a big change 500 years ago.

• *The Palazzo is not worth touring on a quick visit like ours (but if you want to, see page 30; WC in second courtyard). Return to the square*

and head right as you leave the palace door, over towards the big fountain of Neptune by Ammanati that Florentines (including Michelangelo) consider a huge waste of marble— though one of this book's authors…

Find the round bronze plaque in the cobbles 10 steps in front of the fountain.

Savonarola

The Medici family was briefly thrown from power by an austere monk named Savonarola, who made Florence a constitutional republic. He organized huge rallies here on the square where he preached, lit by roaring bonfires. While children sang hymns, the devout brought their rich "vanities" (such as paintings, musical instruments, and playing cards) and threw them into the flames.

But not everyone wanted a return to the medieval past. The Medicis fought back, and arrested Savonarola. For two days, they tortured him, trying unsuccessfully to persuade him to see their side of things. Finally, on the very spot where Savonarola's followers had built bonfires of vanities, the monk was burned. The bronze plaque, engraved in Italian (*"Qui dove…"*), reads: "Here, Girolamo Savonarola and his Dominican brothers were hanged and burned" in the year "MCCCCXCVIII" (1498).

• *Stay cool, we have 100 meters to go. Follow the gaze of the fake* David *into the courtyard of the two-toned horseshoe-shaped building…*

Uffizi Courtyard—The Renaissance Hall of Fame

The top floor of this building, known as the *uffizi* ("offices") during Medici days, is filled with the greatest collection of Florentine painting anywhere. It's one of Europe's top four or five galleries (see next chapter).

The Uffizi courtyard, filled with merchants and hustling young artists, is watched over by statues of the great figures of the Renaissance. Tourists zero in on the visual accomplishments of the Renaissance—they show best on a postcard. Let's pay

tribute to the nonvisual Renaissance as well as we wander through Florence's Hall of Fame.

• *Stroll down the left side of the courtyard from the Palazzo Vecchio to the river, noticing...*

1. **Lorenzo the Magnificent,** excelling in everything but modesty, he set the tone for the Renaissance—great art patron and cunning broker of power;

2. **Giotto,** the first great modern painter (he died from the plague; this statue looks posthumous);

3. **Donatello,** the sculptor who served as a role model for Michelangelo, holds a hammer and chisel;

4. **Leonardo da Vinci,** scientist, sculptor, musician, engineer...and not a bad painter either;

5. **Michelangelo,** pondering the universe and/or stifling a belch;

6. **Dante,** with the laurel-leaf crown and lyre of a poet, says "I am the father of the Italian language." He was the first Italian to write a popular work (*The Divine Comedy*) in non-Latin, using the Florentine dialect, which soon became "Italian" throughout the country;

7. the poet **Petrarch** wears laurel leaves from Greece, a robe from Rome, and a belt from Wal-Mart;

8. **Boccaccio,** author of *The Decameron,* stories told to pass the time during the 1348 Black Plague;

9. the devious-looking **Machiavelli** is hatching a plot—his book, *The Prince,* taught that the end justifies the means, paving the way for the slick and cunning "Machiavellian" politics of today;

10. **Amerigo Vespucci** (in the corner), an explorer who gave his name to a fledgling New World; and finally,

11. **Galileo Galilei** (in the other corner), with the home-made telescope he used to spot the moons of Jupiter.

• *Finish our walk at the Arno River, overlooking the Ponte Vecchio.*

Ponte Vecchio

Before you is the Ponte Vecchio (Old Bridge). A bridge has spanned this narrowest part of the Arno since Roman times. But while Rome "Fell," Florence really didn't, remaining a bustling trade center along the Arno.

In the 1500s, the Medicis booted out the bridge's butchers

and tanners and installed the gold- and silversmiths you'll see and be tempted by today. (A fine bust of the greatest goldsmith, Cellini, graces the central point of the bridge.) Notice the Medicis' protected and  elevated passageway that led from the Palazzo Vecchio through the Uffizi, across the Ponte Vecchio, and up to the immense Pitti Palace, four blocks beyond the bridge. During World War II, the local German commander was instructed to blow the bridge up. But even some Nazis appreciate history—he blew up the buildings at either end, leaving the bridge impassable but intact. *Grazie.*

UFFIZI
GALLERY
TOUR

In the Renaissance, Florentine artists rediscovered the beauty of the natural world. Medieval art had been symbolic, telling Bible stories. Realism didn't matter. But Renaissance people saw the beauty of God in nature and the human body. They used math and science to capture the natural world on canvas as realistically as possible.

The Uffizi Gallery (pron: oo-FEEDZ-ee) has the greatest overall collection anywhere of Italian painting. We'll trace the rise of realism and savor the optimistic spirit that marked the Renaissance.

> *My eyes love things that are fair,*
> *and my soul for salvation cries.*
> *But neither will to Heaven rise*
> *unless the sight of Beauty lifts them there.*
> —Michelangelo

Orientation

Cost: €8, plus 1.55 for optional but recommended reservation fee.

Hours: Tue–Sun 8:15–18:50, until 22:00 on holidays and maybe summer Sat (last entry 45 min before closing), closed Mon.

Reservations: Avoid the two-hour peak-season midday wait by making a telephone reservation. It's easy, slick, and costs only €1.55. Dial 055-294-883 during office hours (Mon–Fri 8:30–18:30, Sat 8:30–12:30) at least a day before your visit and ideally at least a few days in advance for a better selection. With the help of an English-speaking operator, you'll quickly get an entry slot (15-min window) and a six-digit confirmation number. Off-season, it can be possible to get a same-day reservation. Using the same phone number, you can reserve in advance for the Accademia, Bargello, Medici Chapels, and Pitti Palace; of these, the Accademia has the worst lines.

Uffizi Gallery Overview

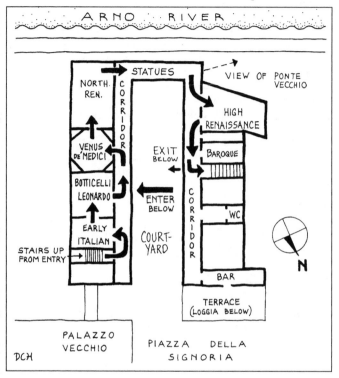

After you've booked your reservation, go to the Uffizi at your appointed time. Walk briskly past the 200-meter-long line—pondering the IQ of this gang—to the special entrance for those with reservations (labeled in English "Entrance for Reservations Only"), give your number, pay (cash only), and scoot right in.

If you haven't called ahead, there are other ways to make an Uffizi reservation (sometimes for the same day, depending on luck and availability): (1) buy Uffizi tickets with reservations at the Museum of San Marco, the Museum of Precious Stones, or another Florence sight; (2) try booking directly at the Uffizi (ask the clerk who stands at the reservations entrance if you can reserve in person; he may direct you to the ticket office); or (3) take a tour of the museum with Walking Tours of Florence (booking required, see "Tours and Talks," page 21).

Getting There: It's on the Arno River between Palazzo Vecchio and Ponte Vecchio, a 15-minute walk from the train station.

Information: To study ahead, see www.arca.net/uffizi/. In Florence, you can get cheap Uffizi guidebooks sold by street vendors. At the Uffizi, there's nothing inside—until the exit, where you'll find a decent card and bookshop (stop by the shop first, public entry opposite museum entrance). There's only one WC; it's on the top floor, near the snack bar and the stairs leading down to the exit.

Length of Our Tour: Two hours.

Cloakroom: At the start, far from the finish.

Cuisine Art: The simple café at the end of the gallery has salads, desserts, fruit cups, and a terrace with a Duomo/Palazzo Vecchio view. A cappuccino here is one of Europe's great $2 treats.

Photography: Cameras without flash are OK.

Starring: Botticelli, Venus, Raphael, Giotto, Titian, Leonardo, and Michelangelo.

The Ascent

• *Buy your ticket, then take the elevator or walk up the four long flights of the monumental staircase to the top floor. Your brain should be fully aerated from the hike up. Past the ticket-taker, look out the window.*

The U-ffizi is U-shaped, running around the courtyard. The entire collection is on this one floor, displayed chronologically. This left wing contains Florentine painting from medieval to Renaissance times. The right wing (which you can see across the courtyard) has Roman and Venetian High Renaissance, the Baroque that followed, and a café terrace facing the Duomo. Connecting the two wings is a short corridor with sculpture. We'll concentrate on the Uffizi's forte, the Florentine section, then get a taste of the art it inspired.

• *Down the hall, enter the first door on the left and face Giotto's giant* Madonna and Child.

MEDIEVAL—WHEN ART WAS AS FLAT AS THE WORLD (1200–1400)

Giotto—*Madonna and Child (Madonna col Bambino Gesu, Santi e Angeli)*

For the Florentines, "realism" meant "three-dimensional." In this room, pre-Renaissance paintings show the slow process of learning to paint a 3-D world on a 2-D canvas.

Before concentrating on the Giotto, look at some others in the room. First look at the crucifixion on your right (as you face the Giotto). This was medieval 3-D—paint a crude two-dimensional work...then physically tilt the head forward. Nice try.

The three similar-looking Madonna-and-Bambinos in this

Giotto and Medieval Art

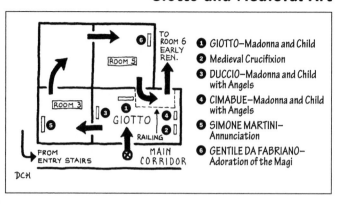

1 GIOTTO–Madonna and Child
2 Medieval Crucifixion
3 DUCCIO–Madonna and Child with Angels
4 CIMABUE–Madonna and Child with Angels
5 SIMONE MARTINI–Annunciation
6 GENTILE DA FABRIANO–Adoration of the Magi

room were all painted within a few decades of each other around the year 1300. The one on the left (as you face Giotto), by Duccio, is the most medieval and two-dimensional. There's no background. The angels are just stacked one on top of the other, floating in a gold never-never land. Mary's throne is crudely drawn—the left side is at a three-quarters angle while the right is practically straight on. Mary herself is a wispy cardboard-cutout figure seemingly floating just above the throne.

On the opposite wall, Cimabue's is a vast improvement. The large throne creates an illusion of depth. Mary's foot actually sticks out toward us. Still, the angels are stacked like sardines, serving as a pair of heavenly bookends.

Now let's look at the Giotto (pron: JOT-oh). Giotto creates a space and fills it. Like a set designer, he builds a three-dimensional

"stage"—the canopied throne—then peoples it with real beings. We know the throne has depth because there are angels in front of it and prophets behind. The steps leading up to it give even more depth. But the real triumph here is Mary herself—big and monumental, like a statue. Beneath her robe, she has a real live body—her knees and breasts stick out at us. This three-dimensionality was revolutionary in its day, a taste of the Renaissance a century before it began.

Giotto was one of the first "famous" artists. In the Middle Ages, artists were mostly unglamorous craftsmen, like carpenters or cable-TV repairmen. They cranked out generic art and could have signed their work with a bar code. Giotto was the first to be recognized as a genius, a unique individual. He died in a plague that devastated Florence. If there had been no plague, would the Renaissance have started 100 years earlier? No.

• *Enter Room 3, to the left of Giotto.*

Simone Martini—*Annunciation* (*Annunciazione con I Santi Ansano e Giulitta*)

After Giotto's spasm of Renaissance-style realism, painting returned to two-dimensionality for the rest of the 1300s. But several medieval artists (including this one from Siena) eased Florence into the Renaissance.

Martini boils things down to the basic figures needed to get the message across: (1) The angel appears to sternly tell (2) Mary that she'll be the mother of Jesus. In the center is (3) a vase of lilies,

a symbol to tell us Mary is pure. Above is the (4) Holy Spirit as a dove about to descend on her. If the symbols aren't enough to get the message across, Martini has spelled it right out for us in Latin: "*Ave Gratia Plena* ... Hail, favored one, the Lord is with you." Mary doesn't look exactly pleased as punch.

This is not a three-dimensional work. The point was not to recreate reality but to teach religion, especially to the illiterate masses. This isn't a beautiful Mary or even a real Mary. She's a generic woman without distinctive features. We know she's pure—not from her face but only because of the halo and symbolic flowers. Before the Renaissance, artists didn't care about the beauty of individual people.

Martini's *Annunciation* has medieval features you'll see in many of the paintings in the next few rooms: (1) religious subject, (2) gold background, (3) two-dimensionality, and (4) meticulous detail.

• *Pass through the next room, full of golden altarpieces, stopping at the far end of Room 5.*

Gentile da Fabriano—*Adoration of the Magi* (*Adorazione dei Magi*)

Look at the incredible detail of the Three Kings' costumes, the fine horses, the cow in the cave. The canvas is filled from top to

bottom with realistic details—but it's far from realistic. While the Magi worship Jesus in the foreground, their return trip home dangles over their heads in the "background."

This is a textbook example of the International Gothic style popular with Europe's aristocrats in the early 1400s: well-dressed, elegant people in a color-ful, design-oriented setting. The religious subject is just an excuse to paint secular luxuries like brocade-pattern clothes and jewelry. And the scene's background and foreground are compressed together to create an overall design that's pleasing to the eye.

Such exquisite detail work raises the question: Was Renais-sance three-dimensionality truly an improvement over Gothic, or simply a different style?

• *Exit to your right and hang a U-turn left into Room 6.*

EARLY RENAISSANCE (MID-1400s)

Uccello—*The Battle of San Romano (La Battaglia di S. Romano)*

In the 1400s, painters worked out the prob-lems of painting real-istically. They used mathematics to create the illusion of three-dimensionality and learned how to paint the human body.

Paolo Uccello almost literally went crazy trying to conquer the problem of perspective. He was a man obsessed with the three dimensions (thank God he was born before Einstein discovered one more). This canvas is not so much a piece of art as an exercise in perspec-tive. Uccello (pron: oo-CHEL-loh) has challenged himself with every possible problem.

The broken lances at left set up a 3-D "grid" in which to place this crowded scene. The fallen horses and soldiers are experiments in "foreshortening"—shortening the things that are farther away from us to create the illusion of distance. Some of the figures are definitely A-plus material, like the fallen gray horse in the center and the white horse at right walking away. But some are more

Early Renaissance

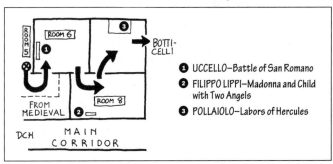

ROOMS 5-6 ROOM 6 →BOTTI-
CELLI

FROM MEDIEVAL

ROOM 8

DCH   MAIN CORRIDOR

❶ UCCELLO—Battle of San Romano
❷ FILIPPO LIPPI—Madonna and Child with Two Angels
❸ POLLAIOLO—Labors of Hercules

like B-minus work—the kicking red horse's legs look like ham hocks at this angle, and the fallen soldier at far right would only be child-sized if he stood up.

And then there's the D-minus "Are-you-on-drugs?" work. The converging hedges in the background create a nice illusion of a distant hillside maybe 75 meters (250 feet) away. So what are those soldiers the size of the foreground figures doing there? And jumping the hedge, is that rabbit 12 meters (40 feet) tall? Uccello got so wrapped up in three-dimensionality he kind of lost...perspective.

• *Enter Room 8.*

Fra Filippo Lippi—*Madonna and Child with Two Angels (Madonna col Bambino e Due Angeli)*

Compare this Mary with the generic female in Martini's *Annunciation.* We don't need the wispy halo over her head to tell us she's

holy—she radiates sweetness and light from her divine face. Heavenly beauty is expressed by a physically beautiful woman.

Fra (Brother) Lippi, an orphan raised as a monk, lived a less-than-monkish life. He lived with a nun who bore him two children. He spent his entire life searching for the perfect Virgin. Through his studio passed Florence's prettiest girls, many of whom decorate the walls here in this room.

Lippi painted idealized beauty, but his models were real flesh-and-blood human beings. You could look through all the thousands of paintings from the Middle Ages and not find anything so human as the mischievous face of one of Lippi's little angel boys.

• *Enter Room 9, with two small works by Pollaiolo in the glass case between the windows.*

Pollaiolo—*Labors of Hercules (Fatiche di Ercole)*

While Uccello worked on perspective, Pollaiolo studied anatomy. In medieval times, dissection of corpses was a sin and a crime (the two were one then), a desecration of the human body, which was the temple of God. But Pollaiolo was willing to sell his soul to the devil for artistic knowledge. He dissected.

These two small panels are experiments in painting anatomy. The poses are the wildest imaginable—to show how the muscles twist and tighten, yes, but also to please International Gothic fans with a graceful linear design.

There's something funny about this room that I can't put my finger on... I've got it—no Madonnas. Not one.

We've seen how Early Renaissance artists worked to conquer reality. Now let's see the fruits of their work, the flowering of Florence's Renaissance.

• *Enter the large Botticelli room and take a seat.*

FLORENCE—THE RENAISSANCE BLOSSOMS (1450–1500)

Florence in 1450 was in a firenz-y of activity. There was a can-do spirit of optimism in the air, led by prosperous merchants and bankers and a strong middle class. The government was reasonably democratic, and Florentines saw themselves as citizens of a strong Republic like ancient Rome. Their civic pride showed in the public monuments and artworks they built. Man was leaving the protection of the church to stand on his own two feet.

Lorenzo de Medici, head of the powerful Medici family, epitomized this new humanistic spirit. Strong, decisive, handsome, poetic, athletic, sensitive, charismatic, intelligent, brave, clean, and reverent, Lorenzo was a true Renaissance Man, deserving of the nickname he went by—"the Magnificent." He gathered Florence's best and brightest around him for evening wine and

The Renaissance Blooms

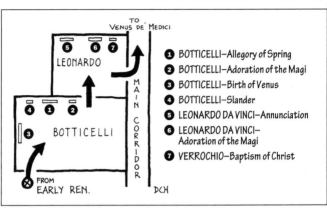

TO
VENUS DE MEDICI

LEONARDO

BOTTICELLI

MAIN CORRIDOR

FROM
EARLY REN.

DCH

❶ BOTTICELLI—Allegory of Spring
❷ BOTTICELLI—Adoration of the Magi
❸ BOTTICELLI—Birth of Venus
❹ BOTTICELLI—Slander
❺ LEONARDO DA VINCI—Annunciation
❻ LEONARDO DA VINCI—Adoration of the Magi
❼ VERROCHIO—Baptism of Christ

discussions of great ideas. One of this circle was the painter Botticelli (pron: bot-i-CHEL-ee).

Botticelli—*Allegory of Spring (Allegoria dell Primavera)*

It's springtime in a citrus grove. The winds of spring blow in (Mr. Blue at right) causing Flora to sprout flowers from her lips. Meanwhile, the figure of Spring walks by, spreading flowers from her dress. At the left are Mercury and the Three Graces, dancing a delicate maypole dance. The Graces may be symbolic of the three forms of love—love of beauty, love of people, and sexual love, suggested by the raised intertwined fingers. (They forgot love of peanut butter on toast.) In the center stands Venus, the Greek goddess of love. Above her flies a blindfolded Cupid, happily shooting his arrows of love without worrying who they'll hit.

Here is the Renaissance in its first bloom, its "springtime" of innocence. Madonna is out, Venus is in. Adam and Eve hiding their nakedness are out, glorious flesh is in. This is a return to the pre-Christian pagan world of classical  Greece, where things of the flesh are not sinful. But this is certainly no orgy—just fresh-faced innocence and playfulness.

Botticelli has painted a scene of exquisite beauty. The lines

of the bodies, especially of the Graces in their see-through night-ies, have pleasing, S-like curves. The faces are idealized but have real human features. There's a look of thoughtfulness and even melancholy in the faces—as though everyone knows that the innocence of spring must soon pass.
• *Look at the next painting to the right.*

Botticelli—*Adoration of the Magi (Adorazione dei Magi)*

Here's the rat pack of confident young Florentines who reveled in the optimistic pagan spirit—even in a religious scene. Botticelli included himself among the adorers, looking vain in the yellow robe at far right. Lorenzo's the Magnificent-looking guy at the far left.

Botticelli—*Birth of Venus (Nascita di Venere)*

According to myth, Venus was born from the foam of a wave. Still only half awake, this fragile newborn beauty is kept afloat on a clam shell while the winds come to blow her to shore, where her handmaiden waits to cover her. The pose is the same S-curve of classical statues (as we'll soon see). Botticelli's pastel colors make the world itself seem fresh and newly born.

This is the purest expression of Renaissance beauty. Venus' naked body is not sensual but innocent. Botticelli thought that physical beauty was a way of appreciating God. Remember Michelangelo's poem: souls will never ascend to Heaven "...until the sight of Beauty lifts them there."

The details show Botticelli's love of the natural world— Venus' windblown hair, the translucent skin, the braided hair of her handmaiden, the slight ripple of the wind's chest muscles,

and the flowers tumbling in the slowest of slow motions, suspended like musical notes, caught at the peak of their brief but beautiful life.

Mr. and Mrs. Wind intertwine— notice her hands clasped around his body. Their hair, wings, and robes mingle like the wind. But what happened to those splayed toes?

• *"Venus on the Half-shell" (as many tourists call this) is one of the masterpieces of Western art. Take some time with it. Then find the small canvas on the wall to the right, near* La Primavera.

Botticelli—*Slander (La Calumnia)*

The spring of Florence's Renaissance had to end. Lorenzo died young. The economy faltered. Into town rode the monk Savonarola, preaching medieval hellfire and damnation for those who embraced the "pagan" Renaissance spirit. "Down, down with all gold and decoration," he roared. "Down where the body is food for the worms." He presided over huge bonfires, where the people threw in their fine clothes, jewelry, pagan books . . . and paintings.

Slander spells the end of the Florentine Renaissance. The setting is classic Brunelleschian architecture, but look what's taking place beneath those stately arches. These aren't proud Renaissance Men and Women but a ragtag, medieval-looking bunch, squatters in an abandoned hall of justice. Here in this chaotic Court of Thieves, the accusations fly and everyone is condemned. The naked man pleads for mercy but the hooded black figure, a symbol of his execution, turns away. Once-proud Venus—straight out of *The Birth of Venus*—looks up to heaven as if to ask "What has happened to us?" The classical statues in their niches look on in disbelief.

Botticelli listened to Savonarola. He burned some of his own paintings and changed his tune. The last works of his life were darker, more somber, and pessimistic of humanity.

The German poet Heine said, "When they start by burning books, they'll end by burning people." Savonarola, after four short years of power, was burned on his own bonfire in the Piazza della Signoria, but by then the city was in shambles. The first flowering of the Renaissance was over.

• *Enter the next room.*

Leonardo da Vinci—*Annunciation*

A scientist, architect, engineer, musician, and painter, Leonardo was a true Renaissance Man. He worked at his own pace rather than to please an employer, so he often left works unfinished. The two in this room aren't his best, but even a lesser Leonardo is enough to put a

museum on the map, and they're definitely worth a look.

Think back to Martini's *Annunciation* to realize how much more natural, relaxed, and realistic Leonardo's version is. He's taken a miraculous event—an angel appearing out of the blue—and made it seem almost commonplace. He constructs a beautifully landscaped "stage" and puts his characters in it. Gabriel has walked up to Mary and now kneels on one knee like an ambassador, saluting her. See how relaxed his other hand is, draped over his knee. Mary, who's been reading, looks up with a gesture of surprise and curiosity. Leonardo has taken a religious scene and presented it in a very human way.

Look at the bricks on the right wall. If you extended lines from them, the lines would all converge at the center of the painting, the distant blue mountain. Same with the edge of the sarcophagus and the railing. Subconsciously, this subtle touch creates a feeling of balance, order, and spaciousness.

Leonardo—*Adoration of the Magi* (unfinished)
This painting may still be under restoration when you visit.

Leonardo's human insight is even more apparent here. The poor kings are amazed at the Christ child—even afraid of him. They scurry around like chimps around fire. This work is as agitated as the *Annunciation* is calm, giving us an idea of Leonardo's range. Leonardo was pioneering a new era of painting, showing not just the outer features but the inner personality.

The next painting to the right, *Baptism of Christ*, is by Verrochio, Leonardo's teacher. Legend has it that Leonardo painted the angel on the far left when he was only 14 years old. When Verrochio saw that some kid had painted an angel better than he ever would...he hung up his brush for good.

Florence saw the first blossoming of the Renaissance. But when the cultural climate turned chilly, artists flew south to warmer climes. The Renaissance shifted to Rome.

• *Exit into the main corridor. Breathe. Sit. Admire the ceiling. Look out the window. See you in five.*

Back already? Now continue down the corridor and turn left into the octagonal Venus de' Medici *room (they only allow 25 people in at a time). If you skip this because there's a line, you'll also be missing the next five rooms, which include masterpieces by Cranach, Dürer, Memling, Holbein, Giorgione, and others.*

CLASSICAL SCULPTURE

If the Renaissance was the foundation of the modern world, the foundation of the Renaissance was classical sculpture. Sculptors, painters, and poets alike turned for inspiration to these ancient Greek and Roman works as the epitome of balance, 3-D, human anatomy, and beauty.

The Venus de' Medici, or *Medici Venus (Venere de' Medici),* ancient Greece

Is this pose familiar? Botticelli's *Birth of Venus* has the same position of the arms, the same S-curved body and the same lifting of the right leg. A copy of this statue stood in Lorenzo the Magnificent's garden, where Botticelli used to hang out. This one is a Roman copy of the lost original by the great Greek sculptor Praxiteles. The *Medici Venus* is a balanced, harmonious, serene statue from Greece's "Golden Age," when balance was admired in every aspect of life.

Perhaps more than any other work of art, this statue has been the epitome of both ideal beauty and sexuality. In the 18th and 19th centuries, sex was "dirty," so the sex drive of cultured aristocrats was channeled into a love of pure beauty. Wealthy sons and daughters of Europe's aristocrats made the pilgrimage to the Uffizi to complete their classical education... where they swooned in ecstasy before the cold beauty of this goddess of love.

Louis XIV had a bronze copy made. Napoleon stole her away to Paris for himself. And in Philadelphia in the 1800s, a copy had to be kept under lock and key to prevent the innocent from catching the Venere-al disease. At first, it may be difficult for us to appreciate such passionate love of art, but if any generation knows the power of sex to sell something—be it art or underarm deodorant—it's ours.

Classical Sculpture and Northern Renaissance

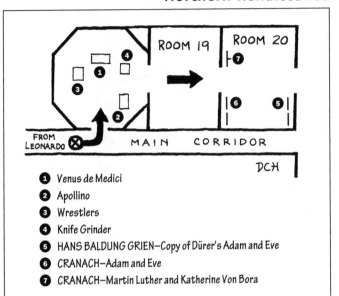

1. Venus de Medici
2. Apollino
3. Wrestlers
4. Knife Grinder
5. HANS BALDUNG GRIEN—Copy of Dürer's Adam and Eve
6. CRANACH—Adam and Eve
7. CRANACH—Martin Luther and Katherine Von Bora

The Other Statues

Venus de Medici's male counterpart is on the right, facing Venus. *Apollino* (a.k.a. "Venus with a Penis") is also by the master of smooth, cool lines: Praxiteles.

The other works are later Greek (Hellenistic), when quiet balance was replaced by violent motion and emotion. *The Wrestlers* to the left of Venus is a study in anatomy and twisted limbs— like Pollaiolo's paintings a thousand years later.

The drama of *The Knife Grinder* to the right of Venus stems from the off-stage action—he's sharpening the knife to flay a man alive.

• *Exit the octagonal room and pass through Room 19 into Room 20.*

NORTHERN RENAISSANCE

Hans Baldung Grien—Copy of Dürer's *Adam and Eve*

The warm spirit of the Renaissance blew north into Germany. Albrecht Dürer (1471–1528), the famous German engraver, traveled to Venice, where he fell in love with all things Italian. Returning home, he painted the First Couple in the Italian style—

full-bodied, muscular
(check out Adam's abs and
Eve's knees), "carved"
with strong shading, fresh-
faced, and innocent in
their earthly Paradise.

This copy by Hans
Baldung Grien of Dürer's
original (now in the Prado)
was a training exercise. Like
many of Europe's artists—
including Michelangelo and
Raphael—Baldung Grien
learned technique by study-
ing Dürer's meticulous
engravings, spread by the
newly invented printing press.

Lucas Cranach—*Adam and Eve*

Eve sashays forward, with heavy-lidded eyes, to offer the for-
bidden fruit. Adam stretches to display himself and his foliage
to Eve. The two canvases are linked by smoldering eye contact,
as Man and Woman awaken to their own nakedness. The Garden
of Eden is about to be rocked by new ideas that are both liberating
and troubling.

Though the German Lucas Cranach (1472–1553) occasionally dabbled in the "Italian style," he chose to portray his Adam

and Eve in the now-retro look
of International Gothic.

They are slimmer than
Dürer's, smoother, more
S-shaped, elegant, graceful,
shapely, and erotic, with the
dainty pinkies of refined aristocrats signing Cranach's paycheck.

Though life-sized, this
Adam and Eve are not lifelike,
not monumental, not full-
bodied or muscular, and are
not placed in a real-world
landscape with distant perspectives. Even so, Cranach was
very much a man of the Renaissance, a friend of Martin Luther,
and a champion of humanism.

Lucas Cranach—*Martin Luther*

Martin Luther—German monk, fiery orator, and religious whistle-blower—sparked a century of European wars by speaking out against the Catholic Church.

Luther (1483–1546) lived a turbulent life. In early adulthood, the newly ordained priest suffered a severe personal crisis of faith, before finally emerging "born again." In 1517, he openly protested against church corruption and was excommunicated. Defying both the pope and the emperor, he lived on the run as an outlaw, watching as his ideas sparked peasant riots. He still found time to translate the New Testament from Latin to modern German, write hymns such as "A Mighty Fortress," and spar with the humanist Erasmus and fellow-Reformer Zwingli.

Now 46 years old, Martin Luther is easing out of the fast lane. Recently married to an ex-nun, he has traded his monk's habit for street clothes, bought a house, had several kids...and has clearly been enjoying his wife's home cooking and home-brewed beer.

Lucas Cranach—*Katherine von Bora* (Luther's wife)

When "Katie" decided to leave her convent, the famous Martin Luther agreed to help find her a husband. She rejected his nominees, saying she'd marry no one...except Luther himself. In 1525, the 42-year-old ex-priest married the 26-year-old ex-nun "to please my father and annoy the pope." Martin turned his checkbook over to "my lord Katie," who also ran the family farm, raised their six children and 11 adopted orphans, and hosted Martin's circle of friends (including Cranach) at loud, chatty dinner parties.

• *Pass through the next couple of rooms, exiting to a great view of the Arno. Stroll through the sculpture wing.*

The Sculpture Wing

A hundred years ago, no one even looked at Botticelli—they came to the Uffizi to see the sculpture collection. Why isn't the sculpture as famous now? They're copies.

• *There are benches at the other end of the wing with a superb view.*

View of the Arno

Enjoy Florence's best view of the Arno and Ponte Vecchio. You can also see the red-tiled roof of the Vasari Corridor, the "secret" passage connecting the Palazzo Vecchio, Uffizi, Ponte Vecchio, and Pitti Palace on the other

side of the river (not visible from here)—a kilometer in all. This was a private walkway, wallpapered in great art, for the Medici family's commute from home to work.

As you appreciate the view (best at sunset), remember that it's this sort of pleasure that Renaissance painters wanted you to get from their paintings. For them, a canvas was a window you looked through to see the wide world.

We're headed down the home stretch now. If your little U-feetsies are killing you and it feels like torture, remind yourself it's a pleasant torture and smile . . . like the statue next to you.

• *In the far corridor, turn left into the first room (#25) and grab a blast of cold from the air-conditioner vent on the floor to the left.*

HIGH RENAISSANCE—MICHELANGELO, RAPHAEL, TITIAN (1500–1550)

Michelangelo—*Holy Family (Sacra Famiglia)*
This is the only completed easel painting by the greatest sculptor in history. Florentine painters were sculptors with brushes. This shows it. Instead of a painting, it's more like three clusters of statues with some clothes painted on.

The main subject is the holy family—Mary, Joseph, and baby Jesus—and in the background are two groups of nudes looking like classical statues. The background represents the old pagan world, while Jesus in the foreground is the new age of Christianity. The figure of young John the Baptist at right is the link between the two.

This is a "peasant" Mary, with a plain face and sunburned arms. Michelangelo shows her from a very unflattering angle—we're looking up her nostrils. But Michelangelo

High Renaissance

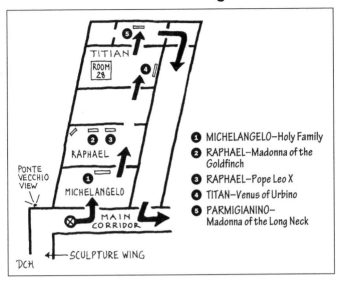

1 MICHELANGELO–Holy Family
2 RAPHAEL–Madonna of the Goldfinch
3 RAPHAEL–Pope Leo X
4 TITAN–Venus of Urbino
5 PARMIGIANINO– Madonna of the Long Neck

himself was an ugly man, and he was among the first artists to recognize the beauty in everyday people.

Michelangelo was a Florentine—in fact he was like an adopted son of the Medicis, who recognized his talent—but much of his greatest work was done in Rome as part of the Pope's face-lift of the city. We can see here some of the techniques he used on the Sistine Chapel ceiling that revolutionized painting—monumental figures, dramatic angles (we're looking up Mary's nose), accentuated, rippling muscles, and bright, clashing colors (all the more apparent since both this work and the Sistine have been recently cleaned). These added an element of dramatic tension lacking in the graceful work of Leonardo and Botticelli.

Michelangelo painted this for Angelo Doni for 70 ducats. When the painting was delivered, Doni tried to talk Michelangelo down to 40. Proud Michelangelo took the painting away and would not sell it until the man finally agreed to pay double... 140 ducats.
• *Enter Room 26.*

Raphael (Raffaello Sanzo)—*Madonna of the Goldfinch (La Madonna del Cardellino)*

Raphael (pron: roff-eye-ELL) brings Mary and Bambino down from their gold never-never land and into the real world of trees, water, and sky. He gives baby Jesus (right) and John the Baptist a

realistic, human playfulness. It's a tender scene painted with warm colors and a hazy background that matches the golden skin of the children.

Raphael perfected his craft in Florence, following the graceful style of Leonardo. In typical Leonardo fashion, this group of Mary, John the Baptist, and Jesus is arranged in the shape of a pyramid, with Mary's head at the peak.

The two halves of the painting balance perfectly. Draw a line down the middle, through Mary's nose and down through her knee. John the Baptist on the left is balanced by Jesus on the right. Even the trees in the background balance each other, left and right. These things aren't immediately noticeable, but they help create the subconscious feelings of balance and order that reinforce the atmosphere of maternal security in this domestic scene—pure Renaissance.

Raphael—*Leo X and Cardinals (Leone X con i Cardinali)*

Raphael was called to Rome at the same time as Michelangelo, working next door while Michelangelo did the Sistine ceiling. Raphael peeked in from time to time, learning from Michelangelo's monumental, dramatic figures. His later work is grittier and more realistic than the idealized, graceful, and "Leonardo-esque" Madonna.

Pope Leo is big, like a Michelangelo statue. And Raphael captures some of the seamier side of Vatican life in the cardinals' eyes—shrewd, suspicious, and somewhat cynical. With Raphael, the photographic realism pursued by painters ever since Giotto was finally achieved.

The Florentine Renaissance ended in 1520 with the death of Raphael. Raphael (see his self-portrait to the left of the Madonna) is considered both the culmination and conclusion of the Renaissance. The realism, balance, and humanism we associate with the Renaissance are all found in Raphael's work. He combined the grace of Leonardo with the power of Michelangelo. With his death, the Renaissance shifted again—to Venice.

• *Pass through the next room and enter Room 28.*

Six Degrees of Leo X

This sophisticated, luxury-loving pope was at the center of an international, Renaissance world that spread across Europe. He crossed paths with many of the Renaissance Men of his generation. Based on the theory that any two people are linked by only "six degrees of separation," let's link Leo X with the actor Kevin Bacon:

- **Leo X's** father was **Lorenzo the Magnificent,** patron of **Botticelli** and **Leonardo.**
- When **Leo X** was age 13, his family took in 13-year-old **Michelangelo.**
- **Michelangelo** inspired **Raphael,** who was later hired by **Leo X.**
- **Raphael** exchanged masterpieces with fellow genius **Albrecht Dürer,** who was personally converted by **Martin Luther** (who was friends with **Lucas Cranach**), who was excommunicated by...**Leo X.**
- **Leo X** was portrayed in the movie *The Agony and the Ecstasy,* which starred **Charlton Heston,** who was in *Planet of the Apes* with **Burgess Meredith,** who was in *Rocky* with **Sylvester Stallone**...who ultimately connects with...**Kevin Bacon.**

Titian (Tiziano)—*Venus of Urbino* (*La Venere di Urbino*)

Compare this Venus with Botticelli's newly hatched Venus and you get a good idea of the difference between the Florentine and Venetian Renaissance. Botticelli's was pure, innocent, and otherworldly. Titian's should have a staple in her belly button. This isn't a Venus, it's a centerfold—with no purpose but to please the eye and other organs. While Botticelli's allegorical Venus is a message, this is a massage.

Titian and his fellow Venetians took the pagan spirit pioneered in Florence and carried it to its logical hedonistic conclusion. Using bright, rich colors, they captured the luxurious life of happy-go-lucky Venice.

While Raphael's *Madonna of the Goldfinch* was balanced with a figure on the left and one on the right, Titian balances his painting in a different way—with color. The canvas is split down the middle by the curtain. The left half is dark, the right half warmer. The two halves are connected by a diagonal slash of luminous gold—the nude woman. The girl in the background is trying to find her some clothes.

By the way, visitors from centuries past also panted in front of this Venus. The poet Byron called it *"the* Venus." With her sensual skin, hey-sailor look, and suggestively placed hand, she must have left them blithering idiots.

• *Find the n-n-n-next painting.*

Parmigianino—*Madonna of the Long Neck (Madonna dal Collo Lungo)*

Raphael, Michelangelo, Leonardo, and Titian mastered reality. They could place any scene onto a canvas with photographic accuracy. How could future artists top that?

"Mannerists" such as Parmigianino tried by going beyond realism, exaggerating it for effect. Using brighter colors and twisting poses (two techniques explored by Michelangelo), they created scenes more elegant and more exciting than real life.

By stretching the neck of his Madonna, Parmigianino (pron: like the cheese) gives her an unnatural swanlike beauty. She has the same pose and position of hands as Botticelli's Venus and the *Venus de' Medici*. Her body forms an arcing S-curve— down her neck as far as her elbow, then back the other way along Jesus' body to her knee, then down to her foot. The baby Jesus seems to be blissfully gliding down this slippery slide of sheer beauty.

In the Uffizi, we've seen many images of female beauty: from ancient goddesses to medieval Madonnas to wicked Eves, from Botticelli's pristine nymphs to Michelangelo's peasant Mary, from Raphael's Madonna-and-baby to Titian's babe. Their physical beauty expresses different aspects of the human spirit.

• *Pass through several rooms, returning to the main corridor.*

The Rest of the Uffizi

As art moved into the Baroque period, artists took Renaissance realism and exaggerated it still more—more beautiful, more emotional, or more dramatic. There's lots of great stuff in the following rooms, and I'd especially recommend Rembrandt's *Self-Portrait*, the enormous canvases of Rubens, and the shocking ultra-realism of Caravaggio's *Bacchus* and *Abraham Sacrificing Isaac*.
• *But first, head to the end of the corridor for a true aesthetic experience.*

The Little Cappuccin Monk (Cappuccino)

This drinkable art form, born in Italy, is now enjoyed all over the world. It's called *The Little Cappuccin Monk* because the coffee's frothy light-and-dark-brown foam looks like the two-toned cowls of the Cappuccin order. Drink it on the terrace in the shadow of the towering Palazzo Vecchio and argue the philosophy of Marx and Hegel—was the Renaissance an economic phenomenon or a spiritual one? *Salute.*

BARGELLO
TOUR

The Renaissance began with sculpture. The great Florentine painters were "sculptors with brushes." You can see the birth of this revolution of 3-D in the Bargello (pron. bar-JEL-oh), which boasts the best collection of Florentine sculpture. It's a small, uncrowded museum and a pleasant break from the intensity of the rest of Florence.

Orientation

Cost: €4.

Hours: Daily 8:15–13:50 but closed first, third, and fifth Sun and second and fourth Mon of each month. Last entry 30 minutes before closing.

Getting There: It's located at Via del Proconsolo 4, a three-minute walk northeast of the Uffizi. Facing the Palazzo Vecchio, go behind the Palazzo and turn left. Look for a rustic brick building with a spire that looks like a baby Palazzo Vecchio. If lost ask, "DOH-vay bar-JEL-oh?"

Information: Nothing in English. Tel. 055-238-8606.

Length of Our Tour: One hour.

Cuisine Art: Inexpensive bars and cafés await in the surrounding streets.

Photography: Cameras without flash are OK.

Starring: Michelangelo, Donatello, Brunelleschi, Ghiberti, and four different *Davids*.

SCULPTURE IN FLORENCE

• *Buy your ticket and take a seat in the courtyard.*

The Bargello, built in 1255, was Florence's city hall. The heavy fortifications tell us that politics in medieval Florence had its occupational hazards. After the administration shifted to the larger Palazzo Vecchio, this became a police station (*bargello*) and then a prison.

The Bargello, a three-story rectangular building, surrounds this cool and peaceful courtyard. The best statues are found in two rooms—one on the ground floor at the foot of the outdoor staircase and another one flight up, directly above it. We'll proceed logically in a chrono kind of way, from Donatello to Verrochio to Michelangelo.

But first, meander around this courtyard and get a feel for sculpture in general and rocks in particular. Sculpture is a much more robust art form than painting. Think of the engineering problems alone of moving these stones from a quarry to an artist's studio. Then the sheer physical strength needed to chisel away for hours on end. A sculptor must be powerful yet delicate, controlling the chisel to chip out the smallest details. Think of Michelangelo's approach to sculpting—he wasn't creating a figure but only liberating it from the rock that surrounded it.

If the Renaissance is humanism, then sculpture is the perfect medium to express it in. It shows the human form, standing alone, independent of church, state, or society.

Finally, a viewing note. Every sculpture has an invisible "frame" around it—the stone block it was cut from. Visualizing this frame helps you find the center of the composition.

• *Climb the courtyard staircase to the next floor up and turn right into the large Donatello room. Pause at Donatello's painted bust of* Niccolo de Uzzano.

Donatello—*Niccolo da Uzzano* (c. 1420)

Not an emperor, not a king, not a pope or prince, this is simply one of Florence's leading businessmen, portrayed in the style of an ancient Roman patrician. In the 1400s, when Florence was inventing the Renaissance that all Europe would soon follow, there was an optimistic spirit of democracy that gloried in everyday people. With wrinkles, quizzical look, and bags under the eyes, Donatello has portrayed this man literally wart (left cheek) and all.

Donatello—*An early David* (marble, 1408)

This is the first of several Davids we'll see in the Bargello. His dainty pose makes him a little unsteady on his feet. He's fully

Donatello Room

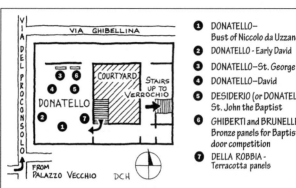

- **❶** DONATELLO– Bust of Niccolo da Uzzano
- **❷** DONATELLO - Early David
- **❸** DONATELLO–St. George
- **❹** DONATELLO–David
- **❺** DESIDERIO (or DONATELLO)– St. John the Baptist
- **❻** GHIBERTI and BRUNELLESCHI– Bronze panels for Baptistery door competition
- **❼** DELLA ROBBIA - Terracotta panels

clothed (but showing some leg through the slit skirt). The generic face and blank, vacant eyes give him the look not of a real man but of an anonymous decoration on a church facade. At age 22, Donatello still had one foot in the old Gothic style. To tell the story of David, Donatello plants a huge rock right in the middle of Goliath's forehead.

• *At the far end of the room,* St. George *stands in a niche in the wall.*

Donatello—*St. George (S. Giorgio,* 1416)
This proud warrior has both feet planted firmly on the ground. A century before Michelangelo sculpted his famous *David,* this was the unofficial symbol of Florence. George, the Christian slayer of dragons, was just the sort of righteous warrior that proud Renaissance Florentines could rally around in their struggles with nearby cities.

He stands on the edge of his niche looking out alertly. He tenses his powerful right hand as he prepares to attack. George has the same relaxed intensity and determination that Michelangelo would use for his *David.* This is the original marble statue. A bronze version stands in its original niche at Orsanmichele Church.

The relief panel below shows George doing what he's been pondering. To George's right, the sketchy arches and trees create the illusion of a distant landscape. Donatello, who apprenticed

Donatello (1386–1466)

Donatello was the first great Renaissance genius, a model for Michelangelo and others. He mastered realism, creating the first truly lifelike statues of people since ancient times. Donatello's work is highly personal. Unlike the ancient Greeks—but like the ancient Romans—he often sculpted real people, not idealized versions of pretty gods and goddesses. Some of these people are downright ugly. In the true spirit of Renaissance humanism, Donatello appreciated the beauty of flesh-and-blood human beings.

Donatello's personality was also a model for later artists. He was moody and irascible, purposely setting himself apart from others in order to concentrate on his sculpting. He developed the role of the "mad genius" that Michelangelo would later perfect.

in Ghiberti's studio, is actually credited with teaching his master how to create 3-D illusions like this.
• *On the floor to your left, you'll find . . .*

Donatello—*David* (bronze, c. 1430)

He's naked. This boyish-approaching-girlish *David* is quite a contrast with his early generic David (and quite different from Michelangelo's powerful version at the Accademia). This smooth-skinned warrior sways gracefully, poking his sword playfully at the severed head of the giant Goliath. He has a *contrapposto* stance similar to Michelangelo's David's, resting his weight on one leg in the classical style, but it gives him a feminine rather than masculine look. Gazing into his coy eyes and at his bulging belly is a very different experience from confronting Michelangelo's tough Renaissance Man.

This *David* paved the way for Michelangelo's. Europe hadn't seen a free-standing male nude like this in a thousand years. In the Middle Ages, the human body was considered a dirty thing, a symbol of man's weakness, something to be covered up in shame. The church prohibited exhibitions of nudity like this one and certainly would never decorate a church with it. But in the

Renaissance, a new class of rich and powerful merchants appeared that bought art for personal enjoyment. This particular statue stood in the courtyard of the Medicis' palace... where Michelangelo, practically an adopted son, grew up admiring it.

As we see the different *Davids* in the Bargello, compare and contrast the artists' styles. How many ways can you slay a giant?
• St. John the Baptist, *done by Donatello or his student, is to the right of the boyish, naked* David.

Desiderio da Settignano (or Donatello)—*St. John the Baptist (S. Giovanni Battista)*

John the Baptist was the wild-eyed, wildcat prophet who lived in the desert preaching, living on bugs 'n' honey, and baptizing Saviors of the World. Donatello, the mad prophet of the coming Renaissance, might have identified with this original eccentric.
• *On the wall next to George, you'll find some bronze relief panels. Don't look at the labels just yet.*

Ghiberti and Brunelleschi—Baptistery Door Competition Entries (two different relief panels, titled *Il Sacrificio di Abramo*)

Some would say these two panels are the first works of the Renaissance. These two versions of *Abraham Sacrificing Isaac* were finalists in the contest held in 1401 to decide who would do the bronze doors of the Baptistery. The contest sparked citywide excitement that evolved into the Renaissance spirit. Lorenzo Ghiberti won, and later did the doors known as the Gates of Paradise. Brunelleschi lost—fortunately for us—

You be the judge. Here are the two finalists for the Baptistery door competition—Ghiberti's and Brunelleschi's. Which do you like the best?

Ghiberti's, on the left, won.

freeing him to design the Duomo's dome. (Teenage Donatello also entered and lost.)

Both artists catch the crucial moment when Abraham, obeying God's orders, prepares to slaughter and burn his only son as a sacrifice. At the last moment—after Abraham passed this test of faith—an angel of God appears to stop the bloodshed.

Is one panel clearly better than the other? Composition: One is integrated and cohesive, the other a balanced knickknack shelf of segments. Human drama: One has bodies and faces that speak. The boy's body is a fine classical nude in itself, so real and vulnerable. Abraham's face is intense and ready to follow God's will. Perspective: An angel zooms in from out of nowhere to save the boy in the nick of time. Detail: One lamb's wool is curlier than the other, one altar is more intricate.

It was obviously a tough call, but Ghiberti's was chosen, perhaps because his goldsmith training made him better suited for the technical end.

• *Along the walls, you'll find several colorful terra-cotta reliefs.*

Luca della Robbia—Terra-cotta Relief Panels

Mary and baby Jesus with accompanying angels look their most serene in these panels by the master of the terra-cotta medium. Polished blue, white, green, and yellow, they have a gentle and feminine look that softens the rough masculine stone of this room.

• *Exit the Donatello room through the same door you entered. Cross to the rooms on the other side of the courtyard. Take your first left, then turn right and climb the red-carpeted stairs to the next floor. At the top of the stairs, turn left, then left again. Verrochio's* David *stands in the center of the room.*

Verrochio—*David* (c. 1470)

Andrea del Verrochio (1435–1488) is best known as the teacher of Leonardo da Vinci, but he was also the premier sculptor between the time of Donatello and Michelangelo. This saucy, impertinent *David* is more masculine than Donatello's, but a far cry from Michelangelo's monumental version. He's definitely the shepherd "boy" described in the Bible. He leans on one leg, not with a firm, commanding stance but a nimble one (especially noticeable from behind). The artist is clearly contrasting the smug smile of the victor with Goliath's "Oh, have I got a headache" expression.

• *Backtrack to the nearby room of glass cases filled with small statues. In the center of the room, you'll find ...*

Pollaiolo—*Hercules and Antaeus* (*Ercole e Anteo*, 1498)

Antaeus was invincible as long as he was in contact with the earth, his mother. So Hercules just picked him up like "The Rock" of the Renaissance and crushed him to death.

More than any early artist from this period, Pollaiolo studied the human body in motion. These figures are not digni-fied Renaissance Men. Yet, in this tan-gled pose of flailing arms and legs, there still is a Renaissance sense of balance—all the motion spins around the center of gravity where their bodies grind together.

• *In the nearby glass cases, you'll see small-scale, alternate versions of the* Mercury *we'll soon see.*

The Rest of the Bargello

Before we lose elevation to visit the final room downstairs, browse around the upper floors. On this floor, you'll find ivories, jewelry, and terra-cotta Mary-baby-and-angel panels by other members of the della Robbia clan. The top floor has armor and medallions.

• *Now descend back to the courtyard on the ground floor. The final room we'll visit is through the door to your left at the bottom of the stairs.*

Lesser Michelangelos

Michelangelo— *Bacchus* (c. 1497)

Bacchus, the god of wine and revelry, raises another cup to his lips, while his little com-panion goes straight for the grapes.

Maybe Michelangelo had a sense of humor after all. Compare this tipsy Greek god of wine with his sturdy, sober *David*, begun two years later. *Bacchus* isn't nearly so muscular, so monumental...or so sure on his feet. Hope he's not driving. The pose, the smooth muscles, the beer belly and swaying hips look more like Dona-tello's boyish *David*.

This was Michelangelo's first major

Ground Floor

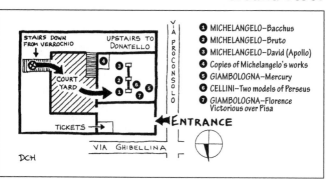

STAIRS DOWN FROM VERROCHIO

UPSTAIRS TO DONATELLO

COURT YARD

TICKETS →

VIA PROCONSOLO

VIA GHIBELLINA

ENTRANCE

DCH

❶ MICHELANGELO—Bacchus
❷ MICHELANGELO—Bruto
❸ MICHELANGELO—David (Apollo)
❹ Copies of Michelangelo's works
❺ GIAMBOLOGNA—Mercury
❻ CELLINI—Two models of Perseus
❼ GIAMBOLOGNA—Florence Victorious over Pisa

commission. He often vacillated between showing man as strong and noble, and as weak and perverse. This isn't the nobility of the classical world, but the decadent side of orgies and indulgence.

• *Just to the left, you'll find . . .*

Michelangelo—*Bruto* (1540)

Another example of the influence of Donatello is this so-ugly-he's-beautiful bust by Michelangelo. His rough intensity gives him the look of a man who has succeeded against all odds, a dignity and heroic quality that would be missing if he were too pretty.

The subject is Brutus, the Roman who, for the love of liberty, murdered his friend and dictator, Julius Caesar (*Et tu . . . ?*). Michelangelo could understand this man's dilemma. He himself had close ties to the Medicis, his adopted family . . . but also to the democratic tradition of his beloved Florence. When the later Medici became corrupt and tyrannical, Michelangelo was torn.

So he gives us two sides of a political assassin. The right profile (the front view) is heroic. But the hidden side, with the drooping mouth and squinting eye, makes him more cunning, sneering, and ominous.

Michelangelo—*David* (also known as *Apollo*, 1530–32)

This restless, twisting man is the last of the *David*s in the Bargello, a good time to think back on those we've seen: Donatello's generic warrior and girlish, gloating *David*; Verrochio's boyish, impish

version; and now this unfinished one by Michelangelo. Michelangelo certainly learned from these earlier versions, even copying certain elements, but what's truly amazing is that his famous *David* in the Accademia is so completely different from the others, so much larger than life in every way.

In the glass cases in the corner are small-scale copies of some of Michelangelo's most famous works. Back near the entrance there's a bust of Michelangelo, capturing his broken nose and brooding nature.

• *On the other side of the room . . .*

Giambologna—*Mercury*

Catch this statue while you can—he's got flowers waiting to be delivered. Despite all the bustle and motion, *Mercury* has a solid Renaissance core: the line of balance that runs straight up the center, from toes to hip to fingertip. His top half leans forward, counterbalanced by his right leg in back. Down at the toes, notice the cupid practicing up for the circus.

Cellini—Models of *Perseus (Perseo)*

The life-size statue of Perseus slaying Medusa, located in the open-air loggia next to Palazzo Vecchio, is cast bronze. Cellini started with these smaller models in wax and bronze to get the difficult process down. When it came time to cast the full-size work, everything was going fine . . . until he realized he didn't have enough metal! He ran around the studio, gathering up pewterware and throwing it in, narrowly avoiding a messterpiece.

Giambologna—*Florence Victorious over Pisa (Firenze Vittoriosa su Pisa)*

This shows the fierce Florentine chauvinism born in an era when Italy's cities struggled for economic and political dominance . . . and Florence won.

MUSEUM OF SAN MARCO
TOUR

Museo di San Marco

Two of Florence's brightest lights lived in the San Marco Monastery, a reminder that the Renaissance was not just a secular phenomenon. At the Museum of San Marco, you'll find these two different expressions of 15th-century Christianity—Fra Angelico's radiant paintings, fusing medieval faith with Renaissance realism, and Savonarola's moral reforms, fusing medieval faith with modern politics.

Orientation

Cost: €4.

Hours: Daily 8:15–13:50, Sat and Sun until 19:00, but closed the first, third, and fifth Sun and the second and fourth Mon of each month.

Getting There: It's on Piazza San Marco, around the corner from the Accademia, and several long blocks northeast of the Duomo (head up Via Ricasoli or Via Cavour).

Information: Tel. 055-238-8608. You can buy Uffizi and Accademia tickets with reservations here.

Length of Our Tour: One hour.

Cuisine Art: Gran Caffè San Marco, on Piazza San Marco, offers pizzas, sandwiches, and pastries (also has self-service section; across the square from the museum entrance).

Starring: Fra Angelico's paintings and Savonarola's living quarters.

Overview

Ground floor: The world's best collection of Fra Angelico paintings.

Upstairs: The monks' cells, decorated by Fra Angelico, including the cell of the most famous resident, Savonarola.

• *Buy ticket and enter the courtyard/cloister.*

San Marco Ground Floor

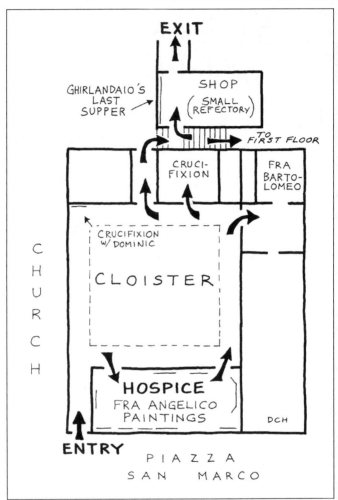

GROUND FLOOR
The Courtyard/Cloister

Renaissance arches frame Gothic cross-vaulting—an apt introduction to a monastery built during the optimistic time (1439) when Renaissance humanism dovetailed with medieval spirituality.

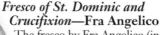

Fresco of St. Dominic and Crucifixion—Fra Angelico

The fresco by Fra Angelico (in the corner of the cloister, straight ahead from the entrance) shows Dominic, the founder of the order, hugging the bloody cross like a groupie adoring a rock star. Monks who lived here—including Fra Angelico, Savonarola, and Fra Bartolomeo—renounced money, sex, ego, and rock music to follow a simple, regimented life, meditating on Christ's ultimate sacrifice.

• *We'll tour the rooms around the courtyard moving counterclockwise. The first one, by the entrance, is the Hospice (Ozpizio).*

The Hospice (Ozpizio), with paintings by Fra Angelico (Beato Angelico)

Fra Angelico (c. 1400–1455)—equal parts monk and painter—fused early-Renaissance technique with medieval spirituality. His works can be admired for their beauty or contemplated as spiritual visions. Browse the room and you'll find serene-faced Marys, Christs, and saints wearing gold halos (often painted on altarpieces), bright primary colors (red-blue-yellow/gold), evenly lit scenes, and meticulous detail—all creating a mystical world of their own, glowing from within like stained-glass windows.

• *Start with the large altarpiece* (The Deposition) *at the near end of the room.*

Deposition of Christ from the Cross (Pala di Santa Trinita)—Fra Angelico

Fra Angelico, trained in medieval religious painting, never closed his eyes to the innovations of the budding Renaissance, using both styles all his life. He'd inherited this altarpiece frame from his former teacher (who painted the pinnacles on top). But he ignored the frame's traditional three-arch (triptych) divisions, boldly "coloring outside the lines" to create a single, realistic scene set in the first great Renaissance landscape.

Christ's body is lowered from the cross, mourned by

haloed women (on the left) and contemporary Florentines (right). There's a clearly defined foreground (the kneeling, curly-headed man and the woman with her back to us), background (the distant city and hills), and middle distance (the trees).

Yes, there are Gothic elements—the altarpiece itself, the halos, the deep-creased robes, and the "body of Christ" being symbolically "displayed" like the communion bread—but it's a truly Renaissance work. Christ's body, kissed by Mary Magdalene, crosses the triptych wall, connecting the women with the central group. The man (in green) lowering Christ bends forward at a strongly foreshortened (difficult to draw) angle.

And the holy scene has been removed from its golden heaven and placed on a lawn, among flowers, trees, cloud masses, real people, and the hillsides of Fiesole overlooking Florence. Fra Angelico, the ascetic monk, refused to renounce one pleasure— his joy in the natural beauty of God's creation.

• *Working counterclockwise around the room, you'll find the following works (among others).*

Triptych of St. Peter the Martyr (Trittico di San Pietro Martire)—Fra Angelico

In this early work, Fra Angelico sets (big) Mary and Child in a gold background flanked by (small) saints standing obediently in their niches. Having recently joined the Dominican community

in Fiesole, young Brother Giovanni (as he was known in his lifetime) now dressed like these famous Dominicans— white robe, blue cape, and tonsured haircut.

Peter the Martyr (next to Mary, with bloody head) exemplified the unbending Domin-ican spirit. Attacked by heretics (see the scene above Peter), he was hacked in the head with a dagger, but died still preaching, writing with his own blood: "*Credo in Deum*" (I believe in God).

• *Continuing counterclockwise...*

Wedding and Funeral (two panels) of the Virgin (Spozialo e Funerali della Vergine)—Fra Angelico

His teenage training was as a miniaturist, so even these small *predella* panels (part of a larger altarpiece) are surprisingly realistic—the folds in the clothes, the gold-brocade hemlines, and the precisely outlined

people, as though etched in glass. Notice the Renaissance perspective tricks he was exploring, setting the wedding in front of receding buildings and the funeral among candles that get shorter at the back of the scene.

Last Judgment (Giudizio Universale)—Fra Angelico

Despite the Renaissance, Florence in the 1420s was still a city in the Christian universe described by Dante. Hell (to the right) is a hierarchical barbecue where sinners are burned, boiled, and tortured by a minotaur-like Satan, who rules the bottom of the pit. The blessed in Heaven (left) play ring-around-the-rosy with angels. In the center, a row of open tombs creates a 3-D Highway to Hell, stretching ominously to that Final Judgment Day.

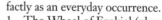

Thirty-five Scenes Painted on Doors of a Silverware Storeroom (Panelli Dell'Armadio degli Argenti)—Fra Angelico and assistants

The first nine scenes in this Life of Christ are by Fra Angelico himself (the rest by assistants). Natural, realistic, and straightforward—like storyboards for a movie—they "show" through action, they don't just "tell" through symbols. (The Latin inscription beneath each panel is redundant.) The miraculous is presented as matter-of-factly as an everyday occurrence.

1. The Wheel of Ezekiel (okay, that's medieval symbolism) prophesies Christ's coming.
2. In the Annunciation, the angel gestures to tell Mary she'll give birth.
3. Newborn Jesus glows, amazing his parents, while timid shepherds sneak a peek.
4. Precocious Jesus splays himself and says, "Cut me."

5. One of the Magi kneels to kiss the babe's foot.
6. In the temple, the tiny baby is dwarfed by elongated priests and columns.
7. Mary and the baby ride, while Joseph carries the luggage.
8. Meanwhile, babies are slaughtered in a jumble of gore, dramatic poses, and agonized faces.
9. The commotion contrasts with the serenity of child Jesus in the temple.

This work by 50-year-old Fra Angelico—master of many styles, famous in Italy, recently returned from a gig in the Vatican—has the fresh, simple, spontaneous storytelling of a children's book.

Lamentation (Compianto sul Cristo morto)—Fra Angelico

The executed Christ, mourned silently by loved ones, was the last thing many condemned prisoners saw during their final night incarcerated in the church where this painting originally hung.

The melancholy mood is understated, suggested by a series of horizontal layers—Christ's body, the line of mourners, the city walls, landscape horizon, layered clouds, and the crossbar. It's as though Christ is being welcomed into peaceful rest, a comforting message from Fra Angelico to the condemned.

"Fra Angelico" (Brother Angelic) is a nickname that describes his reputation for sweetness, humility, and compassion. It's said he couldn't paint a crucifixion without crying. In 1984, he was beatified by Pope John Paul II and made patron of artists.

Altarpiece of the Linen-Drapers (Tabernacolo dei Linaioli)—Fra Angelico

The impressive size and marble frame (by Ghiberti) attest to Fra Angelico's worldly success and collaboration with Renaissance greats. The monumental Mary and Child and the saints on the doors are gold-backed and elegant to please conservative patrons. In the three *predella* panels below, Fra Angelico gets to display his Renaissance chops, showing haloed saints mingling with well-dressed Florentines amid local city- and landscapes. (Find Ghiberti in the left panel, kneeling, in blue.)

• *In the middle of the long wall is the large...*

San Marco Altarpiece (Pala di San Marco)—Fra Angelico

In 1439, Cosimo de' Medici built this monastery, inviting Fra Angelico's Dominican community to move here from Fiesole. Fra Angelico soon became prior (head monk), turning down an offer to be archbishop of Florence.

Cosimo commissioned this painting as the centerpiece of the new church (next door). For the dedication Mass, Fra Angelico theatrically "opens the curtain," revealing a stage set with a distant backdrop of trees, kneeling saints in the foreground, and a crowd gathered around Mary and Child at center stage on a raised, canopied throne. The altarpiece was like a window onto a marvelous world where holies mill about on Earth as naturally as mortals.

Evolution of the *"Sacra Conversazione"*

Fra Angelico (largely) invented what became a common Renaissance theme: Mary and Child surrounded by saints "conversing" informally about holy matters. Four examples in this room show how Fra Angelico, exploring Renaissance techniques, developed the idea over his lifetime.

• *You'll find three of the following four works on the long wall, and the fourth you've seen already.*

Triptych of St. Peter the Martyr (Trittico di San Pietro Martire)

The *Triptych of St. Peter the Martyr*, shown on page 86 (not a true *sacra conversazione*, but included here for contrast), has an unnaturally big Mary flanked by smaller saints in a line. The gold background gives no hint they inhabit the same space, and there is no eye contact in this conversation.

Annalena Altarpiece (Pala d'Annalena)

In the *Annalena Altarpiece*—considered Florence's first *sacra conversazione*—the saints emerge from their niches, gather cautiously in a semicircle, and tentatively acknowledge each other with eyes

and gestures. Everyone's either facing out or in profile, not the natural poses of a true crowd. The background is traditional gold, but now in the form of a curtain hanging behind the throne. Mary and Jesus direct our eye to Mary's brooch, the first in a series of circles radiating out from the center: brooch, halo, canopy arch, circle of saints. Set in a square frame, this painting has the circle-in-a-square composition that marks many *sacra*s.

San Marco Altarpiece (Pala di San Marco)

The *San Marco Altarpiece*, shown on page 89, places the holy saints clearly in the 3-D world we inhabit. The carpet makes a "chessboard" pattern to establish 3-D space (according to the mathematics of perspective laid out in Alberti's then recently published book, *On Painting*). To show just how far we've come from Gothic, Fra Angelico gives us a painting-in-a-painting—a crude, gold-backed crucifixion.

Bosco ai Frati Altarpiece (Pala di Bosco ai Frati)

The *Bosco ai Frati Altarpiece* is Fra Angelico's last great work, and he uses every stylistic arrow in his quiver: detailed friezes of the miniaturist; medieval halos and gold backdrop; monumental, naturally posed figures in the style of Masaccio (especially St. Francis, third from left, with his relaxed *contrapposto*); Alberti-esque per-

spective (established by the floor tiles); and Renaissance love of natural beauty (the trees and sky).

Fra Angelico's bright colors are eye-catching. The gold backdrop sets off the red-pink hand-maidens, which set off Jesus' pale skin. The deep blue of Mary's dress, frosted with a precious gold hem, turns out at her feet to show a swath of the green inner lining, suggesting the 3-D body within.

Despite Renaissance realism, Fra Angelico creates a world of his own—perfectly lit, with no moody shadows, no dirt, frayed clothing, or imperfection. The faces are certainly realistic, but they express no human emotion. These mortals, through sacrifice and meditation, have risen above the petty passions celebrated by "humanist" painters to achieve a serenity that lights them from within.

• *Leave the Hospice and return to the courtyard. Continue counterclockwise and enter the next set of rooms. The small room on the left has paintings and fresco fragments by Fra Bartolomeo. Working clockwise around the room, you'll find these works by . . .*

Fra Bartolomeo (1473–1517)

Fra Bartolomeo lived and worked in this monastery a generation after the "Angelic" brother. *Ecce Homo* shows the kind of Christ that young, idealistic Dominican monks (like Fra Bartolomeo) adored in their meditations—curly-haired, creamy-faced, dreamy-eyed, bearing the torments of the secular world with humble serenity.

St. Dominic (San Domenico)

St. Dominic holds a finger to his lips—"Shh! We have strict rules in my order." Dominic (c. 1170–1221), a friend of St. Francis of Assisi, formed his rules after seeing the austere *perfecti* (perfect ones) of the heretical Cathar sect of southern France. He figured they could only be converted by someone just as extreme, following Christ's simple, possessionless lifestyle. Nearing 50, Dominic made a 5,500-kilometer (3,400-mile) preaching tour—on foot, carrying his luggage—from Rome to Spain to Paris and back. Dominic is often portrayed with the star of revelation over his head.

St. Thomas Aquinas (San Tommaso d'Aquino)

St. Thomas Aquinas (c. 1225–1274), the intellectual giant of the U. of Paris, used logic and Aristotelian models to defend and explain Christianity (building the hierarchical belief system known as Scholasticism). He's often shown with a heavy build and the sun of knowledge burning in his chest.

Portrait of Savonarola (Ritratto di fra' Girolamo Savonarola)

This is the famous portrait—in profile, hooded, with big nose and clear eyes, gazing intently into the darkness—of the man reviled as the evil opponent of Renaissance goodness. Would it surprise you

to learn that it was Savonarola who inspired Fra Bartolomeo's art? Bartolomeo
was so moved by Savonarola's sermons
that he burned his early nude paintings
(and back issues of *Penthouse*), became
a monk, gave up painting for a few
years...then resurfaced to paint the
simple, sweet frescoes we see here.
• *Return to the courtyard and continue
to the next room, which contains the large
wall fresco...*

Crucifixion with Saints
(Crocifissione dell' Angelico)—Fra Angelico

Shortly after the Fiesole monks moved into their new digs here
(c. 1440), Fra Angelico began decorating the walls with frescoes.
This crucifixion, against a bleak background, is one of more than
20 versions in the monastery of Christ's torture/execution. It was
in this room that naughty monks were examined and judged.

Among the group of hermits,
martyrs, and religious extrem-
ists that surround the cross,
locate Dominic (kneeling
at the foot of the cross, in
Dominican white robe, blue
cape, and tonsured hair, with
star on head), Peter the Martyr
(kneeling in right corner, with
bloody head), and Thomas
Aquinas (standing behind Peter, with fleshy face and sun on chest).

The bell in the room is the original church bell, the one
that rang a warning to Savonarola the night he was arrested.
(The mob was so enraged that they exiled the bell for 10 years.)
• *Head upstairs to the first floor.*

FIRST FLOOR

• *At the top of the stairs, orient from Fra Angelico's* Annunciation
*fresco immediately in front of you. A few steps to the left is a corridor
lined with "cells" (monks' bedrooms) decorated with frescoes by Fra
Angelico. Stretching to the right are more cells (by Fra Angelico and
assistants) and the library, displaying old manuscripts. In the far corner
(not visible from here, reached by circling clockwise) is Savonarola's cell.*

Forty-three cells were decorated in the early 1440s under
Fra Angelico's direction, but many were executed by assistants.
We'll concentrate on his best.

San Marco First Floor

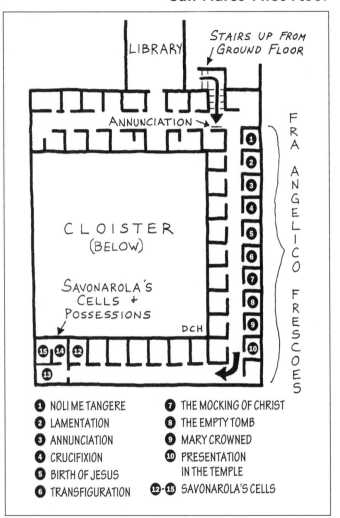

STAIRS UP FROM GROUND FLOOR

LIBRARY

ANNUNCIATION →

FRA ANGELICO FRESCOES

CLOISTER (BELOW)

SAVONAROLA'S CELLS & POSSESSIONS

DCH

❶ NOLI ME TANGERE
❷ LAMENTATION
❸ ANNUNCIATION
❹ CRUCIFIXION
❺ BIRTH OF JESUS
❻ TRANSFIGURATION
❼ THE MOCKING OF CHRIST
❽ THE EMPTY TOMB
❾ MARY CROWNED
❿ PRESENTATION IN THE TEMPLE
⓬-⓯ SAVONAROLA'S CELLS

The Annunciation—**Fra Angelico**

Monks gathered in this corner for common prayers, contemplating Christ's life from beginning (*Annunciation*) to end (the *Crucifixion with St. Dominic*, over your shoulder).

The angel with rainbow wings (sway back and forth and watch them sparkle) greets Mary under an arcade remarkably similar to

the one in the monastery courtyard, literally bringing this scene
home to unimaginative monks.
It was paintings such as this that
made Fra Angelico so famous
that the pope would call him to
paint the Vatican. Yet this, like
the other frescoes here, was
meant only for the private eyes
of humble monks.

• *From* The Annunciation, *take a
few steps to the left and look down
the (east) corridor lined with cells.
The best examples of Fra Angelico's
work are in the 10 cells along the left-hand side.*

Fra Angelico's frescoes
(in monks' cells of the east corridor)

After a long day of prayer, meditation, reading, frugal meals, chop-
ping wood, hauling water, translating Greek, attending Mass, and
more praying—a monk retired to one of these small, bare, lamplit
rooms. His "late-night TV" was programmed by the prior—Fra
Angelico—in the form of a fresco to meditate on before sleep.

Cell #1—*Noli me Tangere* (the first
of 10 rooms on the left-hand side of the
corridor): The resurrected Jesus, appearing as a hoe-carrying gardener, says
"Don't touch me," and awkwardly side-
steps Mary Magdalene's grasp. The flowers and trees represent the blossoming
of new life, and they're about the last
we'll see. Most scenes have stark, bare
backgrounds, to concentrate the monk's
focus on just the essential subject.

Cell #2—*Lamentation*: Christ
and mourners are a reverse image of
the *Lamentation* downstairs. Christ
levitates, not really supported by the
ladies' laps. The colors are muted
grays, browns, and pinks. Dominic
(star on head) stands contemplating,
just as the monk should do by mentally transporting himself there.

Cell #3—*Annunciation:* The painting's arches echo the room's real arch. (And they, in turn, harmoniously "frame" the "arch" of Mary and the angel bending toward each other to talk.) Peter the Martyr (bloody head) looks on.

You can't call these cells a wrap until you've found at least six crosses, three Dominics, two Peters, and a Thomas Aquinas. Ready, go.

Cell #4—*Crucifixion:* That's one. And another Dominic.

Cell #5—*Birth of Jesus:* And there's your second Peter.

Cell #6—*Transfiguration:*
Forsaking Renaissance realism, Fra Angelico emphasizes the miraculous. In an aura of blinding light, Christ spreads his arms cross-like, dazzling the three witnesses at the bottom of the "mountain." He's joined by disembodied heads of prophets, all spinning in a circle echoed by the room's arch.

Cell #7—*The Mocking of Christ:*
From Renaissance realism to Dali surrealism. Dominic, while reading the Passion, conjures an image of Christ—the true king, on a throne with globe and scepter—now blindfolded, spit upon, slapped, and clubbed by . . . a painting of medieval symbols of torment. This must

have been a puzzling riddle from the Master to a novice monk.

Cell #8—*The Empty Tomb:* The worried women are reassured by an angel that "He is risen." Jesus, far away in the clouds, seems annoyed they didn't listen to him.

Cell #9—*Mary Crowned:* . . . while Dominic, Peter, Aquinas, Francis, and others play patty-cake.

Cell #10—*Presentation in the Temple*
• *Continue around the bend—Savonarola's three rooms are at the far end of the corridor.*

Girolamo Savonarola (1452–1498)— His Rooms and Possessions

You'll find a number of Savonarola's possessions scattered about these three rooms (and one back out in the corridor). Browse around while reading about his life.

The **portrait bust** shows the hooded monk whose personal charisma and prophetic fervor led him from humble scholar to celebrity preacher to prior of San Marco to leader of Florence to controversial martyrdom. Reviled as a fanatical, regressive tyrant and praised as a saint, reformer, and champion of democracy, Savonarola was a complex man in turbulent times.

Home-schooled by his Scholastic grandfather, the 30-year-old monk (see his monk's **blue cloak** in the last room in the corridor) was assigned to San Marco (1482) as a lecturer. (See his ecclesiastical folding **chair**—*La sedia del Savonarola*—in the next room.) He was bright, humble . . . and boring. Then, after experiencing divine revelations, he spiced his sermons with prophecies of future events . . . which started coming true. Sermons on Ezekiel, Amos, or Exodus (see his **Bible,** with margin notes) predicted doom for the Medici family, referred in veiled terms to the pope's embezzling and stable of mistresses, and preached hope for a glorious future after city and church were cleansed.

Packed houses heard him rail against the "prostitute church . . . the monster of abomination." Witnesses wrote that "the church echoed with weeping and wailing," and afterward "everyone wandered the city streets dazed and speechless." From his humble **desk,** he corresponded with the worldly pope, the humanist Pico della Mirandola, and fans, such as Lorenzo the Magnificent, who begrudgingly admired his courage.

Lorenzo died, the bankrupt Medicis were exiled, and Florence was invaded by France . . . as Savonarola had prophesied. In the power vacuum, Savonarola was a moderate voice whose personal moral authority was unquestioned (as the simple possessions such as **wool clothes** and **rosary** attest). He proposed a democratic constitution in the old Florentine tradition (see the **relief under the portrait bust**), and city leaders adopted it with Savonarola as head (1494). They cut taxes, reduced street crime, shifted power from rich Medicis to citizens, and even boldly proposed banning Vespas from tourist zones. They also passed strict morality laws (against swearing, blasphemy, gambling, and ostentatious clothes), which were often enforced by gangs of thuggish teenagers.

At the height of the Christian Republic, during Lent of 1497, followers built a huge "bonfire of vanities" on the Piazza della Signoria where they threw wigs, carnival masks, dice, playing cards, musical instruments, and discredited books and paintings.

In 1498, several forces undermined Savonarola's Republic: scheming Medici fans, crop failure, rival cities, a pissed-off pope threatening excommunication for Savonarola and political isolation for Florence, and a public tiring of puritanism. Gangs of opponents (called *Arrabbiati*, Rabid Dogs) battled Savonarola's supporters (the "Weepers"). Meanwhile, Savonarola was slowly easing out of public life, refusing to embroil the church in a lengthy trial, retiring to his routine of study, prayer, and personal austerity; see his **hair-shirt girdle** and **stick (*palo*)** for self-flagellation.

During Lent, a Franciscan monk challenged a Dominican to a public ordeal by fire to prove Savonarola right or wrong. (The righteous one would supposedly survive.) The Franciscan chickened out, but a bloodthirsty mob—with the blessing of city leaders and the pope—marched on San Marco to arrest Savonarola. *Arrabbiati* fought monks with clubs (imagine it in the **courtyard** out the window), while the church bells clanged and the monks shouted, "*Salvum fac populum tuum, Domine!*" ("Save thy people, Lord!") Savonarola was handed over to the authorities in the **library doorway** (back near Fra Angelico's *Annunciation;* see the appropriate *Kiss of Judas* **fresco** in the cell nearby). He was taken to the Palazzo Vecchio, where he was tortured, tried, and sentenced.

On May 23, 1498 (see the painting *Supplizio* **[Torture]** *del Savonarola in Piazza della Signoria*), before a huge crowd in the square in front of the Palazzo Vecchio (where today there's a **memorial plaque** embedded in the pavement in front of the Neptune fountain), Savonarola was publicly  defrocked, then publicly forgiven by a papal emissary. Then he was hanged—not American execution–style, where the neck snaps—but slowly strangled, dangling from a rope, while teenage boys hooted and threw rocks. The crowd looked on the lifeless body of this man who had once captivated their minds, as they lit a pyre under the scaffold. The flames rose up, engulfing the body, when suddenly... his arm shot upward!—like a final blessing or curse—and the terrified crowd stampeded, killing several. His ashes were thrown in the Arno.

Looking out the window onto the San Marco courtyard, ponder the two manifestations of Dominican spirituality—Fra Angelico's humility and Savonarola's moral conscience.

• *To exit, return to the stairway and descend. Take a right at the bottom into a bookshop decorated with a fine Ghirlandaio* Last Supper *fresco, then exit. On the street, turn right, then right again, and you'll see the Duomo.*

DUOMO MUSEUM TOUR

Museo dell' Opera del Duomo

Brunelleschi's dome, Ghiberti's bronze doors, and Donatello's statues—these three define the 1400s in Florence (the "Quattrocento") when the city blossomed and classical arts were reborn. All three are featured at the Duomo Museum...oh yes, and a Michelangelo *Pietà* intended as his sculptural epitaph. While copies now decorate the exteriors of the cathedral, Baptistery, and bell tower, the original sculptured masterpieces of the complex are now restored and displayed safely indoors, filling the Duomo Museum. This newly refurbished museum is a delight that most visitors to Florence overlook.

Orientation

Cost: €6.

Hours: Mon–Sat 9:00–19:30, Sun 9:00–13:40, closed on holidays. Last entry 45 minutes before closing. (This is one of the few museums in Florence open on Monday.)

Getting There: The museum is across the street from the Duomo on the east side, at Via del Proconsolo 9.

Information: Tel. 055-230-2885. If you find all this church art intriguing, look through the open doorway of the Duomo art studio, which has been making and restoring church art since the days of Brunelleschi (a block toward the river from the Duomo at 23a Via dello Studio).

Length of Our Tour: 90 minutes.

Starring: Brunelleschi, Ghiberti, Donatello, and Michelangelo.

GROUND FLOOR—THE MEDIEVAL CATHEDRAL

• *Browse the first few small rooms.*

Roman sarcophagi, Etruscan fragments, a **chronological chart,** and broken **Baptistery statues** attest to the 2,000-year history of Florence's cathedral, Baptistery, and campanile (bell tower, called

Duomo Museum Ground Floor

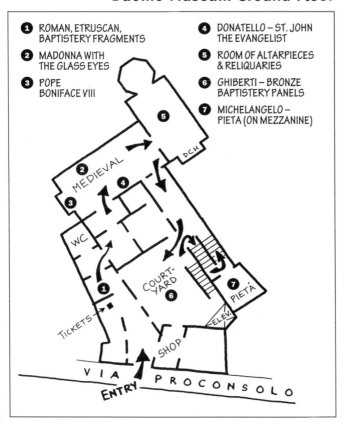

❶ ROMAN, ETRUSCAN, BAPTISTERY FRAGMENTS

❷ MADONNA WITH THE GLASS EYES

❸ POPE BONIFACE VIII

❹ DONATELLO – ST. JOHN THE EVANGELIST

❺ ROOM OF ALTARPIECES & RELIQUARIES

❻ GHIBERTI – BRONZE BAPTISTERY PANELS

❼ MICHELANGELO – PIETA (ON MEZZANINE)

Giotto's Tower). The Baptistery was likely built on the site of a pagan Roman temple. It was flanked by a humble church that, by the 1200s, was not big enough to

contain the exuberant spirit of a city growing rich from the wool trade and banking. In 1296, the cornerstone was laid for a huge church—today's Cathedral, or Duomo—intended to be the biggest in Christendom.

• *The first large room is lined with statues from the original facade (1296–1587). On the long wall, you'll find . . .*

Madonna with the Glass Eyes

The church was dedicated to Mary—starry-eyed over the birth of baby Jesus—who sat, crowned like a chess-set queen, above the main door, framed with a dazzling mosaic halo. She's flanked by

St. Zenobius, Florence's first bishop during Roman times, whose raised hand consecrates the former pagan ground as Christian.

This room recreates the original facade, designed by the church's architect, Arnolfo di Cambio. It looked much like today's colorful neo-Gothic facade—faced with white, pink, and green marble, pointed arches, three horizontal stories, gleaming with gold mosaics, and studded with the statues in this room.

But only the ground story was ever finished, the work stalled by the plague, stylistic debates, and the construction of the cathedral itself. The upper two-thirds remained bare brown brick all through medieval and Renaissance times, until 1587, when the still-incomplete facade was torn down.

Large, Seated Statue of Pope Boniface VIII

Despised by Dante for meddling in politics, this pope paid 3,000 florins to get his image in a box seat on the facade. Though the statue is stylized, it realistically shows his custom-made, extra-tall hat and bony face. (Most of the room's statues are straight-backed to hang on the facade.)

• *On the long wall opposite the Madonna, find . . .*

Donatello—*St. John the Evangelist (San Giovanni Evangelista)*

A hundred years later, di Cambio's medieval facade became a showcase for Renaissance sculptors.

John sits gazing at a distant horizon, his tall head rising high above the massive body. Starting at John's deep-furrowed hemline, the stone gets smoother as you go up, like intelligence rising from the rock. At 22 years old, Donatello (c. 1386–1466) sculpted this just before becoming a celebrity for his Rebirth-inducing statue of *St. George* (original in Bargello, copy on exterior of Orsanmichele Church).

John, the visionary, foresees a new age . . . and the coming Renaissance. The right hand is massive—as relaxed as though it were dangling over the back of a chair, but full of powerful tension. Clearly, this is the hand of Michelangelo's *David*, but a hundred years earlier. (Ciuffagni's *St. Matthew*, nearby, is also a Donatello knockoff.)

Donatello, like most early Renaissance artists, was a blue-collar worker, raised as a workshop apprentice among knuckle-dragging musclemen. He proudly combined physical skill with technical know-how to create beauty (Art + Science = Renaissance Beauty). His statues are thinkers with big hands who can put theory into practice.

• *Enter an adjoining room.*

Room of Altarpieces and Reliquaries

These medieval altarpieces, which once adorned chapels and altars inside the Duomo, show saints and angels suspended in a gold never-never land. In the adjoining room, the ornate reliquaries hold bones and objects of the saints—Peter's chains, Jerome's jawbone, and so on—many bought from a single, slick 14th-century con artist preying on medieval superstition.

In the 1400s, tastes changed, and these symbols of crude, superstitious medievalism were purged from the Duomo and stacked in storage. Soon artists replaced the golden heavenly scenes with flesh-and-blood humans inhabiting the physical world of rocks, trees, and sky...the Renaissance.

• *In the ground-floor courtyard, you'll find...*

Ghiberti—Six Bronze Panels from the Baptistery Doors called the "Gates of Paradise" (1425–1452)

The Renaissance began in 1401 with a citywide competition to build new doors for the Baptistery. Lorenzo Ghiberti (c. 1378–1455) won the job and built the doors (now on the Baptistery's north side), which everyone loved. He then was hired to make another set of doors—these panels—for the main entrance facing the Duomo. These "Gates of Paradise" revolutionized the way Renaissance people saw the world around them.

Of the 10 panels from the Gates of Paradise, the museum displays six, with the rest still being cleaned. (Copies now adorn the Baptistery itself.) Restoration is difficult, because the corrosive oxides gather inside, between the bronze panel and gilding. (See the pitting in the Joseph and Benjamin panel.) The cleaned panels are under glass to protect against natural light, and gassed with nitrogen against oxygen and humidity.

• *Start with Adam and Eve and work counterclockwise.*

Adam and Eve (*La Creazione e Storie di Adamo ed Eva*)

Ghiberti tells several stories in one panel—a common medieval technique—using different thickness in the relief. In the sketchy background (very low relief), God in a bubble conducts the Creation. In the center (a little thicker), Eve springs from Adam's side. Finally, in the lower left (in high relief), an elegantly robed God pulls Adam—as naked as the day he was born—from the mud.

Ghiberti welcomed the innovations of other artists. See the angel flying through an arch (right side). This arch is in very low relief but still looks fully 3-D because it's rendered sideways, using painters' perspective tricks—a relief technique Ghiberti learned from one of his employees, the young Donatello.

Jacob and Esau (*Storie di Giacobbe ed Esau*)

Several stories of the feuding brothers are placed in a single unified setting—an open-air loggia of Brunelleschian arches and tiled pavement. Suddenly, the "background" arches and the space they create are as interesting as the people.

Nearing 50, Lorenzo met young Leon Battista Alberti, who turned him on to the (Brunelleschian) mathematics of linear perspective, changing the course of the later panels. At the center of this panel is the "vanishing point" on the distant horizon, where all the arches and floor tiles converge. This calm center gives us an eye-level reference point for all the figures. Those closest to us are big, clearly defined, and at the bottom of the panel. Distant figures are smaller, fuzzier, and higher up.

Ghiberti has placed us about six meters (20 feet) away from the scene, part of this casual crowd of holy people—some with their backs to us—milling around an arcade.

Joseph *(Storie di Giuseppe e Beniamino)*

With just the depth of a thumbnail, Ghiberti creates a temple in the round inhabited by workers. This round temple wowed Florence. Armed with the rules of perspective, Ghiberti rendered reality with a mathematical precision we don't normally notice in everyday life, when our eyes and mind settle for ballpark estimates. For Florentines, suddenly the world acquired a whole new dimension—depth.

David and Saul

This tangle of soldiers (Israelites fighting Philistines) is very un-Renaissance. Though Ghiberti dabbled in linear perspective, International Gothic remained his favorite style. The many moving figures blend together to form a pattern like silk brocade that is really quite beautiful, and the complexity suggests the confusion of battle.

David beheads Goliath (foreground) rather awkwardly, since both of them are actually facing each other in profile. In fact, Ghiberti's panels show only elements of the coming Renaissance style, with just a few figures at odd angles with extreme foreshortening. In general, they retain a dreamy, elegant, medieval formality.

Labors of Adam, and Cain and Abel *(Il lavoro dei progenitorie e Storie di Caino e Abele)*

On one mountain, we see Cain and Abel offering a sacrifice at the top, Adam waving at the bottom, and the first murder in between. In early panels such as this one, Ghiberti used only a

sketchy landscape as a backdrop for human activities.

Ghiberti, the illegitimate son of a goldsmith, labored all his working life (over 50 years) on the two Baptistery doors. These were major manufacturing jobs, employing a large workshop of artists and artisans for each stage of the process: making the door frames that hold the panels, designing and making models of the panels, casting the design in bronze, gilding the panels (by bathing them in powdered gold dissolved in mercury, then heating until the gold and bronze blended), polishing the panels, mounting them, installing the doors...and signing paychecks for everyone along the way. Ghiberti was as much businessman as artist.

Solomon and the Queen of Sheba

The receding arches stretch into infinity, giving the airy feeling we could see forever. All the arches and stair steps converge at the center of the panel, where the two monarchs meet, uniting their respective peoples. Ghiberti's subject was likely influenced by the warm ecumenical breeze blowing through Florence in 1439, as religious leaders convened here to finally heal the Great Schism between French- and Italian-based popes.

If the Renaissance began in 1401 with Ghiberti's doors, it ended in 1555 with Michelangelo's *Pietà*.

• *From the courtyard, go back inside, then up the old stairs to the first landing.*

Michelangelo—*Pietà* (1547–1555)

Eighty-year-old Michelangelo (1475–1564) was designing his own tomb, with this as the centerpiece. He was depressed by old age, the recent death of his soulmate, and the grim reality that sculpting this statue was writing his own obituary.

The broken body of the crucified Christ is tended by three mourners— Mary his mother (the shadowy figure on our right), Mary Magdalene (on the left, polished up by a pupil), and Nicodemus, the converted Pharisee, whose face is clearly that of Michelangelo himself. The polished body of Christ stands out from the unfinished background. Michelangelo (as Nicodemus), who spent a lifetime bringing statues to life by "freeing" them from the stone, looks down sadly and tenderly at what could be his final creation, the once-perfect body of Renaissance Man that is now twisted, disfigured, and dead.

Seen from the right side, the four figures seem to interact

with each other, their sketchy faces changing emotions from grief to melancholy to peaceful acceptance. Seen face-on, they form a powerful geometric shape of a circle inside a triangle, split down the middle by Christ's massive but very dead arm.

Fifty years earlier, a confident Michelangelo had worked here on these very premises, skillfully carving *David* from an imperfect block. But he hated this marble for the *Pietà*; it was hard and grainy and gave off sparks when hit wrong. (The chisel grooves in the base remind us of the sheer physical effort of a senior citizen sculpting.) Worst of all, his housekeeper kept bugging him with the same question Pope Julius II used to ask about the Sistine Chapel—"When will you finish?" Pushed to the edge, Michelangelo grabbed a hammer and attacked the statue, hacking away and breaking off limbs, then turned to the servant and said, "There! It's finished!" (An assistant later repaired the damage.)

• *Continue upstairs to the first floor, entering a large room lined with statues and two balconies. Donatello's four prophets are at the far end.*

FIRST FLOOR—THE QUATTROCENTO
Room of the Cantorie—Donatello's Prophets

The room displays the original 16 statues (by several sculptors) that ring the bell tower's third story (where copies stand today). Donatello did five of them (plus some others in collaboration).

Donatello ("Little Donato") invented the Renaissance style Michelangelo would later perfect—powerful statues that are ultra-realistic, even ugly, sculpted in an "unfinished" style by an artist known for experimentation and a prickly, brooding personality, who was famous but lived like a peasant, married only to his work.

Donatello—*Habakkuk (Abacuc)*

Donatello's signature piece shows us the frail man beneath the heavy mantle of a prophet. His rumpled cloak falls diagonally down the front, dividing the body lengthwise. From the deep furrows emerges a bare arm with wiry tendons and that powerful right hand. His long muscled neck leads to a bald, squash-like head (the Italians call the statue *Lo Zuccone*).

The ugly face, with several days' growth of beard, crossed eyes, and tongue-tied mouth, looks crazed. This is no confident Charlton Heston prophet, but a man who's spent too much time alone, fasting in the wilderness,

Duomo Museum First Floor

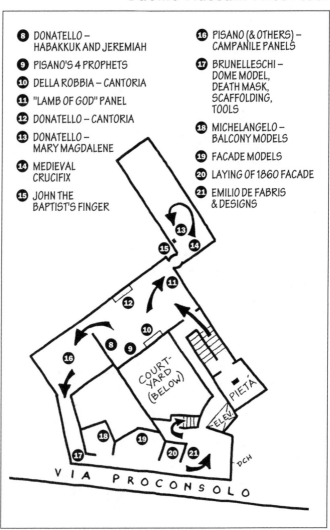

8 DONATELLO – HABAKKUK AND JEREMIAH

9 PISANO'S 4 PROPHETS

10 DELLA ROBBIA – CANTORIA

11 "LAMB OF GOD" PANEL

12 DONATELLO – CANTORIA

13 DONATELLO – MARY MAGDALENE

14 MEDIEVAL CRUCIFIX

15 JOHN THE BAPTIST'S FINGER

16 PISANO (& OTHERS) – CAMPANILE PANELS

17 BRUNELLESCHI – DOME MODEL, DEATH MASK, SCAFFOLDING, TOOLS

18 MICHELANGELO – BALCONY MODELS

19 FACADE MODELS

20 LAYING OF 1860 FACADE

21 EMILIO DE FABRIS & DESIGNS

searching for his calling, and now returns to babble his vision on a street corner.

Donatello—the eccentric prophet of a new style—identified with this statue, talking to it, swearing at it, yelling at it: "Speak!"

• *Nearby, look for . . .*

Donatello—*Jeremiah (Geremia)*

Watching Jerusalem burn in the distance, the ignored prophet reflects on why the Israelites wouldn't listen to his warning. He purses his lips bitterly, and his downturned mouth is accentuated by his plunging neck muscle and sagging shoulders.

The folds in the clothes are very deep, suggesting the anger, sorrow, and disgust Jeremiah feels but cannot share, as it is too late.
• *Along the long, left-hand wall are ...*

Andre and Nino Pisano's Four Prophets

Pisano's prophets are elegant but smaller and two-dimensional, with flat backs to stand obediently in their niches. The faces are generic and calm. Donatello's statues are agitated from within, with rumpled clothes, bare arms, and youthful, beardless, eccentric faces. They need elbow room to squirm around and shift their weight. Movement, realism, and human drama were Donatello's great contributions to sculpture. No wonder that Donatello's *Habakkuk* and *Jeremiah*—sculpted when 35-year-old Donatello was at the height of his powers—replaced Pisano's Gothic works on the front of the campanile. Compared with Donatello's, the other prophets in the room look old, musty, shaggy, and a bit befuddled, unprepared for the new age of the Renaissance.
• *The two balconies in room 12 are the Cantorie—Donatello's on the right (from the entrance), della Robbia's on the left. Della Robbia's is a reconstruction from casts, with the original 10 panels below.*

Luca della Robbia—*Cantoria* (1431–1438)

After almost 150 years of construction, the cathedral was nearly done, and they began preparing the interior for the celebration. Brunelleschi hired a little-known sculptor, 30-year-old Luca della Robbia, to make this choir box—a balcony for singers next to the

organ in the cathedral—and it summed up the exuberance of the Quattrocento. The panels are a celebration of music, song, and dance of toddlers, children, and teenagers.

"Praise the Lord" (*Laudate Dominum*, abbreviated "D.N.M."), reads the banner along the top. "Praise him in his holy place, in the firmament (*Firmamento*) for his mighty deeds (*Virtu*) and greatness (*Magnitudinus*)." Della Robbia's relief panels bring these words from Psalm 150 to life like an MTV video:

"Praise with the sound of trumpets" (*sono Tubae;* see the upper-left panel with trumpeting teens). "Praise him with psalter and zither" (*Psaltero et Cythera;* in the second and third panels, babysitters put down infants and pick up guitars and autoharps), "with tambourines" (*Timpano;* fourth panel), "and dancing" (*Choro;* seven kids dance ring-around-the-rosy as della Robbia sculpts a scene in the round on an almost-flat surface, showing front, back, and in-between poses), "with pipes and strings" (*Organo;* a child Apollo pumps a hand organ), "and with jubilant cymbals" (*Cimbales;* the kids make a joyful racket). "Everybody praise the Lord!"

Della Robbia's choir box was a triumph, a celebration of Florence's youthful boom time. Perhaps sensing he could never top it, the young sculptor hung up his hammer and chisel and concentrated on the colorful glazed terra-cotta, for which he's best known. (Find the **round "Lamb of God" panel** over your left shoulder, above a doorway nearby, by Luca's little brother, who took over the workshop.)

Donatello—*Cantoria*

If della Robbia's balcony looks like afternoon recess, Donatello's is an all-night rave. It's the perfect complement to della Robbia's polished, gleaming innocence. Donatello's

figures are sketchier, murky, and filled with frenetic activity, as the dancing kids hurl themselves around the balcony.

Recently returned from a trip to Rome, Donatello carved in the style of classical friezes of dancing *putti* (chubby, playful toddlers). This choir box stood in a dark area of the Duomo, so Donatello chose colorful mosaics and marbles to catch the eye, while purposely leaving the dancers unfinished, shadowy, tangled figures flitting inside the columns. In the dim light, worshippers swore they saw them move.

Pop. 100,000 . . . but Still a Small Town

Ghiberti won the bronze-door competition. Brunelleschi lost and took teenage Donatello with him to Rome. Donatello returned to join Ghiberti's workshop. Ghiberti helped Brunelleschi with dome plans. Brunelleschi, Donatello, and Luca della Robbia collaborated on the Pazzi Chapel. And so on, and so on.

• *Enter an adjoining room full of bishops' robes, a half-ton silver altarpiece, and . . .*

Donatello—*Mary Magdalene (Maddalena)*

Carved out of white poplar, originally painted with realistic colors (like the **medieval crucifix** displayed nearby), this statue is less a Renaissance work of beauty than a medieval object of intense devotion.

Mary Magdalene—the prostitute rescued from the streets by Jesus—folds her hands in humble prayer. Her once-beautiful face and body have been scarred by the fires of her own remorse, fasting, and repentance. The matted hair sticks to her face; veins and tendons line the anorexic arms and neck. The rippling animal-skin dress and hair suggest the emotional turmoil within. But from her hollow eyes, a new beauty shines, an enlightened soul that doesn't rely on the external beauty of human flesh.

The man who helped re-birth the classical style now shocked Florence by turning his back on it. Picking up a knife, he experimented in the difficult medium of wood carving, where subtlety can get lost when the wood splits off in larger-than-wanted slivers.

Sixty-five-year-old Donatello had just returned to Florence, after years away. His city had changed. Friends were dying (Brunelleschi died before they could reconcile after a bitter fight), favorite pubs were overrun with frat boys, and Florence was gaga over Greek gods in pretty, gleaming marble. Donatello fell into a five-year funk, completing only two statues, including this one.

• *In the display case to Mary's right, you'll find . . .*

John the Baptist's Finger in a Reliquary
(Artisti fiorentino: Reliquario di un osso di dito di S. Giovanni Battista)

The severed index finger of the beheaded prophet is the most revered relic of all the holy body parts in this museum.

• *Pass back through the large room of the Cantorie and into the next room. Work clockwise from the entrance.*

Andrea Pisano (and others)—
The Campanile Panels (c. 1334–59)

These 28 hexagonal and 28 diamond-shaped, blue-glazed panels decorated Giotto's Tower, seven per side (where copies stand today). The original design scheme was perhaps Giotto's, but most were executed by his successor, Andrea Pisano, and assistants.

The panels celebrate technology, showing workers, inventors, and thinkers. Allegorically, they depict man's long march to "civilization"—a blend of art and science, brain and brawn. But realistically, they're snapshots of that industrious generation that helped Florence bounce back ferociously from the Black Death of 1347–1348.

The lower, **hexagonal panels** (reading clockwise from the entrance) show God starting the chain of creation by inventing (1) man and (2) woman, then (3) Adam and Eve continuing the labors, (4) Jabal learning to domesticate sheep, (5) Jubal blowing a horn, inventing music...

• *Continuing along the next wall . . .*

(6) Tubalcain the blacksmith, and (7) Noah inventing wine and Miller Time. (8) An astronomer sights along a quadrant to chart the heavens and the (round, tilted-on-axis, pre-Columbus) Earth, (9) a master builder supervises his little apprentices building a brick wall, (10) a doctor holds a flask of urine to the light for analysis, etc.

• *On the fourth wall, check out . . .*

(20) The invention of sculpture, as a man chisels a figure to life.

The upper **diamond-shaped panels,** of marble on blue majolica (tin-glazed pottery tinged blue with copper sulfate), add religion (Sacraments and Virtues) to the civilization equation.

• *Enter the next, narrow room to find tools, scaffolding, and, at the end of the corridor, a wooden model of the cathedral dome's lantern.*

Brunelleschi's Dome—*Model of the Lantern*
(Cupola di S. Maria dei Fiori)

Brunelleschi's dome (look at the model, or out the window at the real thing) put mathematics in stone, a feat of engineering that was functional and beautiful. It rises 100 meters (330 feet) from the ground, with eight white, pointed-arch ribs, filled in with red brick, and capped with a "lantern" to hold it all in place.

The dome had to cover a gaping 43-meter (140-foot) hole in the roof of the church (a drag on rainy Sundays), a hole too wide to be spanned by the wooden scaffolding traditionally used to support a dome while it was being built. (An earlier architect suggested supporting the dome with a great mound of dirt inside the church ... filled with coins, so peasants would later cart it away for free.) In addition, the eight-sided "drum" the dome was to rest on was too weak to support a heavy dome, and there were no side buildings on the church on which to attach Gothic-style buttresses.

The solution was a dome within a dome, leaving a hollow space between to make it lighter. And the dome had to be self-supporting, both while being built and when finished, so as not to require buttresses.

Brunelleschi used wooden models such as these to demonstrate his ideas to skeptical approval committees.

Scaffolding

Although no scaffolding supported the dome, they needed exterior scaffolding for the stone and brick masons. The support timbers were stuck into postholes in the drum (some are visible on the church today).

The dome rose in rings. First, they'd stack a few blocks of white marble to create part of the ribs, then connect the ribs with horizontal crosspieces, then fill in the space with red brick in a herring-bone pattern. When the ring was complete and self-supporting, they'd move the scaffolding up and do another section.

Tools

The dome weighs 80 million pounds—as much as the entire population of Florence—so Brunelleschi had to design special tools and machines to lift and work all that stone. (The lantern alone—which caps the dome—is a marble building nearly as tall as the Baptistery.) You'll see sun-dried bricks, brick molds, rope, a tool belt, compasses, stone pincers, and various pulleys for lifting. Brunelleschi also designed a machine (not on display) where horses turned a shaft that reeled in rope, lifting heavy loads.

The dome was completed in 14 short years, capping 150 years of construction on the church. Brunelleschi enjoyed the dedication ceremonies, but died before the lantern was completed. His legacy is a dome that stands as a proud symbol of man's ingenuity, proving that art and science can unite to make beauty.

• *Next to the lantern model, find . . .*

Brunelleschi's Death Mask *(Anonimo: Maschera funebre)*

Filippo Brunelleschi (1377–1446) was uniquely qualified to create the dome. Trained in sculpture, he gave it up in disgust after losing the Baptistery gig. In Rome, he visualized placing the Pan-

theon on top of the Duomo, and dissected its mathematics and engineering.

Back home, he astounded Florence with a super-realistic painting of the Baptistery, as seen from the Duomo's front steps. Florentines lined up to see the painting (now lost) displayed side by side with the real thing, marveling at the 3-D realism. (Brunelleschi's mathematics of linear perspective were later expanded and popularized by Alberti.)

In 1420, Brunelleschi was declared *capomaestro* of the dome project. He was a jack-of-all-trades and now master of all as well, overseeing every aspect of the dome, the lantern, and the machinery to build them. Despite all his planning, it's clear from documentary evidence that he was making it up as he went along, exuding confidence to workers and city officials while privately improvising.

• *In the next room, behind glass, you'll see . . .*

Michelangelo—Two Wooden Models
for the Duomo's Balcony

But the church wasn't done. Even today, there's bare brick on much of the drum at the base of the dome. In 1507, a competition

was held to cover that brick with a marble balustrade. Michelangelo lost. Baccio d'Agnolo won, and covered part of the southeast section before others with better taste stopped him.
• *The next room deals with . . .*

The Facade from the 16th to the 19th Centuries

In 1587, the medieval facade by di Cambio was considered hopelessly outdated and was torn down like so much old linoleum. But work on a replacement never got off the ground, and the church front sat bare for nearly 300 years while they debated proposal after proposal by many famous architects. Most versions champion the Renaissance style to match Brunelleschi's dome rather than Gothic to fit the church.
• *Enter the next room.*

Laying of the First Stone of the Facade in 1860

In the 1800s, with the Romantic movement, there was a renaissance of the Gothic style (so to speak). In 1860, a ceremonial first stone was laid—using the hammer and trowel displayed here—by King Vittorio Emmanuel II, the future leader of a newly unified modern Italy.
• *In the last room . . .*

The 19th-Century Facade

Emilio de Fabris (portrait) won the competition with a neo-Gothic facade echoing the original work of di Cambio, and the new-old facade was dedicated in 1887. Notice that even de Fabris changed **designs** as he went—the spikes along the roofline in some of the designs are not there today.

Critics may charge that this facade is too retro, but it was the style of the church beloved by Ghiberti, Donatello, Brunelleschi, and the industrious citizens of Florence's Quattrocento, who saw it as Florence's finest art gallery.

MEDICI CHAPELS TOUR

Capelli dei Medici

The Medici Chapels (pron. MED-uh-chee) contain tombs of Florence's great ruling family, from Lorenzo the Magnificent to those less so. The highlight is a chapel designed by Michelangelo at the height of his creative powers. This is the Renaissance Man's greatest "installation," a room completely under his artistic control, featuring innovative architecture, tombs, and sculpture. His statues are a middle-aged man's brooding meditation on mortality, the fall of the Medici Golden Age, and the relentless passage of time—from *Dawn* to *Day* to *Dusk* to *Night*.

Orientation

Cost: €6.

Hours: Daily 8:15–17:00 but closed the second and fourth Sun and the first, third, and fifth Mon of each month.

Getting There: It's in the church of San Lorenzo—the one with the smaller dome on Florence's skyline (5-min walk northwest of Duomo). The bustling outdoor market almost obscures the chapel entrance at the back (west end) of the church.

Information: Tel. 055-238-8602.

Length of Our Tour: One hour.

Photography: Not allowed.

Starring: Michelangelo's statues *Day*, *Night*, *Dawn*, and *Dusk*.

Overview

The Medici Chapels consist of three burial places: the unimpressive Crypt, the large and gaudy Chapel of Princes, and—the highlight—Michelangelo's New Sacristy, a room completely designed by him with architecture, tombs, and statues to honor four Medicis.

• *Buy tickets and enter at the back (west) end of the church of San Lorenzo. Immediately past the turnstile, you're in ...*

The Crypt

This gloomy, low-ceilinged room with gravestones underfoot reminds us that these "chapels" are really tombs. You'll see lots of "Lorenzos" here (the family's patron saint)... but none that are "Magnificent" (he's later). Historians will search for the slab of **Cosimo the Elder** (look for "Cosmus Magnus Dux Etr" in the first chapel to right of entry), a shrewd banker and politician, grandfather of Lorenzo the Magnificent, and founder of the first Medici dynasty.

• *Head upstairs—either staircase—into the large, domed, multicolored...*

Chapel of Princes
(*La Capella dei Principi*), 1602–1743

The impressive **dome** overhead (seen from outside, it's the big, red-brick "mini-Duomo") tops an octagonal room that echoes the Baptistery and Duomo drum. It's lined with six tombs of now-forgotten Medici rulers. It's decorated everywhere with the **Medici coat of arms**—a shield with six balls representing the pills of doctors (*medici*), their original occupation. Along with many different colored marbles, geologists will recognize jasper, porphyry, quartz, alabaster, coral, mother-of-pearl, and lapis lazuli.

Sixteen shields ring the room at eye level, the Tuscan cities ("Civitas") ruled by Florence's dukes. Find Florence, with its fleur-de-lis ("Florentiae") and Pisa ("Pisarum"), both just left of the altar.

The bronze **statues** honor two of the "later" Medicis (1531–1743), the cultured but oppressive dukes who ruled Florence after the city's glorious Renaissance. Ferdinando I (ruled 1587–1609), in ermine cape and jewels, started the work on this Chapel of Princes and tore down the Duomo's medieval facade. His son, Cosimo II (ruled 1609–1621, to the right), appointed Galileo "first professor" of science at Pisa U., inspiring him to label the moons of Jupiter "the Medici Stars."

Apart from the **altar**—only finished in 1939 for a visit from Hitler and Mussolini—there is no Christian symbolism in this spacious but stifling temple to power, wealth, and mediocre Medicis.

New Sacristy

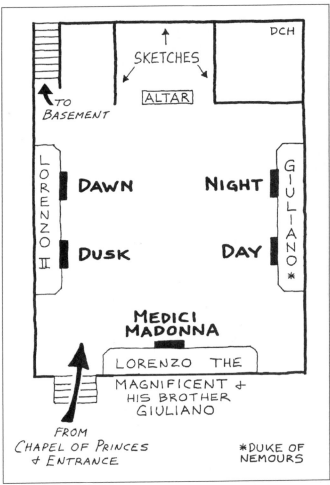

DCH

SKETCHES

ALTAR

TO BASEMENT

LORENZO II

DAWN

DUSK

NIGHT

DAY

GIULIANO *

MEDICI MADONNA

LORENZO THE MAGNIFICENT & HIS BROTHER GIULIANO

FROM CHAPEL OF PRINCES & ENTRANCE

*DUKE OF NEMOURS

• *Continue down the hall, passing statues of Roman armor with worms sprouting out, to Michelangelo's New Sacristy.*

New Sacristy *(Sacrestia Nuova)*, by Michelangelo

The entire room—architecture, tombs, and statues—was designed by Michelangelo (1520–34) to house the bodies of four of the Medici family. Michelangelo, who spent his teen years in the Medici household and personally knew three of the four buried here, was emotionally attached to the project. This is the work of a middle-aged man (age 45–59) reflecting on his contemporaries dying around him and on his own mortality.

• *There are tombs decorated with statues against three of the walls, and an altar on the fourth. Start with the tomb on the left wall (as you enter and face the altar).*

Tomb of Lorenzo II, Duke of Urbino

Lorenzo II—the grandson of Lorenzo the Magnificent—is shown as a Roman general, seated, arm resting on a Medici-bank money box, and bowing his head in contemplation. He had been the model for Machiavelli's *The Prince*, and when he died without a male heir at 27 (of tuberculosis and syphilis), the line of great princes stretching back to Cosimo the Elder died with him.

His sarcophagus, with a curved, scrolled lid, bears the reclining statues that Michelangelo named *Dusk* and *Dawn*. **Dusk** (the man), worn out after a long day, slumps his chin on his chest and reflects on the day's events. **Dawn** (the woman), stirs restlessly after a long night, with an anguished face, as though waking from a bad dream. *Dusk* and *Dawn*, with their counterparts *Day* and *Night* (opposite wall), represented to Michelangelo the swift passage of time, which kills everyone and causes our glorious deeds on earth to quickly fade.

During the 14 years he worked here, Michelangelo suffered the deaths of his father, favorite brother, and his unofficial stepbrother, Pope Leo X Medici. In addition, plagues in 1522 and 1527 killed thousands in Florence. In 1527, his adoptive city of Rome was looted by mercenaries. Michelangelo's letters reveal that, turning 50, he was feeling old, tired ("If I work one day, I need four to recuperate"), and depressed (he called it *mio pazzo*, "my madness"), facing the sad fact that the masterpiece of his youth—the grand tomb of Pope Julius II—was never going to be completed.

Overachievers in severe midlife crises may wish to avoid the Medici Chapels.

• *On the opposite wall…*

Tomb of Giuliano, Duke of Nemours

Overshadowed by his famous father (Lorenzo the Magnificent) and big brother (Pope Leo X), **Giuliano** led a wine-women-and-

song life, dying young without a male heir. His statue as a Roman general, with scepter, powerful Moses-esque pose, and alert, intelligent face, looks in the direction of the Madonna statue, as though asking forgiveness for a wasted life. The likeness is not at all accurate. Michelangelo said, "In a thousand years, no one will know how they looked."

Giuliano's "active" pose complements the "contemplative" one of Lorenzo, showing the two elements (thought + action) that Plato and Michelangelo believed made up the soul of man.

Night (the woman) does a cross-over sit-up in her sleep, toning the fleshy abs that look marvelously supple and waxlike, not like hard stone. She's highly polished, shimmering, and finished with minute details. Michelangelo's females—muscle-men with coconut-shell breasts—are generally more complete and (some think) less interesting than his men.

Theories abound that Michelangelo was homosexual. While his private sex life (or lack thereof) ulti-mately remains a mystery, his public expressions of affection were clearly weighted towards men. Some say he was less interested in female bodies and felt he could easily sum them up in a statue.

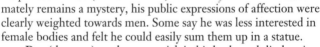

Day (the man) works out a crick in his back, each limb twisting a different direction, turning away from us. He looks over his shoulder with an expression (suspicious? angry? arrogant?) for-ever veiled behind chisel marks suggestive of Impressionist brush strokes. In fact, none of the four reclining statues' faces expresses a clear emotion, all turned inward, letting body language speak.

If, as some say, Michelangelo purposely left these statues "unfinished" while liberating them from their stone prison, it certainly adds mystery and a contrast in color and texture. *Night*'s moonlit clarity and *Day*'s rough-hewn grogginess may also reflect Michelangelo's own work schedule—a notorious day-sleeper and guilt-ridden layabout ("Dear to me is sleep") who, when inspired (as a friend wrote), "works much, eats little, and sleeps less."

Among *Night*'s symbols (the crescent moon on her forehead,

owl under knee, and poppies underfoot) is a grotesque **mask** with, perhaps, a self-portrait. Michelangelo, a serious poet (so much so he almost considered sculpting his "day job"), has *Night* say in one of his poems: "As long as shame and sorrow exist/I'd rather not see or hear/So speak softly and let me sleep."

Day, *Night*, *Dawn*, and *Dusk*—brought to life in this room where Michelangelo had his workshop, and where they've been ever since—meditate eternally on Death, squirming restlessly, unable to come to terms with it.

Tomb of Lorenzo the Magnificent and his Brother Giuliano

As the tomb was never completed, all that really marks where The Magnificent One's body lies is the marble base that the Madonna and saints stand on. Perhaps Michelangelo was working up to the grand finale to honor the man who not only was the greatest Medici but who also plucked a poor 13-year-old Michelangelo from an obscure apprenticeship to dine at the Medici table with cardinals and kings.

Lorenzo's beloved younger brother, Giuliano, died in 1478 in a "hit" by a rival family, stabbed to death before the altar of the Duomo during Easter Mass. (Lorenzo, wounded, drew his sword and backpedaled to safety. Enraged supporters grabbed the assassins—including two priests planted there by the pope— and literally tore them apart.)

The **Medici Madonna**, unlike many Michelangelo women, is thin, vertical, and elegant, her sad face veiled under chisel marks. She tolerates the squirming, two-year-old Jesus—who still seems to want to breast-feed—aware of the hard life her son has ahead of him. Mary's right foot is still buried in stone, so this unfinished statue was certainly meant to be worked on more. The saints **Cosmas** and **Damian** were done by assistants.

The Unfinished Project

The Chapel project (1520–1534) was plagued by delays: design changes, late shipments of Carrara marble, the death of patrons, Michelangelo's other obligations (including the Laurentian Library next door), his own depression, and...revolution.

In 1527, Florence rose up against the Medici pope and

The Medicis in a Minute and a Half

The Medici family—part *Sopranos*, part Kennedys, part John-D-and-Catherine-T art patrons—dominated Florentine politics for 300 years (c. 1434–1737). Originally a hardworking, middle-class family in the cloth, silk, and banking business, they used their wealth, blue-collar popularity, and philanthropy to rise into Europe's nobility, producing popes and queens.

1400s: The Princes

Cosimo the Elder (ruled 1434–1464), a shrewd moneylender, had free-spending popes and nobles in his pocket, becoming the richest man in Europe and virtual dictator of Florence. He was the patron of Brunelleschi, Donatello, Ghiberti, and Fra Angelico.

Lorenzo the Magnificent (ruled 1469–1492), Cosimo's grandson, epitomized the Medici ruling style: publicly praising Florence's constitution while privately holding the purse strings. A true Renaissance Man, Lorenzo's personal charisma, public festivals, and support of da Vinci, Botticelli, and teenage Michelangelo made Florence Europe's most enlightened city.

1494–1532: Exile in Rome

After Lorenzo's early death, the family was exiled by the Florentines, a victim of bank failure, Savonarola's reforms, and the Florentine tradition of democracy. They built a power base in Rome under Lorenzo's son (Pope Leo X, who made forays into Florence) and nephew (Pope Clement VII, who finally invaded Florence and crushed the republic).

1537–1737: The Grand Duchy—Mediocre Medicis

Backed by Europe's popes and kings, the "later" Medicis—descendants of Cosimo the Elder's brother—ruled Florence and Tuscany as just another duchy. Politically repressive but generous

declared an independent republic. Michelangelo, torn between his love of Florence and loyalty to the Medicis of his youth, walked a fine line. He continued to work for the pope while simultaneously designing fortified city walls to defend Florence from the pope's troops. In 1530, the besieged city fell, Republicans were rounded up and executed, and Michelangelo went into hiding (perhaps in the chapel basement, down the steps to the left of the altar). Fortunately, his status both as artist and staunch Florentine spared him from reprisals.

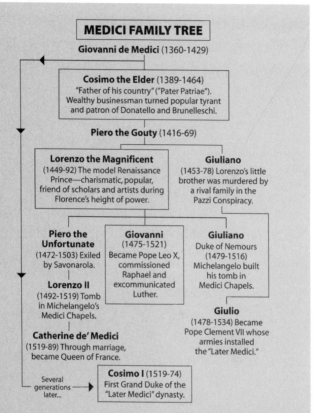

MEDICI FAMILY TREE

Giovanni de Medici (1360-1429)

Cosimo the Elder (1389-1464)
"Father of his country" ("Pater Patriae").
Wealthy businessman turned popular tyrant
and patron of Donatello and Brunelleschi.

Piero the Gouty (1416-69)

Lorenzo the Magnificent
(1449-92) The model Renaissance
Prince—charismatic, popular,
friend of scholars and artists during
Florence's height of power.

Giuliano
(1453-78) Lorenzo's little
brother was murdered by
a rival family in the
Pazzi Conspiracy.

Piero the Unfortunate
(1472-1503) Exiled
by Savonarola.

Lorenzo II
(1492-1519) Tomb
in Michelangelo's
Medici Chapels.

Catherine de' Medici
(1519-89) Through marriage,
became Queen of France.

Giovanni
(1475-1521)
Became Pope Leo X,
commissioned
Raphael and
excommunicated
Luther.

Giuliano
Duke of Nemours
(1479-1516)
Michelangelo built
his tomb in
Medici Chapels.

Giulio
(1478-1534) Became
Pope Clement VII whose
armies installed
the "Later Medici."

Several
generations
later...

Cosimo I (1519-74)
First Grand Duke of the
"Later Medici" dynasty.

patrons of the arts (the Uffizi, Pitti Palace, Cellini, Galileo), they married into Europe's royal families (Catherine and Marie de Medici were queens of France) while Florence declined as a political and economic power.

In 1534, a new pope enticed Michelangelo to come back to Rome with a challenging new project: painting the *Last Judgment* over the altar in the Sistine Chapel. Michelangelo left, never to return to the Medici Chapels. Assistants gathered up statues and fragments from the chapel floor (and the Madonna from Michelangelo's house) and did their best to assemble the pieces according to Michelangelo's designs.

• *The apse is the area behind the altar. This has the best view of the chapel as a whole.*

Sketches on the Walls of the Apse

Michelangelo's many design changes and improvisational style come to life in these (dimly lit and hard to see behind Plexiglas) black chalk and charcoal doodles, presumably by Michelangelo and assistants.

• *Starting on the left wall and working clockwise at about eye level . . .*

I think I saw hash marks counting off days worked, a window frame for the Laurentian Library, scribbles, a face, an arch, a bearded face, and (on the right wall) squares, a nude figure crouching in a doorway, a twisting female nude with her dog, and a tiny, wacky cartoon Roman soldier with shield and spurs. You really do get a sense of Michelangelo and staff working, sweating, arguing, and just goofing off as the hammers pound and dust flies.

The Whole Ensemble—Michelangelo's Vision

The New Sacristy was the first chance for Michelangelo, the quintessential well-rounded Renaissance Man, to use his arsenal of talents—as sculptor, architect, and Thinker of Big Ideas—on a single, multimedia project. The resulting "installation" (a 20th-century term) produces a powerful overall effect that's different for everyone—"somber," "meditative," "redemptive," "ugly."

The room is a cube topped with a Pantheon-style dome, with three distinct stories—the heavy tombs at ground level, upper-level windows with simpler wall decoration, and the dome, better lit and simpler still. The whole effect draws the eye upward, from dark and "busy" to light and airy. (It's intensified by an optical illusion—Michelangelo made the dome's coffers, the upper windows, and round lunettes all taper imperceptibly at the top to make them look taller and higher.)

The white walls are lined in gray-brown-green stone. The half columns, arches, and triangular pediments are traditional Renaissance forms, but with no regard for the traditional "orders" of the time (matching the right capital with the right base, the correct width-to-height ratio of columns, upper story taller than lower, etc.). Michelangelo had Baroque-en the rules, baffling his contemporaries and pointing the way to a new, more ornate style, using old forms as mere decoration.

Finally, Michelangelo, a serious neo-Platonist, wanted this room to symbolize the big philosophical questions that death presents to the survivors. Summing up these capital-letter concepts (far, far more crudely than was ever intended), the room might say:

Time (the four reclining statues) kills Mortal Men (statues of Lorenzo and Giuliano) and mocks their Glory (Roman power symbols). But if we Focus (Lorenzo and Giuliano's gaze) on God's Grace (Madonna and Child), our Souls (both Active and Contemplative parts) can be Resurrected (the Chapel was consecrated to this) and rise from this drab Earth (the dark, heavy ground floor) up into the Light (the windows and lantern) of Heaven (the geometrically perfect dome) where God and Plato's Ideas are forever Immortal.

And that, folks, is a Mouthful.

DANTE'S HOUSE TOUR

Casa di Dante

"Halfway into my trip through Life," begins *The Divine Comedy*, "I awoke to find myself"...in a cheap hotel room, far from loved ones, having a midlife crisis, obsessing over an old flame, and wondering in which direction my soul was headed. Dante's greatest poem parallels his legendary life.

The Casa di Dante traces this life from exuberant youth in Florence through embittered exile to the consolation he found in writing the epic poem that (some say) invented modern poetry and helped kick off the Renaissance.

Orientation

Cost: €3.
Hours: Mon and Wed–Sat 10:00–17:00, Sun 10:00–14:00, closed Tue.
Getting There: It's at Via S. Margherita 1, a block west of the Bargello.
Length of Our Tour: One hour.
Photography: Allowed without a flash.
Starring: Dante and *The Divine Comedy*.

FIRST FLOOR— VITA NUOVA (NEW LIFE)

There appeared before my eyes the glorious lady of my mind—Beatrice, dressed in crimson. At that very moment—and I speak the truth— my heart trembled, my veins tingled, and I heard a voice say: "Ecce deus....Behold a god stronger than I."

From that moment on, Love dominated me. And when anyone asked me any question about anything whatsoever, the only response my mouth could manage was: "Love!"

— Dante, *Vita Nuova (New Life)*

• *The first room you enter is Room II. As a general rule, follow the displays clockwise around the rooms.*

Room II: Dante's Early Years

Dante Alighieri (1265–1321) was born to poor but noble parents with deep roots in the growing town of Florence (see **Alighieri coat of arms** on the wall). Baptized in the Baptistery (see **Baptistery photos** in the display case), he was raised on medieval sermons about winged devils snacking on sinners—images he'd write about decades later (Inferno XXXIV. 61–63).

Schooled in Latin, logic, and rhetoric at the University of Bologna, he devoured the troubadour love poetry of his day (**poetry manuscripts,** next display case), mostly written in scholarly Latin.

His own poetic soul was stirred at age 18 in a chance meeting with teenage Beatrice Portinari (see **Portinari coat of arms** on the wall). Her beauty stunned him; her goodness inspired him to think good thoughts. Though they would meet only a few times, barely spoke to each other, and never even got close to doing it, Beatrice's beauty would inspire Dante all his life. Unfortunately, Beatrice blew Dante off, married a rich banker, and died young, but she lives on as his muse in early poetry (*Vita Nuova*) and his spiritual guide in *The Divine Comedy*. Heartbroken, Dante consoled himself with philosophy, politics, and an arranged marriage with Gemma Donati (see **Donati coat of arms**).

Room I: Florence in Dante's Time

Dante's energetic generation (c. 1300) transformed Florence from a rural, feudal village to an urban, democratic center of trade and banking. Dante saw cornerstones laid for the Duomo, Palazzo Vecchio, and Santa Croce, but never saw them completed. (Most of the room's displays are, in fact, post-Dante: Even this "Casa di Dante" isn't his real house but a reconstruction in his old neighborhood.)

Dante loved Florence. Even today, he would recognize the nearby **Badia Fiorentina church** (see **sketch**), the **Bargello tower** (see **photo**), the **Castagna Tower** (out the window; it's the rough brick wall in your face), and **San Martino** (out the window, to the right), his humble family church.

Room III: The Public Life of Dante in Florence

Citizen Dante proudly championed the new democratic—and controversial—ideas blossoming in Florence. At the **Battle of Compaldino (diorama of toy soldiers),** 25-year-old Dante joined Florence's "citizens' army" (on the right, many bearing red-and-white shields with the fleur-de-lis of Florence) against aristocratic Arezzo (left). There's Dante himself on horseback, in the second row (in green-black-and-white Alighieri family colors, dipping his flag just to be different). Arezzo charged first, driving the Florentines back. But Florence rallied and won, killing 1,700 and capturing 2,000.

Back at home, Dante joined a workers' guild (see **coat of arms** of "Arte dei Medici e Speziali," by the entrance), served as ambassador to **San Gimignano (photo),** and was elected to the City Council **("Dante Prior" manuscript).** Dante and his party were fighting to make Florence independent of popes, emperors, foreigners, and tyrants of any sort.

On June 19, 1300, Dante rose in the Council of Hundreds **("Dante speaks out" manuscript)** and demanded that Florence's armies leave the service of **Pope Boniface VIII (picture).** A power struggle ensued between Dante's White Guelphs (pro-independence), the Black Guelphs (pro-pope), and Ghibellines (pro-emperor, that is, foreign kings). In October, Dante headed off to Rome to negotiate with the pope. He would never see Florence again.

The Blacks seized control, banished all Whites, and decreed **(The Podesta condemns . . .)** that should Dante ever return to Florence, he "shall be burned with fire till he be dead" **(Book of the Nail).** Midway in his journey through life, 35-year-old Dante suddenly awoke from his dreams of success to find himself wandering in the "dark forest" of banishment for life.

SECOND FLOOR—EXILE

"This is the road to the city of desolation.
This is the road of eternal damnation.
Abandon hope, all ye who enter in."
  —Written on the door to Hell,
    from Inferno III

Room IV: Dante's Life in Exile from 1301 to 1311
The painting on the wall *(Dante in Exile)* imagines a weary, melancholy Dante resting by the seashore. Unable to return home to Florence, he was on the road the rest of his life, traveling through Italy

and Europe, suffering through poverty, disillusionment, fear for his life, and showers down the hall. His wife, Gemma, never joined him, remaining safe in Florence with their four kids (including baby Beatrice).

He slept on the couches of old college friends, political allies, and poetry fans **(castle photos),** while trying to negotiate a truce **(Epistle for conciliation, Epistle to "the wicked Florentines").** When Florence finally gave him the chance to return if he'd renounce his beliefs, he refused **(Epistle to a Florentine friend, refusing 1315 amnesty),** saying, "Can a man who is anything like a philosopher stoop to such humiliation?"

In 1308, he began writing *The Divine Comedy* **(facsimile of Trivulziana Codex 1337,** the earliest known edition). Here, he settles old scores and grinds political axes, placing his enemies in hell and his heroes in paradise. He puts  Pope Boniface VIII among the Greedy in Hell, planted head down in the ground while demons sauté his feet, "for betraying, then raping, the Fairest Woman (Florence) that ever was." Dante rants on: "You deify gold and silver, your greed saddens the world.... Pastors like you, fornicating with the kings of the earth!" (Inferno XIX).

The Divine Comedy was his therapy/catharsis/consolation for all the abuse he suffered in life, but what makes it a "Comedy" is that he rose above his bitterness.

The trip through Hell ends with...

> *We trudged upward from the dark den till at last I*
> *looked up and glimpsed a light through a round hole.*
> *Through this we climbed and came forth, to look once*
> *more upon the stars.*
> > —Inferno XXXIV. 133–39

Room V: Dante's Life in Exile from 1311 until His Death in 1321

In *The Divine Comedy,* Purgatory begins with:
The wind at my back, I shake out more sail and leave
that ocean of despair behind.
> —Purgatorio I. 1–3

Dante wrote a famous essay (see pages from **La Monarchia**) backing Holy Roman Emperor Henry VII against the pope.

The Divine Comedy:
Hell, Purgatory, and Paradise

The Plot

In the year 1300, a middle-aged man (Dante) wakes up lost in a forest, where he's attacked by wild animals. He's rescued by the ghost of the old Roman poet Virgil, who leads him through a gate, tunneling down into the earth.

This is Hell (*Inferno* in Italian)—a huge, funnel-shaped pit, terraced along the sides in "rings" that wind, like a drain, slowly down to the center of the earth. As they descend, Dante chats with sinners being tortured by demons in true "poetic justice"—murderers are plunged in boiling blood, flatterers are immersed in human feces, and hypocrites wear heavy lead coats with a pretty gold trim.

He hears tales of woe from former enemies (Pope Boniface VIII), celebrities from history (Mohammed, Brutus), legendary figures (Ulysses, Jason), and even old friends (his poor, beloved mentor Brunetto Latini is among the Sodomites because...he was one). Though they are sinners, Dante the writer withholds judgment, portraying them as vulnerable, humorous, three-dimensional people.

At the bottom of the pit (the center of the earth) sits Satan, a winged ogre immersed in a frozen lake, gnawing on souls. Dante and Virgil skip quickly by him and begin their climb up through

But Henry suddenly died **(Death of Emperor Arrigo VII),** just as he was about to liberate Florence from its Black Guelphs (pro-pope), snuffing out Dante's last chance of returning home

Dante settled in Verona, where he was received like royalty by Cangrande ("Big Dog") Scaligeri **(Monument to Cangrande),** to whom he dedicated the Paradiso.

His last years were spent in relative comfort in Ravenna (see the fanciful painting *Dante introducing* **[curly-haired]** *Giotto to the* **[seated]** *Duke of Ravenna*). The luminous gold mosaics of Ravenna's churches **(Mosaic in the apse of**

the other side of the (round) earth. Thirty-six hours after they first entered Hell, they emerge from the earth at the opposite pole and "see the stars."

They climb Mount Purgatory, winding up this cone-shaped, wedding-cake mountain ringed with terraces (the inverse of the pit of Hell). They talk with souls who are being purged of their sins so they can one day enjoy peace. Near the top, as they approach the Garden of Eden, Virgil (a non-Christian) must say goodbye, giving way to Dante's new guide—his old girlfriend, Beatrice, who appears as a radiant angel.

As Beatrice looks up to the heavens, Dante looks at her, and the two begin to float upward through the layers of Paradise that encircle the earth. They pass the moon, Mercury, Venus, the Sun, and so on, meeting blessed souls such as Francis of Assisi and St. Peter. Finally, they soar out into "the Empyrean" and gaze upon the indescribable glory of God.

Dante's whole adventure takes place in the three days from Good Friday to Easter, 1300.

The Allegory
It is the Christian's journey through life, from Fall to Redemption, resulting in wisdom and perspective after experiencing every element—good, bad, and ugly—in the Christian universe.

Sant' Apollinare, in the second case) must have inspired Dante's last poetic visions, where God is described as "Light Supreme . . . the point of rest . . . in a spinning sphere" (Paradiso XXXIII).

In 1321, he sailed as an ambassador to meet with the Doge in Venice. On the voyage home, he caught malaria and died, age 56, in a fever. He lies buried in Ravenna **(Dante's sepulchre),** despite later appeals for his body by Michelangelo and others **(The Florentine Academy demands).** His hometown honored him posthumously with a monument **(Dante's cenotaph in Santa Croce).**

Dante leaves Purgatory with a fantastic mixed metaphor:
> *Born again in the holy waters, sprouting buds*
> *like a tree in springtime, I emerged pure and*
> *prepared to leap up to the stars.*
> —Purgatorio XXXIII. 142–45

THIRD FLOOR—DANTE ETERNAL

In *The Divine Comedy*, Paradise begins with:
The glory of God permeates the universe as dazzling light. Immersed in it, I saw such things as man has never known and no man could describe.
—Paradiso I. 1–6

• *Immediately at the top of the stairs (before crossing the balcony), you'll find hanging on the wall...*

The Divine Comedy (La Commedia Divina)

Here, in small print, is the entire poem, from the first line (*Nel mezzo del cammin di nostra vita;* In the middle of the road of our life) to the last (*L'amor che muove il sole e l'altre stelle;* The love that moves the sun and the other stars). It's surprisingly readable, written in conversational Tuscan rather than formal Latin. Thanks to Dante's popularity, writers everywhere began writing in their native tongues, and Tuscan became modern Italian.

There are three sections (Hell, Purgatory, and Paradise), each with 33 cantos (plus one extra to make an even 100) written in three-line stanzas. (For Dante, 3 symbolized the Trinity.) All told, the poem is about 14,000 lines or 140,000 words long.

The rhyme scheme is *aba bcb cdc* etc., giving the comforting feeling of a regular rhyme, but one that changes before it gets boring. Dante seamlessly matched the sound of words (rhyme and rhythm) with their meaning, creating a philosophical treatise that could be sung by dockworkers.

Dante's original title was simply *The Comedy*, until a printer in 1555 decided it was "Divine," and the name stuck.

Room VI: Dante's Iconography throughout the Centuries

After his death, Dante's poems became famous, but so did he—for his passionate love for Beatrice, bold stand for democracy, tragic exile, and redemption through art.

The earliest portrait of Dante, done by his friend Giotto **(Portrait of Dante, detail of Giotto's workshop fresco)** was the model for all later portrayals—ear-flap headdress, long straight nose, and proud jutting chin. Later versions crown him with the laurel leaves given to great athletes, physical and verbal.

Dante meets Beatrice (a painting on the wall) captures that life-changing moment when 18-year-old Dante—posing awkwardly to try to look cool—exchanges a passing glance with crimson-clothed Beatrice.

Thirty years later, Dante would still see Beatrice as his spiritual guide: "Through a cloud of flowers tossed by angels, came a chariot, bearing the Lady in a white veil. A strange power flowed out from her, and I felt the overpowering might of that old, old love...." (Purgatorio XXX).

Beatrice had awakened Dante to a New Life—the physical beauty of the world and of human emotions—and he spent his life describing it in words. His words inspired painters to capture that beauty on canvas...which is why Dante is sometimes called the father of the Renaissance.

Room VII: Dante's Fortune throughout the Centuries

The large painting (***Dante and His Poem,*** **by Dominico, etc.**) is Florence's attempt to honor her native son 150 years later. Dante, with *Divine Comedy* in hand, stands in a barren wilderness, gesturing to the gate leading to Hell. Behind him, Mount Purgatory rises like a wedding cake, with winged Beatrice at the entrance. Above, the sky is arced into the solar system of Dante's Heaven. To the

right is Florence's skyline, showing the Duomo, Giotto's Tower, and Palazzo Vecchio—ironically, all monuments Dante was not allowed to see built.

Dante's screenplay of the Christian universe was filmed in Technicolor by many famous artists. Clockwise around the room you'll find ***Last Judgments*** (***Giudizio Universale***) by **Giotto, Beato Fra Angelico** (in San Marco monastery), **Luca Signorelli**

(Orvieto Cathedral), and **Michelangelo** (Sistine Chapel, Vatican), plus images by **Delacroix** and **Blake.**

That initial pulse of energy that motivated Dante lives on today, with **translations** in many languages, all trying to capture the journey of the human soul that defies description. Even Dante, who after some 140,000 words, is finally face-to-face with God at the very end of *The Divine Comedy*, says that, at that moment, his powers of description failed him. But he feels something, something that "moves" him, sending him spinning, like a planet in orbit, or turning like a tiny cogwheel in the great clockwork of the universe. And that something is... "Love!"

> *So I wrestled with the mystery, but my own wings could not take me that high. Then, a great flash of understanding hit me. Just as a wheel in perfect balance is set turning, I felt my own will and desire moved by...Love— the Love that moves the sun and the other stars.*
> —Paradiso XXXIII

SANTA MARIA NOVELLA
TOUR

Santa Maria Novella was the church of the Dominicans (Domini Canes, or the Hounds of God), whose mission was to hunt down heresy. Many wealthy families paid for chapels inside the church that today are appreciated for their fine art.

Masaccio's fresco *The Trinity*, the first painting of modern times to portray three-dimensional space (1427), blew a "hole in the wall" of this church. From then on, a painting wasn't just a decorated panel, but a window into the spacious 3-D world of light and color. With Masaccio's *Trinity* as the centerpiece, the church traces Florentine art from the medieval to the Quattrocento (1400s) to the onset of Baroque.

Orientation

Cost: €2.60.

Hours: Mon–Thu and Sat 9:30–17:00, Fri and Sun 13:00–17:00.

Dress Code: Shorts are allowed, but please no short shorts or bare arms.

Getting There: It's on Piazza Santa Maria Novella, a block south of the train station.

Note: Art lovers can seek out the adjacent chapels (separate fee and entry to the left of the church's facade); the highlight is the chapel of the Spaniards, featuring Bonaiuto's fresco *Allegory of the Dominican Order.*

Around the corner from the church is a fancy perfumery that's fun to visit (free, Mon–Sat 9:30–19:30, closed Sun, Via della Scala 16); see page 221 for details.

Length of Our Tour: One hour.

Photography Allowed without a flash.

Starring: Masaccio, Giotto, Brunelleschi, Ghirlandaio, and Filippino Lippi.

Santa Maria Novella

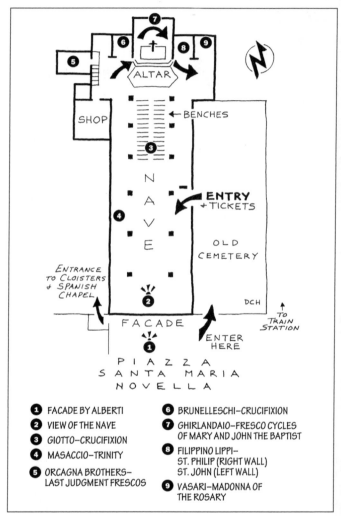

- **1** FACADE BY ALBERTI
- **2** VIEW OF THE NAVE
- **3** GIOTTO—CRUCIFIXION
- **4** MASACCIO—TRINITY
- **5** ORCAGNA BROTHERS—LAST JUDGMENT FRESCOS
- **6** BRUNELLESCHI—CRUCIFIXION
- **7** GHIRLANDAIO—FRESCO CYCLES OF MARY AND JOHN THE BAPTIST
- **8** FILIPPINO LIPPI—ST. PHILIP (RIGHT WALL) ST. JOHN (LEFT WALL)
- **9** VASARI—MADONNA OF THE ROSARY

1. Exterior—The Facade

The green-and-white marble facade by Leon Battista Alberti (1456–70) contains elements of Florence's whole history: Romanesque (horizontal stripes, like the baptistery), Gothic (pointed arches on the bottom level), Renaissance (geometric squares and circles on the upper level), and even proto-Baroque (the scrolls).

The church itself is cross-shaped, with a high central nave and low-ceilinged side aisles—the scrolls on the facade help bridge the two levels.

• *Enter the courtyard to the right of the main door, passing through the cemetery, where you'll pay to enter. Masaccio's Trinity is on the opposite wall from the entrance. But we'll start our tour at the central doorway in the facade, looking down the long nave to the altar.*

2. Interior—View Down the Nave from the Main Entrance

The long, 100-meter (330-foot) nave looks even longer thanks to a 14th-century perspective illusion. The columns converge as you approach the altar, their number increases, the arches get lower and the floor gets higher— creating a tunnel effect. Gothic architects were aware of the rules of perspective, just not how to render it on a 2-D canvas.

• *Hanging from the ceiling in the middle of the nave is . . .*

3. Giotto (1266?–1337)— *Crucifixion* (c. 1300)

Giotto's altarpiece originally stood on the main altar. Stately and under-stated, it avoids the gruesome excesses of many medieval crucifixes. The tragic tilt of Christ's head, the parted lips, and the stretched rib cage tell more about human suffering than the excessive spurting of blood.

On either side of the crossbar, Mary and John sit in a golden iconic heaven, but they are fully human, turned at three-quarter angle, with knowing, sympathetic expressions. Giotto, the proto-Renaissance experimenter in perspective, creates the illusion that Christ's hands are actually turned out, palms down, not hammered flat against the cross.

• *Masaccio's* Trinity *is on the left wall, about midway along the nave (opposite the entrance). For the best perspective, stand about 8 meters (20 feet) from it, then take four steps to your left. Masaccio positioned it to be seen by the faithful as they dipped fingers into a (missing) font and crossed themselves—"Father, Son, and Holy Ghost."*

4. Masaccio (1401–1428)— *The Trinity* (1425–1427)

In his short but influential five-year career, Masaccio was the first painter to portray Man in Nature—real humans with real emotions, in a spacious three-dimensional world. (Unfortunately for tourists, he did the best 3-D space here, and the best humans in the Brancacci Chapel across the river.)

With simple pinks and blues (now pretty faded), Masaccio creates the illusion that we're looking into a raised, cube-shaped chapel (about 3 meters by 3 meters by 3 meters) topped with an arched ceiling and framed at the entrance with classical columns. Inside the chapel, God the Father stands on an altar, holding up the cross of Christ. (Where's the dove of the Holy Spirit? Why is God's "white collar" crooked?) John looks up at Christ while Mary looks down at us. Two donors (husband and wife, most likely) kneel on the front step outside the chapel, their cloaks spilling out of the niche. Below this fake chapel sits a fake tomb with the skeleton of Adam; compare it with the real tomb and niche to the right.

The checkerboard ceiling creates a 3-D tunnel effect, with rows of panels that appear to converge at the back, the panels getting smaller, lower, and closer together. Earlier painters had played with tricks like this, but Masaccio went further. He gave such thought to the proper perspective that we, as viewers, know right where we stand in relation to this virtual chapel.

He knew that, in real life, the rows of checks would, if extended, stretch to the distant horizon. Lay a mental ruler along them, and you'll find the "vanishing point"—where all the lines intersect—all the way down below the foot of the cross. Masaccio places us there, with that at eye level, looking "up" into the chapel.

Having fixed where the distant horizon is and where the viewer is, Masaccio draws a checkerboard grid in between, then places the figures on it (actually underneath it) like chess pieces. What's truly amazing is that young Masaccio seemed to grasp this stuff intuitively—a "natural," eyeballing it and sketching freehand what later artists would have to work out with a pencil and paper.

What Masaccio learned intuitively, Brunelleschi analyzed mathematically and Alberti (who did the facade) codified in his famous 1435 treatise, *On Painting*. Soon, artists everywhere were drawing Alberti checkerboards on the ground, creating spacious, perfectly lit, 3-D scenes filled with chess-piece humans.

• *The Orcagna Chapel is at the far end of the left transept. As you approach, view the chapel from a distance. This is the illusion that Masaccio tried to create—of a raised chapel set in a wall—using only paint on a flat surface. Climb the steps to enter.*

5. Orcagna Brothers (a.k.a. the di Cione brothers)—Frescoes of the Last Judgment: *Inferno, Purgatorio, and Paradiso* (1340–1357)

In 1347–1348, Florence was hit with the terrible Black Death (bubonic plague) that killed half the population. Here, in the Orcagna Chapel, the fading frescoes from that grim time show hundreds of figures, and not a single smile.

It's the Day of Judgment (center wall), and God (above the stained-glass window)

spreads his hands to divide the good and evil. God has selected Dante as the interior decorator for heaven and hell. (Find Dante all in white, with his ear-flap cap, among the crowd to the left of the window, about a third of the way up.) Notice that God is bigger than the angels, who dwarf the hallowed saints, who are bigger than ordinary souls such as Dante, mirroring the feudal hierarchy of king, nobles, knights, and serfs.

In *Heaven* (left wall), Hotel Paradiso is *completo*, stacked with gold-haloed saints. *Hell* (faded right wall) is a series of layers, the descending rings of Dante's Inferno. A river of fire runs through it, dividing *Purgatory* (above) and *Hell* (below). At the bottom of the pit, where dogs and winged demons run wild, naked souls in caves beg for mercy and get none.

• *In a chapel to the left of the church's main altar, you'll find . . .*

6. Brunelleschi—*Crucifixion*

Filippo Brunelleschi (1377–1446)—architect, painter, sculptor—
used his skills as an analyst of nature to carve (in wood) a perfectly

realistic *Crucifixion*, neither prettified
nor with the grotesque exaggeration
of medieval religious objects. His
Christ is buck naked, not particularly
muscular or handsome, with bulging
veins, armpit hair, tensed leg muscles,
and bent feet. The tilt of Christ's
head frees a tendril of hair that directs
our eye down to the wound and the
dripping blood, dropping straight
from his side to his thigh to his calf—
a strong vertical line that sets off the
curve of Christ's body.

Brunelleschi carved this to outdo his friend Donatello's crucifix in Santa Croce. Donatello's is an agonized peasant;
Brunelleschi's a dignified noble.

• *In the choir area behind the main altar are Ghirlandaio's 21
frescoes, stacked seven to a wall. We'll concentrate on just the six
panels on the bottom.*

7. Ghirlandaio—Fresco Cycles of Mary and John the Baptist (1485–1490)

At the peak of Florence's power, wealth, and confidence,
Domenico Ghirlandaio (1449–1494) painted portraits of his
fellow Florentines in their Sunday best, inhabiting video-game
landscapes of classical buildings, rubbing shoulders with saints
and angels. The religious subjects get lost in the colorful scenes
of everyday life—perhaps a metaphor for how Renaissance
humanism was marginalizing religion.

• *Start with the left wall and work clockwise along the bottom.
The first scene is . . .*

Ghirlandaio— *Expulsion of Joachim from the Temple*

Proud, young Florentine
men (the group at left)
seem oblivious to bearded,
robed saints rushing from
the arcade. There's
Ghirlandaio himself (in
the group on the right)

looking out at us, with one hand proudly on his hip and the other gesturing, "I did this." The scene is perfectly lit, almost shadow-free, allowing us to look deep into the receding arches.
• *Continue clockwise to the next scene.*

Ghirlandaio—*Birth of the Virgin*

Five beautiful young women, led by the pregnant daughter of Ghirlandaio's patron, parade up to newborn Mary. The pregnant

girl's brocade dress is a microcosm of the room's decorations. Dancing babies in the room's classical frieze celebrate Mary's birth, obviously echoing della Robbia's beloved Cantoria in Florence's Duomo Museum.

True, Ghirlandaio's works are "busy"—each scene crammed with portraits, designs, fantasy architecture, and great costumes—but if you mentally frame off small sections, you discover a collection of mini-masterpieces.

• *On the center wall, flanking the stained-glass window, are two matching panels.*

Ghirlandaio—*Giovanni Tornabuoni Kneeling and Francesca Tornabuoni (his wife) Kneeling*

Giovanni Tornabuoni, who paid for these frescoes, was a successful executive in the Medici Company (and Lorenzo the Magnificent's uncle). However, by the time these frescoes were being finished, the Medici bank was slipping seriously into the red, and soon the family had to flee Florence, creditors on their heels.
• *On the right wall . . .*

Ghirlandaio—*Mary Meets Elizabeth*

In a spacious, airy landscape (with the pointed steeple of S. M. Novella in the distance), Mary and Elizabeth embrace, uniting their respective entourages. The parade of ladies in contemporary

dress echoes the one on the opposite wall. This panel celebrates youth, beauty, the city, trees, rocks, and life.

A generation after Brunelleschi and Alberti, all artists—including the near-genius Ghirlandaio—had mastered perspective

tricks. Here, Alberti's famed checkerboard is laid on its side, making a sharply receding wall to create the illusion of great distance.

Ghirlandaio employed many assistants in his productive workshop: "Johnson, you do the ladies' dresses. Anderson, you're great at birds and trees. And Michelangelo... you do young men's butts." The three small figures leaning over the wall (above Mary and Elizabeth) were likely done by 13-year-old Michelangelo, an apprentice here before being "discovered" by Lorenzo the Magnificent. Relaxed and natural, they cast real shadows, as true to life as anyone in Ghirlandaio's perfect-posture, face-the-camera world.

Ghirlandaio was reportedly jealous (and talented Michelangelo contemptuous), but, before they parted ways, Michelangelo learned how to lay fresco from the man who did it as well as anyone in Florence.

Ghirlandaio—*The Birth of John the Baptist*
Set in a typical (rich) Florentine bedroom, John's birth is attended by none other than Lorenzo de Medici's mom (second figure from right), with the broad face, thin lips, and scooped nose Lorenzo would inherit.
• *In the chapel to the right of the altar, Filippino Lippi did the frescoes on the left and right walls. Look first at the right wall, lower level (there's a decent view from the altar steps)...*

8. Filippino Lippi—
St. Philip at the Temple of Mars

In an elaborate shrine, a statue of the angry god Mars waves his broken lance menacingly. The Christian Philip points back up and says, "I'm not afraid of him—that's a false god." To prove it, he opens a hole in the base of the altar, letting out a little dragon, who promptly farts (believe it when you see it), causing the pagan king's son to swoon and die. The overcome spectators clutch their foreheads and noses.

If Ghirlandaio was "busy," Lippi is downright hyperactive, filling every square inch with something frilly—rumpled hair, folds in clothes, dramatic gestures, twisting friezes, wind-blown flags, and gassy dragons.

• *On the left wall, lower level . . .*

Lippi—*St. John the Evangelist Raising Drusiana from the Dead*

The miracle takes place in a spacious 3-D architectural setting, but Lippi has all his actors in a chorus line across the front of the stage. Filippino Lippi (1457–1504, the son of the more famous Fra Filippo Lippi), was apprenticed to Botticelli, whose bright colors, shadowless lighting, and elegant curves were exaggerated by Filippino.

The sober, dignified realism of Florence's Quattrocento was ending. Michelangelo would extend it, building on Masaccio's spacious, solemn, dimly lit scenes. But Lippi championed a style (later called Mannerism, leading to Baroque) that loved color and dramatic excitement.

• *In the next chapel to the right of the altar, on the central wall, find . . .*

9. Giorgio Vasari— *Madonna of the Rosary*

The picture-plane is saturated with images from top to bottom. Saints and angels twist and squirm around Mary (the red patch in the center), but their body language is gibberish, just an excuse for Vasari to exhibit his technique.

Giorgio Vasari (1511–1574), best known as the writer of *The Lives of the Artists,* was a prolific artist himself. As a Mannerist, he copied the "manner" of, say, a twisting Michelangelo statue, but violated the sober spirit, multiplying by 100 and cramming the canvas. I've tried to defend Vasari from the art critics who unanimously call his art superficial and garish . . . but doggone it, they're right.

With Vasari, who immortalized the Florentine Renaissance with his writing, that Renaissance ended.

BRANCACCI CHAPEL TOUR

In the Brancacci Chapel, Masaccio created a world in paint that looked like the world we inhabit. For the first time in a thousand years, Man and Nature were frozen for inspection. Masaccio's painting techniques were copied by many Renaissance artists. And his people—sturdy, intelligent, and dignified—helped shape Renaissance Men and Women's own self-image. They have an expression of understated astonishment, like people awakening to a new and wonderful world—the Renaissance.

Orientation
Cost: €3.10
Hours: Mon and Wed–Sat 10:00–17:00, Sun 13:00–17:00, closed Tue. During visiting hours, enter through the paid entrance to the right of the church. Otherwise, enter the church (free admission, but the chapel is often blocked off or blacked out); the chapel is in the right transept.
Dress Code: Shorts and bare shoulders are OK if you enter through the paid entrance. If you enter through the church, modest dress is requested.
Getting There: The Chapel is in the Church of Santa Maria del Carmine, on Piazza del Carmine, in the Oltrarno neighborhood south of the Arno River.
Starring: Masaccio, Masolino, and Filippino Lippi.

Overview
The chapel has 12 frescoes, telling the story of Peter—half are by Masaccio and half by Masolino or Filippino Lippi. Although Masaccio is the star, the panels by his colleagues are interesting and a good contrast in styles. Masaccio's works are sprinkled among the others, mostly on the left and center walls.

Brancacci Chapel

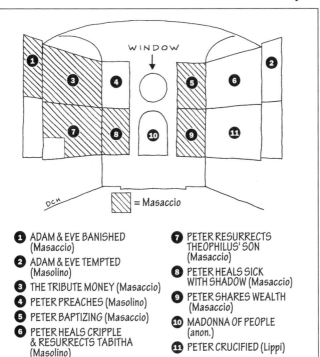

WINDOW

= Masaccio

❶ ADAM & EVE BANISHED (Masaccio)

❷ ADAM & EVE TEMPTED (Masolino)

❸ THE TRIBUTE MONEY (Masaccio)

❹ PETER PREACHES (Masolino)

❺ PETER BAPTIZING (Masaccio)

❻ PETER HEALS CRIPPLE & RESURRECTS TABITHA (Masolino)

❼ PETER RESURRECTS THEOPHILUS' SON (Masaccio)

❽ PETER HEALS SICK WITH SHADOW (Masaccio)

❾ PETER SHARES WEALTH (Masaccio)

❿ MADONNA OF PEOPLE (anon.)

⓫ PETER CRUCIFIED (Lippi)

We'll see them roughly in the order they were painted, from upper left to lower right—the upper six by Masaccio and Masolino (1424–1425), the lower ones by Masaccio (1426–1427) and Filippino Lippi (1481–1485).

• *Start with the left wall, the small panel in the upper left.*

Masaccio—*Adam and Eve Banished from Eden*

Renaissance Man and Woman—as nude as they can be—turn their backs on the skinny, unrealistic, medieval Gate of Paradise and take their first step as mortal humans in the real world. For the first time in a thousand years of painting, these figures cast a realistic shadow, seemingly lit by the same light we are—the natural light through the Brancacci Chapel's window.

Eve wails from deep within. (I thought Eve's gaping mouth was way over the top, until later that night, when on a TV newscast I saw the very same expression on someone dealing with a brother's death.) Adam buries his face in shame. These simple human gestures speak louder than the religious symbols of medieval art.

• *Compare Masaccio's* Adam and Eve *with the one on the opposite wall, by his colleague Masolino.*

Masolino—*Adam and Eve Tempted by the Serpent*

Masolino's elegant, innocent
First Couple float in an ethereal
Garden of Eden with no clear
foreground or background (Eve
hugs a tree or she'd float away).
Their bodies are lit evenly by
a pristine, all-encompassing,
morning-in-springtime light
that casts no shadows.

In 1424, Masolino da
Panicale (1383–1435) was hired by the Brancacci family to decorate this chapel with the story of Peter (beginning with the Original Sin that Peter's "Good News" saves man from). Masolino, a 40-year-old contractor with too many other commitments, invited 23-year-old Masaccio (1401–1428) to help him. The two set up scaffolding and worked side by side—the older, workmanlike master and the young, intuitive genius—in a harmonious collaboration. They just divvied up the panels, never (or rarely) working together on the same scene.

• *Return to the left wall, upper level. From here, we'll work clockwise around the chapel. After* Adam and Eve, *the second panel is . . .*

Masaccio—*Jesus, Peter, and the Disciples Pay the Tribute Money*

The tax collector (in red miniskirt, with his back to us) tells Jesus he must pay a temple tax. Jesus gestures and says, "OK, but the money's over there." Peter, his right-hand man (gray hair and beard, brown robe), says, "Yeah, over there." Peter goes over there to the lake (left side of panel), takes off his robe, stoops down at an odd angle, and miraculously pulls a coin from the mouth of a fish. He puts his robe back on and (right side of panel) pays the man.

Some consider this the first modern painting, placing real humans in a real setting, seen from a single viewpoint—ours. Earlier painters had done far more detailed landscapes than Masaccio's sketchy mountains, lake, trees, clouds, and buildings, but they never fixed where the viewer was in relation to these things.

Masaccio tells us exactly where we stand—near the crowd, farther from the trees, with the sun to our right casting late-afternoon shadows. We're no longer detached spectators, but an extension of the scene. Masaccio lets us stand in the presence of the human Jesus. While a good attempt at three-dimensionality, Masaccio's work is far from perfect. Later artists would perfect mathematically what Masaccio eyeballed intuitively.

The disciples all have strong, broad-shouldered bodies, but each face is unique. Blonde, curly-haired, clean-shaven John is as handsome as the head on a Roman coin (Masaccio had just returned from Rome). Thomas (far right, with a five o'clock shadow) is intense. Their different reactions—with faces half in shadow, half in light—tell us they're divided over paying the tax.

Masaccio's people have one thing in common—a faraway look in the eye, as though hit with a spiritual two-by-four. They're deep in thought, reflective, and awestruck, aware they've just experienced something miraculous. But they're also dazzled, glazed over, and a bit disoriented, like tourists at the Brancacci Chapel.

• *Continuing clockwise, we move to the next panel, on the center wall.*

Masolino—*Peter Preaches to a Crowd*

Masolino and Masaccio, different in so many ways, were both fans of Giotto (1266?–1337), who told stories with simple gestures and minimal acting, adding the human drama by showing the reaction

of bystanders. Here, the miraculous power of the sermon is not evident in Peter (who just raises his hand) but in the faces of the crowd. The lady in the front row is riveted, while others close their eyes to meditate. The big nun (far right) finds it interesting enough to come a little closer, while the tonsured monk's mouth slips open in awe. The gentleman to the left is skeptical but wants to hear more.

Masolino never mastered 3-D space like Masaccio. Peter's extreme profile is a cardboard cutout, his left leg stands too high to plant him realistically on flat ground, the people in the back have their gazes fixed somewhere above Peter, and the "Masacciesque" mountains in the background remain just that, background.

• *Continuing clockwise to the other side of the window . . .*

Masaccio—*Peter Baptizing Converts*

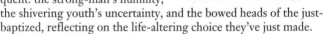

A muscular man kneels in the stream to join the cult of Jesus. On the bank (far right), another young man waits his turn, shivering in his jockstrap. Among the crowd, a just-baptized man wrestles with his robe, while the man in blue, his hair still dripping, buttons up.

The body language is eloquent: the strong-man's humility, the shivering youth's uncertainty, and the bowed heads of the just-baptized, reflecting on the life-altering choice they've just made.

Masaccio builds these bodies with patches of color (an especially effective technique in fresco, where colors can bleed together). He knew that a kneeling man's body, when lit from the left (the direction of the chapel window), would look like a patchwork of bright hills (his pecs) and dark crevasses (his sternum). He assembles the pieces into a sculptural, 3-D figure, "modeled" by light and shade.

Again, Masaccio was the first artist to paint real humans—with 3-D bodies and individual faces, reflecting inner emotions—in a real-world setting.

• *Continue clockwise to the right wall.*

Masolino—*Peter Heals a Cripple* (left side) and *Resurrects Tabitha* (right side)

Masolino takes a crack at the 3-D style of his young partner, setting two separate stories in a single Florentine square, defined by an arcade on the left and a porch on the right. Crude elements of the future Renaissance style abound—the receding buildings establish the viewer's point of reference; the rocks scattered through the square define 3-D space; there are secular details in the background (mother and child, laundry on a balcony, a monkey on a ledge); and the cripple (left) is shown at an odd angle (foreshortening). Masaccio may have helped on this panel.

But there's no denying that the stars of the work are the two sharp-dressed gentlemen strolling across the square, who help

divide (and unite) the two stories of Peter.
The patterned coat is a textbook example
of the International Gothic style that was
the rage in Florence—elegant, refined,
graceful, with curvy lines creating a complex,
pleasing pattern. The man is walking at three-
quarters angle, but Masolino shows the coat
from the front to catch the full display.
The picture is evenly lit, with only a hint
of shadow, accentuating the colorful clothes
and cheerful atmosphere.

In mid-project (1426), Masolino took
another job in Hungary, leaving Masaccio to finish the lower half
of the chapel. Masolino never again explored the Renaissance style,
building a successful career with the eternal springtime of
International Gothic.

• *We move to the lower level. Start on the left wall with the second panel
and work clockwise.*

Masaccio—*Peter Resurrects the Son of Theophilus*

Peter (in that same brown
robe...like Masaccio,
who was careless about his
appearance) raises the boy
from the world of bones,
winning his freedom from
stern Theophilus (seated
in niche to the left).

The courtyard
setting is fully 3-D,
Masaccio having recently
learned a bit of perspective mathematics from his (older) friends
Brunelleschi and Donatello. At the far right of the painting, there
are three of the Quattrocento (1400s) giants who invented painting
perspective (from right to left): Brunelleschi, who broke reality

down mathematically; Alberti,
who popularized the math
with his book, *On Painting;*
and Masaccio himself (looking
out at us), who opened everyone's eyes to the psychologic-
ally powerful possibilities.

Little is known of Masac-
cio's short life. "Masaccio" is a
nickname (often translated as

"Big, Clumsy Thomas") describing his personality—stumbling through life with careless abandon, not worrying about money, clothes, or fame...a lovable doofus.

Next to Masaccio's self-portrait is a painting within a painting of Peter on a throne. On a flat surface with a blank background, Masaccio has created a hovering hologram, a human more 3-D than even a statue made in medieval times.

"Wow," said Brother Philip, a 20-year-old Carmelite monk stationed here when Masaccio painted this. Fra Filippo ("Brother Philip") Lippi was inspired by these frescoes and went on to become a famous painter himself. At age 50, while painting in a convent, he fell in love with a young nun, and they eloped. Nine months later, "Little Philip" was born, and he too grew to be a famous painter—Filippino Lippi...who, in 1481, was chosen to complete the Brancacci Chapel.

Filippino Lippi retouched a damaged section of this fresco, painting the group in the far left (five heads but only eight legs).
• *Moving clockwise to the center wall ...*

Masaccio—*Peter Heals the Sick with his Shadow*

Peter is a powerful Donatello statue come to life, walking towards us along a Florentine street. Next to him, in the red cap, is bearded Donatello, Masaccio's friend and mentor.

Masaccio inspired more than painters. He gave ordinary people a new self-image of what it is to be human. Masaccio's people are individuals, not generic Greek gods, not always pretty (like the old bald guy) but still robust and handsome in their own way. They exude a seriousness that makes them very adult. Compare these street people with Masolino's two well-dressed dandies, and you see the difference between Florence's working-class, urban, "democratic" spirit (Guelphs) and the courtly grace of Europe's landed gentry (Ghibellines).
• *The next panel, on the other side of the altar, is ...*

Masaccio—*Peter Shares the Wealth with the Poor*

Early Christians practiced a form of communal sharing. The wealthy Ananias lied about his contribution, and now does a face-plant of repentance at Peter's feet. Peter takes the missing share and gives it to a poor lady who can't even afford baby pants. The shy baby, the grateful woman, and the admiring man on

crutches show Masaccio's blue-collar sympathies.

The scene reflects an actual event in Florence—a tax-reform measure to make things equal for everyone. Florentines were championing a new form of government where, if we all contribute our fair share through taxes, we don't need kings and nobles.

• *The altar under the window holds a painting that is not by Masaccio, Masolino, or Lippi.*

Anonymous (possibly Coppo di Marcovaldo)—*The Madonna of the People*

This medieval altarpiece replaces the now-destroyed fresco by Masaccio that was the centerpiece of the whole design—Peter's crucifixion.

With several panels still unfinished, Masaccio traveled to Rome to meet up with Masolino. Masaccio died there (possibly of poison) in 1428, at age 27. After his death, the political and artistic climate changed, the chapel was left unfinished (the lower right wall), and some of his frescoes were scraped off whole (his *Crucifixion of Peter*) or in part—we saw in *Peter Resurrects the Son of Theophilus* that several exiled Brancaccis were erased from history, later to be replaced by Medicis.

Finally, in 1481, new funding arrived and Filippino Lippi, the son of the monk-turned-painter, was hired to complete the blank panels and retouch some destroyed frescoes.

• *The right wall, lower section, contains two panels by Filippino Lippi. The first and biggest is . . .*

Filippino Lippi—*Peter Crucified*

Lippi completes the story of Peter with his upside-down crucifixion. Lippi tried to match the solemn style of Masaccio, but his figures are less statuesque, more colorful, and more detailed, and the compositions are busier. Still, compared with Lippi's other hyperactive works found elsewhere, he's reined himself in admirably to honor the great pioneer.

In fact, while Masaccio's perspective techniques were

enormously influential, learned by every Tuscan artist, his sober style was not terribly popular. Another strain of Tuscan painting diverged from Masaccio—from the adult Fra Filippo Lippi to Botticelli, Ghirlandaio, and Filippino Lippi— mixing in the bright colors, line patterns, and even lighting of International Gothic. But Masaccio's legacy remained strong, emerging in the grave, statuesque, harsh-shadow creations of two Florentine giants— Leonardo da Vinci and Michelangelo.

SCIENCE MUSEUM TOUR

Istituto e Museo di Storia della Scienza

Enough art, already! Forget the Madonnas and Venuses for a while to ponder weird contraptions from the birth of modern science. The same spirit of discovery that fueled the artistic Renaissance helped free the sciences from medieval mumbo jumbo. The Science Museum is a historical overview of technical innovations from, roughly, A.D. 1000 to 1900, featuring early telescopes, clocks, experiments, and Galileo's finger in a jar.

English majors will enjoy expanding their knowledge. Art lovers can admire the sheer beauty of functional devices. Engineers will be in hog heaven among endless arrays of gadgets. Everyone will be fully amused by my feeble attempts to explain technical concepts.

Orientation

Cost: €6.50.
Hours: Mon and Wed–Fri 9:30–17:00, Tue and Sat 9:30–13:00, closed Sun.
Getting There: It's at Piazza dei Giudici 1, one block east of the Uffizi, on the north bank of the Arno River.
Information: Tel. 055-239-8876.
Length of Our Tour: Ninety minutes.
Photography: Not allowed.
Starring: Galileo's telescopes, experiment models, and finger.

Overview

There are two floors of rooms. The collection is not really chronological, but if you follow the rooms in order, you get a good overview. Find the displays by their room number (I, II, III, etc.) and exhibit number (I.1, I.2, I.3, etc.).

• *Buy your ticket on the ground floor, then climb stairs to the first floor. Before entering Room I, pick up a free loaner guidebook in English.*

FIRST FLOOR
Rooms I, II, and III

The objects displayed in these first few rooms measured the world around us—the height of distant mountains, the length of a man's arm, the movement of the stars across the sky. This was the bold, first step in science, to actually observe nature and measure it. What they found is that nature—apparently so ever-changing and chaotic—actually behaves in an orderly way, mirroring rather simple mathematical formulas.

Room I: Mathematical Instruments
• *In the center of Room I, you'll find an . . .*

Exhibit I.1—Arabic Celestial Globe (*Globo Celeste Arabio*, 1080)

Looking down on this map of the heavens, you have a God's-eye view of the night sky. Find familiar constellations like the fish, hunter, snake, and bear (our "Big Dipper"). Arab traders mapped the dome of heaven that arches overhead to help them navigate by the stars.

The universe only got bigger with each new bit of knowledge.
• *In the first glass case to the left, on the middle shelf, find exhibit #10.*

Exhibit I.10—Quadrant (*Quadranti Solari*)

You'd grab this wedge-shaped quadrant by its curved edge, point it away from you, and sight along the top edge toward, say, a distant tower or star. Then read the scale etched along the curved edge to find how many degrees above the horizon the object is.

A quadrant measures the triangle formed by you, the horizon, and a distant object. Once you know some of the triangle's six variables (3 angles and 3 sides), you can figure the others. (That's trigonometry.) Armed with this

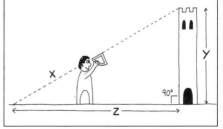

knowledge, you could use the quadrant to measure all kinds of things. On land, calculate how high or how far away a building is. At sea, figure your position in relation to the sun and stars.

Most of the instruments in Rooms I, II, and III are variations on the earliest, simplest device—the quadrant. (A *quad*-rant is one-*fourth* of a 360-degree circle, or 90 degrees.)
• *Just above the quadrant, find…*

Exhibits I.2 through I.5—Arabic Astrolabes (*Astrolabi Arabi*)

Astrolabes, invented by the ancient Greeks and pioneered by medieval Arab sailors, combined a quadrant with a map of the sky (a star chart), allowing you to calculate your position against the stars without doing all the math. You'd hang the metal disk from your thumb and sight along the central crossbeam, locate a star, then read its altitude above the horizon on the measuring scale etched around the rim.

Next, you entered this information in by turning the little handle on the astrolabe's face. This set the wheels-within-wheels into motion, and you'd watch the constellations spin across a backdrop of coordinates. Keep turning until the astrolabe mirrors the current heavens. With your known coordinates dialed in, the astrolabe calculated the unknowns, and you could read out your position along the rim.

In addition, knowing the position of the stars and sun told you the current time of day (see the 24-hour clock around the rim), which was especially useful for Muslims in their daily prayers.
• *In the glass case in the far right corner of the room, on the middle shelf, find…*

Exhibit I.102—Michelangelo's Compass (*Compasso detto di Michelangelo*)

Maybe Michelangelo once used this (it's said to be his), and I suppose it's even conceivable he used it to measure, say, *David*'s hand or to draw a circle on the Sistine ceiling. Regardless, dividers like this were a common way for Renaissance Men and Women to measure the world and marvel at its harmonious proportions.
• *Enter the next room…*

Room II: More Quadrants, Sextants, Octants, and Various Combinations

In the 1500s, improvements were made on the relatively crude quadrants and astrolabes, spurred by the need to navigate the open oceans.

• *Straight ahead, just to the left of the exit doorway, find . . .*

Exhibit II.27—Quadrant
(Quadrante Universale, 1608)

Like a Popeil's Pocket-Navigator, this all-purpose unit has 1,001 uses. The quadrant measures angles. A magnetic compass points to north. A sundial (in the compass's removable cap) tells the time of day, as the sun casts a shadow from the vertical piece onto a scale of hours.

On the backside of the quadrant, a big half-dial arcs across rows of numbers, allowing even non–trig majors to calculate the trajectory of cannon balls. The movable arm even passed through a table of zodiac signs to cast your horoscope—how the stars' alignment affects you personally.

• *On the bottom shelf of the glass case back by the entrance doorway, is . . .*

Exhibit II.88—Calculator
(Macchina Calcolatrice, 1664)

This calculator (mechanical, of course, not electrical) could add and subtract. Enter the numbers you're adding on the dials, and the dials turn gears inside that spin a tube marked with numbers in concentric rings. The answer appears in the digital readout.

Rooms IV and V: Galileo

Galileo Galilei (1564–1642) is known as the father of modern science. His discoveries pioneered many scientific fields, and he was among the first to blend mathematics with hands-on observation of nature to find practical applications. Raised in Florence, he achieved fame teaching at the University of Pisa before retiring back to Florence. The museum displays several of his actual posses-sions (lens, 2 telescopes, compass, and thermometer), models illustrating his early experiments, and his finger.

• *Preserved in a jar in the glass case is . . .*

Exhibit IV.10—Galileo's Finger
(Dito Medio della Mano Destra di Galileo)

Galileo is, perhaps, best known as a martyr for science. He popularized the belief (conceived by the Polish astronomer, Nicolaus
Copernicus, in the early 1500s) that the Earth orbited around
the sun. At the time, the Catholic Church preached an Earth-
centered universe, and, at the age of 70, Galileo was hauled
before the Inquisition in Rome and forced to kneel and publicly
proclaim that the Earth did not move around the sun. As he
walked away, legend has it, he whispered to his followers,
"But it *does* move!"

His students preserved this finger bone, displayed on a
marble pedestal, as a kind of sacred relic in this shrine to science.
Galileo's beliefs eventually triumphed over the Inquisition, and,
appropriately, we have his middle finger raised upward for all
those blind to science.

• *The big wooden ramp is an ...*

Exhibit IV.13—Inclined Plane

Legend has it that Galileo dropped cannonballs from the Leaning Tower of Pisa to see whether heavier objects fall faster than
lighter ones, as the ancient writer Aristotle (and most people)
believed. In fact, Galileo probably did not drop objects from the
Leaning Tower, but he likely rolled them down a wooden ramp
like this reconstructed one.

Rolling balls of different weights down the ramp, he timed
them as they rang the bells posted along the way. (The bells are
spaced increasingly farther apart, but a ball—accelerating as it
drops—will ring them in a regular time.) What Galileo found is
that—if you discount air resistance—all objects fall at the same
speed, regardless of their weight. (It's the air resistance that
makes a feather fall slower than a cannonball, not the weight.)

He also found that falling objects accelerate (speed up) at a
regular rate (9.8 meters per second faster every second) summed
up in a mathematical formula (distance is proportional to the
time squared).

Exhibit IV.15—Model of Water-Lifting Device
(Macchina da Alzare Acqua)

The horses walk in a circle, rocking the two crossbars back and
forth. The crossbars alternately lift and lower buckets in wells,
allowing two horses to draw water from four wells. Galileo was
among the first research scientists to suggest practical applications of his principles.

• *Returning to the glass case, in the upper left, find ...*

Exhibit IV.5—Pendulum Clock Model
(Modello dell'Applicazione del Pendolo all' Orologio)
During a church service in Pisa, Galileo looked up to see the cathedral's chandelier swaying slowly back and forth, like a pendulum. He noticed that a wide-but-fast arc took the same amount of time as a narrow-but-slow arc. "Hmmm. Maybe that regular pendulum motion could be used to time things...."

Exhibit IV.7—Thermometer
(Termoscopio, 19th Century)
Galileo also invented the thermometer (similar to this one), though his glass tube filled with air would later be replaced by thermometers of mercury.
• *Enter Room V, filled with telescopes. Galileo's two telescopes are in the glass cases to the right of the entrance.*

Room V: Galileo's Telescopes
Galileo built these **telescopes (Exhibits V.1 and V.2),** based on reports he'd read from Holland. He was the first person to seriously study the heavens with telescopes. Though these only magnified the image about 30 times ("30 power," which is less than today's binoculars), he saw Jupiter's moons, Saturn's rings, the craters of the moon (which he named "seas"), and blemishes (sunspots) on the supposedly perfect sun.

A telescope is essentially two "magnifying glasses" (convex lenses) in a tube, one at either end. The farther apart the lenses, the greater the magnification, prompting the 4.5-meter (15-foot) **telescope hanging on the wall.** (The longest ever built was 50 meters, or 160 feet, but the slightest movement jiggled the image.)
• *Also in the glass case, displayed in an ivory frame, is...*

Exhibit IV.1—Galileo's Telescope Lens
(Lente obiettiva di Galileo)
Galileo was the first earthling to see the moons of Jupiter. With a homemade telescope, he looked through this lens (it wasn't cracked then) and saw three moons lined up next to Jupiter. This discovery also irked the Church, which insisted that only Earth had a satellite. You could see Jupiter's moons with your own eyes if you simply looked through the telescope, but few church scholars bothered to do so, content to believe what they'd read in ancient books.

Room VI: Lenses and Prisms
A curved glass lens can bend light, magnifying an image.
A **lens-grinding machine (Exhibit VI.55)** could make higher-quality lenses than human hands could.

The study of optics in the 1600s initially had few practical applications beyond optical illusions for the amusement of nobles. Party guests could look at a reflection and see a **man and woman switching genders (Exhibit VI.53)** or walk from side to side to see **Christ become Mary become a saint (VI.54).**

Room VII: Mapping the Cosmos

• *The large contraption in the center of Room VII is an . . .*

Exhibit VII.30—Armillary Sphere
(*Sfera Armilhare Tolemaica,* c. 1590)

This is a three-meter-high (10-foot), gilded-wood model of the universe as conceived by ancient Greeks and medieval Europeans. You'd turn a crank (which is now missing), and watch the stars and planets orbit around the Earth in the center. (Earth's map of North America is pretty accurate, but you're on your own past Reno.) Next to the Earth is the orbit of the moon, then Mercury, Venus, the sun, and so on to the stars in the outer ring. This Earth-centered view of the universe—which matches our common-sense observations of the night sky— was codified by Ptolemy, a Greek-speaking Egyptian of the second century A.D.

Ptolemy (silent *P*) summed up Aristotle's knowledge of the heavens and worked out the mathematics explaining its movements. His math was complex, especially when trying to explain the planets, which occasionally lag behind the stars in their path across the night sky. (We now know it's because fast-orbiting Earth passes the outer planets in their longer, more time-consuming orbits around the sun.)

Ptolemy's system dominated Europe for 1,400 years. It worked most of the time and fit well with medieval Christianity's human-centered theology. But, finally, Nicolas Copernicus (and Galileo) made the mental leap to a sun-centered system. This simplified the math, explained the movement of planets, and— most importantly—changed earthlings' conception of themselves forever.

• *On the wall near the entrance, find the large . . .*

Exhibit VII.40—Map of the World
(*Mappamondo* **by Fra Mauro,**
15th century)

With Columbus' voyages, the
Europeans' world suddenly got
bigger and rounder. This map
portrays the spherical world on a flat
surface. South is up. At the bottom,
find *Europa, Norvegia* (Norway), and
Rossia (Russia). Africa's tip is on top,
with India and China to the left.

Room VIII: Microscopes

The inner world was expanding, too. One day, a Dutchman
picked something from his teeth, looked at it under his crude
microscope, and discovered a mini-universe, crawling with thousands of "very little animalcules, very prettily a-moving" (i.e.,
bacteria and protozoa). Antoni van Leeuwenhoek (1632–1723)
popularized the microscope, finding that fleas have fleas, semen
contains sperm, and one-celled creatures are our fellow animals.

This room displays
simple (*semplice*) and com-
pound (*composto*) micro-
scopes. A simple one is just
a single convex lens—what
we'd call a magnifying glass.
A compound is two (or more)
lenses in a tube, working like
a telescope, where one lens
magnifies the object and the

eyepiece lens magnifies the magnified image. Van Leeuwenhoek
opted for a simple microscope, since early compound ones often
blurred and colored things around the edges. His glass bead–size
lens could make a flea look 275 times bigger.

Rooms IX and X: Thermometers, Barometers, etc.

Even nature's most changeable force—the weather—was analyzed
by human reason.

You'll see many interesting **thermometers (*termometri*)—**
spiral ones, tall ones, and skinny ones on distinctive bases. All
operate on the basic principle that heat expands things. So, a
liquid in a closed glass tube will expand and rise upward as the
temperature rises.

Galileo's early thermometer held air, which is too easily
affected by changing air pressure. So they experimented with

various liquids in a vacuum tube—first water, then alcohol (notice the **lava lamp–style thermometers—*termometri Infingardi*)** where heated alcohol makes the glass balls rise).

Finally, G. D. Fahrenheit (1656–1736) tried mercury, the densest liquid, which expands evenly. He set his scale to the freezing point (32 degrees) and boiling point (212 degrees) of water. Anders Celsius (1701–1744) also used water as the standard, but called the freezing point 0 and boiling point 100.

• *In Room X, to the left of the entrance, find…*

Exhibit X.5—Column Barometer

To make a barometer, take a long, skinny glass tube like the one in the wood frame, fill it with liquid mercury, then turn it upside down and put the open end into a bowlful of more mercury. Some of the mercury in the tube will drop down into the bowl (leaving a vacuum at the top of the tube), but some will stay, sup-

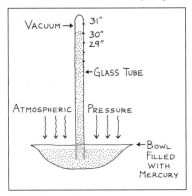

ported by air pressure. The air in the room is "pushing back" by pressing down on the surface of the bowl of mercury.

Changing air pressure signals a change in the weather. Hot air expands, pressing down harder on the bowl of mercury, pushing the mercury column up above 75 centimeters (30 inches), "pushing away" clouds, and pointing to good, dry weather (called *Gran Secco* on this device). Low pressure lets the mercury drop, warning of "big rains" *(Gran Pioggia)*. Your home barometer probably has a round dial with a needle, but it operates on a similar principle.

• *To the right of the entrance…*

Exhibit X.55—Hygrometer

When it's humid (lots of water vapor in the air), your hair gets limp. When it's dry, it frizzes. In various humidity gauges displayed here, when it's humid, the thread or paper absorbs moisture, getting heavier and tilting the scale that measures the humidity.

Room XI: Reflecting Telescopes

The telescopes we saw in Room V were "refracting telescopes," made with lenses that bend (refract) light. The big ones in this room—thick-barreled, often with the eyepiece on the side— are more modern **reflecting telescopes.** They use mirrors to bounce the light rays back and forth through several (refracting) lenses to increase the magnification, thus avoiding the long tubes and distortion of refractors.

Finally, the big double-lensed contraption in the corner (**Exhibit XI.5—*Grande Lente Ustoria***) was owned by the Medici Grand Duke of Florence, who, I believe, used it to burn bugs.
• *Take a break before heading upstairs.*

SECOND FLOOR
Room XII: Clocks

In an ever-changing universe, what is constant enough to measure the passage of time? The sun and stars passing over every 24 hours work for calendar time, but not for hours, minutes, or seconds. Medieval man used sundials, or the steady flow of water or sand through an opening, but these were only approximate.

By the 1600s, with overseas trade booming, there was a crying need for an accurate and durable clock to help in navigation. Sighting by the stars told you your latitude but was less certain on whether you were near Florence, Italy (latitude 44), or Portland, Maine (also latitude 44). You needed a way to time Earth's 24-hour rotation, to know exactly where you were on that daily journey—i.e., your longitude. Reward money was offered for a good clock that could be taken to sea, and science sprang into action.
• *The big clock to the left of the entrance is a . . .*

Exhibit XII.37—Big Clock

Tick. Tock.

This clock is powered by the big, suspended weights that slowly "fall." The energy turns a series of cogwheels that slowly move the clock hands around the dial. The whole thing is regulated by a horizontal ring (at the top) rocking back and forth, once a second. Though big and crude, this "grandfather"-type clock has the three essentials:

1. Power (falling weights).
2. An "escapement" (the cogs that transform the "falling" power into turning power).
3. A regulator that keeps the gears turning evenly. (This one has a rocking ring, while others used a swinging pendulum.)

• *In the glass case ahead in the left corner, find ...*

Exhibit XII.1—Spring Clock

A clock powered by dangling weights won't work on a rocking ship. This clock is powered by a metal spring that slowly uncoils. (The spring is also the power behind most **watches.**) The power is regulated by a pendulu m—Galileo's contribution. Unfortunately, a rocking pendulum on a rocking ship won't work either.

The longitude problem was finally solved—and a £20,000 prize won—by John Harrison of England (1693–1776), whose "chronometer" (not in this museum) was a spring-driven clock in a suspension device to keep it horizontal. It was accurate within three seconds a day, far better than any in this room.

• *In the glass case along the right wall ...*

Exhibit XII.33—The Writing Hand
(*La Mano che scrive*)

A clockwork mechanism powers this mechanical hand of time that writes profundities in Latin (*Huic Domui Deus ...* This is the House of God ...). The hand gets an A for ingenuity and a B-minus for penmanship.

During the so-called Age of Reason (1600s) and Age of Enlightenment (1700s), the clock was the perfect metaphor for the orderly workings of God's well-crafted universe.

• *To the left of the glass case, find the big, black ...*

Exhibit XII.28—"Perpetual Motion" Machine

This big, black clock rolls a ball down a spiral ramp, powering the very device that will launch it back up again. And so on, and so on, ad infinitum ... or so hoped those pursuing the elusive machine that could power itself. In fact, in every energy exchange (as stated in the second law of thermodynamics), a certain amount is transformed into nonrecyclable heat, meaning a perpetual motion machine is impossible. This principle of entropy (trend toward dissipation of energy) leads philosophers to ponder the eventual cold, lifeless fate of the universe itself.

• *Head to the large Room XIV.*

Room XIV: Electricity (or more precisely, Electromagnetism)

Lightning, magnets, and static cling mystified humans for millennia. Little did they know that these quite different phenomena are all generated by the same invisible force—electromagnetism.

• *In the glass case to the right of the entrance, find several compasses.*

The **magnetic compass (Bussola, XIV.1** and others) was first used by the ancient Chinese (what wasn't?), then Arab traders brought it to Europe by the 1100s. They found that a dangling chunk of lodestone, a naturally occurring magnetic rock, always pointed north. (Not directly to the North Pole, but to the "magnetic pole" in upper Canada.) The magnet was aligning itself with the electric field that surrounds the Earth (which is generated by the motion of molten metal in the Earth's interior, plus the solar wind).

In the 1700s, electricity began to be studied, harnessed . . . and played with. The big **static electricity–generating machine** (in the center of the room) was a popular party amusement. You turned a (missing) crank to spin the glass disk, which rubbed against cloth, generating static electricity. The electricity could be stored in the glass Leyden Jar (a jar coated with metal and filled with water). The metal rod sticking out the top of the jar gave off a small charge when touched, enough to create a spark, shock a party guest, or tenderize a turkey (as Ben Franklin attempted one Thanksgiving). But a static generator like this could never produce enough electricity for practical use.

• *In the glass case to the left of the entrance are several early batteries.*

Alessandro Volta (1745–1827) built the first **battery** in Europe (**XIV.117** and **XIV.134** are similar), which generates electricity from a chemical reaction. He stacked metal disks of zinc and copper between disks of cardboard soaked with salt water. The zinc slowly dissolves, releasing electrons into the liquid. Hook a wire to each end of the battery, and the current flows. When the zinc is gone, your battery is dead.

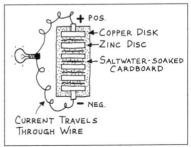

+ POS.
←COPPER DISK
←ZINC DISC
←SALTWATER-SOAKED CARDBOARD
— NEG.
CURRENT TRAVELS THROUGH WIRE

The **electric motor** (*Motore elettrico,* **XIV.132**) generates electricity by moving a magnet through a coil of copper wire, a principle perfected by England's Michael Faraday in 1831. This invention soon led to production of electricity on a large scale.

Room XV: Pneumatic (Air) and Hydraulic (Water) Pumps

Exhibit XV.21—Archimedes Screw Model
(*Modelli di vite d'Archimed*)

Back in third-century-B.C. Greece, Archimedes— the man who gave us the phrase "Eureka!" ("I've found it!")—invented a way to pump water that's still occasionally used today. It's a screw in a cylinder. (This small model has the outer

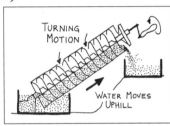

cylinder removed to show the inner workings.) Simply turn the handle and the screw spins, channeling the water up in a spiral path. Dutch windmills powered big Archimedes screws to push water over dikes, to reclaim land from the sea.

• *On the wall near the exit doorway, find a . . .*

Plaque Showing the Magdeburg Vacuum Experiment (*Pneumatica*)

Sixteen horses couldn't pull apart two half globes held together by . . . absolutely nothing.

Otto von Geuricke (1602–1686), the great showman of early science, staged the experiment to publicly demonstrate the power of a vacuum. He placed two 12-foot metal hemispheres together, then removed the air inside (see various **pneumatic pumps** along the left wall), creating a vacuum. The horses could not pry them apart, not with the ton of air pressure—the "ocean" of air all around us—that the globe was "immersed" in. (We all carry a ton of air around on our shoulders, but it's balanced by the same amount pushing in from the side.)

Rooms XVI and XVII: Models for Demonstrating Newton's Mechanics

Isaac Newton (1642–1727) explained all of the universe's motion ("mechanics")—from spinning planets to rolling rocks—in a few simple mathematical formulas.

Exhibit XVI.6—Double Rising Cone
(*Doppio Cono Saliente*)
The double cone rolls up the incline, seemingly defying gravity and Newton's laws. Ah, but Newton would remind us, the cone's center of gravity is always descending.

The **collision balls in Room XVII** (the big wooden frame with hanging balls), a popular desktop toy in the 1970s, demonstrate Newton's three famous laws.

1. Inertia. The balls just sit there unless something moves them, and once they're set in motion, they'll keep moving the same way until something stops them.

2. Force = Mass times Acceleration. The harder you strike the balls, the farther they go. Use two balls to strike with, and you pack twice the punch.

3. For every action, there's an equal and opposite reaction. When one ball swings in and strikes the rest, one ball at the other end swings out, then returns and strikes back.

Room XVIII: Medicine
Back when the same guy who cut your hair removed your appendix, surgery was crude. In the 1700s, there were no anesthetics beyond a bottle of wine, and no knowledge of antiseptics. First (in the glass case in the center of the room, far side, **Exhibit XVIII.1—*Cranio***), they hit you over the head with this (OK, not really). Then they amputated (**Exhibit XVIII.5—*Amputazione***) with these hacksaws (really). Check out the needles for pre-laser eye surgery (**Exhibit XVIII.2—*Occhio***)... no thanks.

The almost life-size wax **obstetrics models**—showing various breech-style complications—are a pregnant woman's nightmare.

Room XIX: Pharmacy

Exhibit XIX.1—Pharmaceutical Jars (late 1700s)
Read the labels on the jars to see what was considered therapeutic in the 1700s: cocaine (*Coca Boliviana*), licorice (*Anice*), poisonous plants (*Belladonna*), tea (*The*), ipecac (*Ipecacuana*), and something I believe translates as flies' nuts (*Noci Mosca*).

Room XX: Chemistry
• *On the wall, find the . . .*

Exhibit XX.34—Affinity Table
(Tabula Affinitatum, 18th century)

This is a precursor of modern periodic tables of the elements. Antoine Lavoisier (1743–94) was the Galileo of chemistry, introducing sound methodology and transforming the mumbo jumbo of medieval alchemy into hard science. He introduced the standardized terminology of suffixes that describe the different forms a single element can take (sulfur, sulf-ide, sulf-ate, sulf-uric, etc.).

Room XXI: Weights and Measures
• *In the glass case ahead to the left, find . . .*

Exhibit XXI.27—One Meter Rod *(Metro)*
Much of the purpose of science is to use constants to measure an ever-changing universe. Here's one constant, the meter, established in 1790 as the fundamental unit by which all distances are measured.

The rod is exactly one meter. Or 39.37 inches. Or 1/1,000th of the distance from the Science Museum to *David.* Or 1/10,000,000th of the distance from the equator to the North Pole. Or, according to the updated definition of 1960, a meter is the length of 1,650,763.73 wavelengths in a vacuum of the orange-red radiation of krypton 86.

Ain't science wonderful?

DAY TRIPS

Pisa • San Gimignano • Siena

Florence offers great day-trip possibilities: Pisa for its tipsy tower and classy Field of Miracles, San Gimignano for its prickly medieval skyline, and Siena for its red-bricked soul. If you can only choose one, it's Siena—no contest.

Allow a minimum of half a day to visit Pisa (2 hrs round-trip by train from Florence) or San Gimignano (1.5 hrs round-trip by bus). For Siena, save a whole day—and an overnight if possible—"to experience the near-mystical twilight at the town's main square (2.5 hrs round-trip by bus, 3.5 hrs by train). Some travelers make Siena their home base and do Florence as a day trip.

PISA

Pisa was a regional superpower in its medieval heyday (11th, 12th, and 13th centuries), rivaling Florence and Genoa. Its Mediterranean empire, which included Corsica and Sardinia, helped make it a wealthy republic. But the Pisa fleet was beaten (in 1284, by Genoa) and its port silted up, leaving the city high and dry, with only its Field of Miracles and its university keeping it on the map.

Pisa's three important sights (the cathedral, the baptistery, and the bell tower) float regally on the best lawn in Italy. Even as the church was being built, the Piazza del Duomo was nicknamed the "Campo dei Miracoli," or Field of Miracles, for the grandness of the undertaking. The style throughout is Pisa's very own "Pisan Romanesque," surrounded by Italy's tackiest ring of souvenir stands. This spectacle is tourism at its most crass. Wear gloves.

The tower recently reopened after a decade of restoration and topple prevention. To ascend, you'll have to make a reservation when you buy your €15 ticket (for details, see "Sights," below).

Florence Day Trips

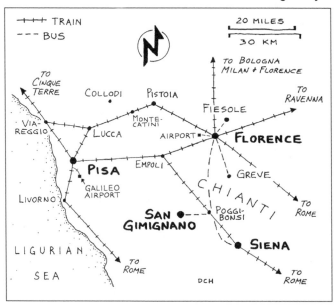

Planning Your Time

Seeing the tower and the square and wandering through the church are 90 percent of the Pisan thrill. Pisa is a touristy quickie. By car, it's a headache. By train, it's a joy. Train travelers may need to change trains in Pisa anyway. Hop on the bus and see the tower. If you want to climb it, go straight to the ticket booth to snare an appointment—usually for a couple of hours later (or check www.duomo.pisa.it before you go to see if you can book online). Sophisticated sightseers stop more for the Pisano carvings in the cathedral and baptistery than for a look at the tipsy tower. There's nothing wrong with Pisa, but I'd stop only to see the Field of Miracles and get out of town. By car, it's a 45-minute detour from the freeway.

Orientation

Tourist Information: One TI is at the train station (summer: Mon–Sat 9:00–19:00, Sun 9:30–15:30; winter: Mon–Sat 9:00–19:00 and possibly closed Sun; to your left as you exit station, tel. 050-42291) and another is near the Leaning Tower (Mon–Fri 9:00–18:00, Sat–Sun 10:30–16:30, outside the medieval wall, hidden behind souvenir stands in a nook of the wall, about 100 meters to the left of the gate before you enter the Field of Miracles, tel. 050-560-464). Another TI is at the airport (tel. 050-503-700).

Arrival in Pisa

By Train: To get to the Field of Miracles from the station, you can **walk** (25–30 min, get free map from TI at station, they'll mark the best route on your map), take a **taxi** (€8, at taxi stand at station or call 050-541-600), or catch a **bus.** The latest information on the bus route to the Field of Miracles is posted in the train information office in Pisa's station lobby (or ask at TI). It's likely bus #3 (3/hr) which leaves from in front of the station, across the street at the big hotel. Buy an €0.80 ticket from the *tabacchi*/magazine kiosk in the station's main hall or at any *tabacchi* shop (good for 1 hr, round-trip OK, 10-minute ride one-way to tower). Confirm the bus route number or risk taking a long tour of Pisa's suburbs. The correct bus will let you off at Piazza Manin, in front of the gate to the Field of Miracles. To return to the station, catch the bus across the street from where you got off (confirm the stop with a local or at the TI).

The train station no longer has a baggage check. If necessary, you could store your bag at the airport (€6/per piece per day); it's only a 5-minute ride on bus #3 (same bus route as to the Field of Miracles but catch bus going in opposite direction) and still make it to the tower on the same bus ticket.

By Car: To get to the Leaning Tower, follow signs to the Duomo or Campo dei Miracoli, located on the north edge of town. If you're coming from the Pisa Nord autostrada exit, you won't have to mess with the city center, but you will have to endure some terrible traffic. There's no option better than the €1-per-hour pay lot just outside the town wall a block from the tower.

By Plane: From Pisa's airport, take bus #3 into town (€0.80, 3/hr, 5 min) or a taxi (€6).

Prices

Pisa has a scheme to get you into its neglected secondary sights: the baptistery, cathedral museum (Museo dell' Opera del Duomo), Camposanto cemetery, and fresco museum (Museo delle Sinopie).

For any one monument, you'll pay €5; for two monuments the cost is €6; for four monuments it's €8.50; and for the works (including the cathedral) you'll pay €10.50. By comparison, the cathedral alone is a bargain (€2). You can buy any of these tickets at the usually crowded ticket office (behind tower and cathedral entrance), or more easily at the Camposanto cemetery, Museo dell' Opera del Duomo, or Museo delle Sinopie (near the baptis-tery, almost suffocated by souvenir stands); note that you can buy a ticket just for, say, the cathedral at any of these points.

For marathon sightseers there's a €13 Universalis ticket that covers all of the above sights, the Museo Nazionale di San Matteo, and many others, purchasable only at the Tower of Santa Maria, behind the baptistery.

No matter what ticket you get, you'll have to pay another €15 to climb the Leaning Tower. Tickets for the ascent are sold only at the crowded ticket office behind the Tower and Duomo.

Sights—Pisa

▲▲**Leaning Tower**—Started in the 12th-century, this most famous example of Pisan Romanesque architecture was leaning even before its completion. Notice how the architect, for lack of a better solution, kinked up the top section. The 294 tilted steps to the top were closed for years as engineers worked to keep the bell tower from toppling. The formerly clean and tidy area around the tower was turned into a construction zone as engineers used steam pipes to dry out the subsoil and huge weights to stabilize (but not straighten out) the tower.

Now 30 people an hour can clamber to the top for €15 (Mon–Sat 8:00–17:20, Sun 9:00–17:00). To make the necessary reservation, go straight to the ticket office behind the tower. You choose a time slot (40 minutes) for your visit at the time of purchase; it will likely be a couple of hours before you're able to go up (you could see the rest of the monuments and grab lunch while waiting). There are plans to set up online booking; check www.duomo.pisa.it or call 050-560-547 for the latest. Note that even though the ticket office sign says the visit is guided, that only means you'll be accompanied by a museum guard to make sure you don't stay up past your scheduled 40-minute appointment time. Not including the climb, you'll have about 25 minutes for vertigo on top.

▲▲**Cathedral**—The huge Pisan Romanesque church (known as the Duomo), with its carved pulpit by Giovanni Pisano, is artistically more important than its more famous bell tower (€2, open daily, summer: Mon–Sat 10:00–20:00, Sun 13:00–19:40; spring and fall: Mon–Sat 10:00–17:40, Sun 13:00–17:40; winter: Mon–Sat 10:00–12:45 & 15:00–16:45, Sun 15:00–16:45). Shorts are OK as long as they're not short shorts. Big backpacks are not allowed, nor is storage provided (but ticket-taker might let you leave bag at entrance).

Baptistery—The baptistery, the biggest in Italy, is interesting for its great acoustics (open daily, summer: 8:00–19:40; spring and fall: 9:00–17:40; winter: 9:00–16:40; located in front of cathedral). If you ask nicely and leave a tip, the ticket-taker uses the place's echo power to sing haunting harmonies with himself. The pulpit,

Pisa

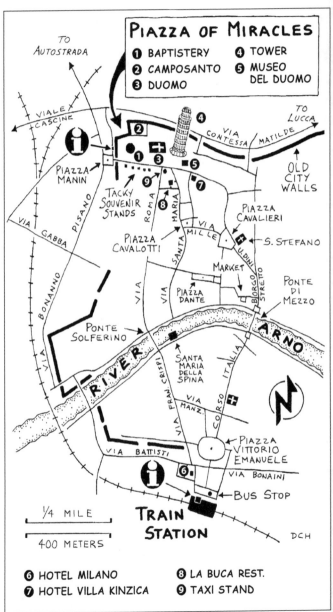

PIAZZA OF MIRACLES
1 BAPTISTERY   4 TOWER
2 CAMPOSANTO   5 MUSEO DEL DUOMO
3 DUOMO

1/4 MILE
400 METERS

6 HOTEL MILANO   8 LA BUCA REST.
7 HOTEL VILLA KINZICA 9 TAXI STAND

by Nicolo Pisano (1260), inspired Renaissance art to follow, but the same artist's pulpit and carvings in Siena were just as impressive to me—in a more enjoyable atmosphere. Notice that even the baptistery leans nearly two meters (5 feet).

Other Sights at the Field of Miracles—For Pisan art, see the **Museo dell' Opera del Duomo,** displaying treasures of the cathedral, including sculptures (12th–14th century), paintings, silverware, and ancient Egyptian, Etruscan, and Roman artifacts (same hours as baptistery; housed behind tower, Piazza Arcivescovado 18).

Skip the **Camposanto** cemetery bordering the cathedral square, even if its "Holy Land dirt" does turn a body into a skeleton in a day (same hours as baptistery).

The **Museo delle Sinopie,** housed in a 13th-century hospital, features the sketchy frescoes that were preparatory work for the frescoes in the cemetery (same hours as baptistery, hidden behind souvenir stands, across street from baptistery entrance).

The much-advertised **Panoramic Walk on the Wall,** which includes just a small section of the medieval wall, isn't worth your time or €2.20 (March–Dec daily 10:00–18:00, entrance near baptistery, at Porta Leone).

More Sights—The **Museo Nazionale di San Matteo,** in a former convent, displays 12th- to 15th-century sculptures, illuminated manuscripts, and paintings by Martini, Ghirlandaio, Masaccio, and others (€4.20, Tue–Sat 8:30–19:00, Sun 9:30–13:30, closed Mon, on river near Piazza Mazzini at Lungarno Mediceo, tel. 050-541-865).

Walking between the station and Field of Miracles in the pedestrian zone from Via G. Oberdan to Piazza Vittorio Veneto shows you a student-filled, classy, Old World town with an Arno-scape much like its rival upstream. A little **fruit market** is pinched and squeezed into Piazza Vettovaglie (Mon–Sat 7:00–18:00, near river, between station and tower). A **street market** attracts shoppers Wednesday and Saturday mornings between Via del Brennero and Via Paparrelle (just outside of wall, about 6 blocks east of tower).

Sleeping and Eating in Pisa
(€1 = about $1, country code: 39, zip code: 56100)

S = Single, **D** = Double/Twin, **T** = Triple, **Q** = Quad, **b** = bathroom, **s** = shower only, **CC** = Credit Cards accepted, **no CC** = Credit Cards not accepted, **SE** = Speaks English, **NSE** = No English. Unless otherwise noted, breakfast is included (but usually optional). English is generally spoken.

Consider **Hotel Milano,** near the station, offering 10 spacious rooms with faded-but-clean bedspreads (D-€47, Db-€65, breakfast extra, CC, air-con, Via Mascagni 14, tel. 050-23162, fax 050-44237, e-mail: hotelmilano@csinfo.it). Or try the pricier **Hotel Villa Kinzica,** with 33 modern rooms within a block of the Field of Miracles—ask for a room with a view of the tower (Db-€104, CC, elevator, most rooms air-con, attached restaurant, Piazza Arcivescovado 2, tel. 050-560-419, fax 050-551-204).

Eating: For a quick lunch or dinner, the pizzeria/trattoria **La Buca**—just a block from the tower—has a good reputation among locals (Sat–Thu 12:00–15:30 & 19:00–23:00, closed Fri, CC, at Via Santa Maria and Via G. Tassi, tel. 050-560-660).

Bar Costa Gelateria has a good assortment of homemade gelato a block from the Museo dell' Opera del Duomo on Via Santa Maria 100 (daily 8:00–24:00, tel. 050-551-016).

For a cheap, fast, and tasty meal a few steps from the train station, try cheery **La Lupa Ghiotta Tavola Calda.** It's got everything you'd want from a *ristorante* at half the price with faster service (you can build your own salad—5 ingredients for €4.50, Mon and Wed–Sat 12:00–15:30 & 19:00–24:00, Tue 12:00–15:30, Sun 19:00–24:00, Viale Bonaini 113, tel. 050-21018).

Transportation Connections—Pisa

By train to: Florence (hrly, 1 hr), **La Spezia** (hrly, 1 hr, gateway to Cinque Terre), **Siena** (change at Empoli: Pisa–Empoli, hrly, 30 min; Empoli–Siena, hrly, 1 hr). Even the fastest trains stop in Pisa, and you might be changing trains here whether you plan to stop or not. Train info: tel. 848-888-088.

By car: The drive between Pisa and Florence is that rare case where the non-autostrada highway (free, more direct, and at least as fast) is a better deal than the autostrada.

SAN GIMIGNANO

The epitome of a Tuscan hill town, with 14 medieval towers still standing (out of an original 72!), San Gimignano is a perfectly preserved tourist trap, so easy to visit and visually pleasing that it's a good stop. In the 13th century, back in the days of Romeo

 and Juliet, towns were run by feuding noble families. They'd periodically battle things out from the protection of their respective family towers. Pointy skylines were the norm in medieval Tuscany. But in San Gimignano,

fabric was big business, and many of its towers were built simply to hang dyed fabric out to dry.

While the basic three-star sight here is the town of San Gimignano itself, there are a few worthwhile stops. From the town gate, shop straight up the traffic-free town's cobbled main drag to Piazza del Cisterna (with its 13th-century well). The town sights cluster around the adjoining Piazza del Duomo. Thursday is market day (8:00–13:00), but for local merchants, every day is a sales frenzy.

Tourist Information: The TI is in the old center on Piazza Duomo (daily March–Oct 9:00–13:00 & 15:00–19:00, Nov–Feb 9:00–13:00 & 14:00–18:00, changes money, tel. 0577-940-008, www.sangimignano.com, e-mail: prolocsg@tin.it). To see virtually all of the city's sights, consider a €10.50 combo-ticket (covers Collegiata, Torre Grossa, Museo Civico, archaeological museum, and more).

Sights—San Gimignano

Collegiata—This Romanesque church, with round windows and wide steps, is filled with fine Renaissance frescoes (€3.50, Mon–Fri 9:30–19:30, Sat 9:30–17:00, Sun 13:00–17:00).

Torre Grossa—The city's tallest tower can be scaled (€4.25, 60 meters/200 feet tall, March–Oct daily 9:30–19:20, Nov–Feb Sat–Thu 10:30–16:20, closed Fri), but the free *rocca* (castle), a short hike behind the church, offers a better view and a great picnic perch, especially at sunset.

Museo Civico—This museum, on Piazza Popolo, has a classy little painting collection with a 1422 altarpiece by Taddeo di Bartolo, honoring Saint Gimignano. You can see the saint with the town in his hands surrounded by events from his life (€3.75, €6.25 combo-ticket with Torre Grossa, same hours as Torre Grossa).

Sleeping and Eating in San Gimignano
(€1 = about $1, country code: 39, zip code: 53037)

Carla Rossi offers rooms and apartments—most with views—throughout the town (Db-from €60, most around €100, no CC, no breakfast, Via di Cellole 81, tel. & fax 0577-955-041, cellular 36-8352-3206, www.appartamentirossicarla.com, e-mail: cabusini@tin.it, SE). For a listing of private rooms, stop by or call **Associazione Strutture Extralberghiere** (Db-€52, no CC, no breakfast, Piazza della Cisterna, tel. 0577-943-190).

Eating: Osteria del Carcere has good food and prices (Via del Castello 13, no CC, just off Piazza della Cisterna, tel. 0577-941-905). Shops guarded by wild boar statues sell boar by the gram; carnivores buy some boar (*cinghiale;* pron. cheen-GAH-lay), cheese, bread, and wine and enjoy a picnic in the garden by the castle.

Transportation Connections—San Gimignano

To: Florence (hrly buses, 75 min, change in Poggibonsi; or catch the frequent 20-min shuttle bus to Poggibonsi and train to Florence), **Siena** (5 buses/day, 1.25 hrs, or can change in Poggibonsi to catch train to Siena), **Volterra** (6 buses/day, 2 hrs, change in Poggibonsi and Colle di Val d'Elsa). In San Gimignano, bus tickets are sold at the bar just inside the town gate. The town has no baggage-check service.

Drivers: You can't drive within the walled town of San Gimignano, but a car park awaits just a few steps outside.

SIENA

Siena was medieval Florence's archrival. And while Florence ultimately won the battle, Siena still competes for the tourists. Sure, Florence has the most heavyweight sights. But Siena offers a unique magic and is my favorite one-day side trip from Florence.

Siena seems to be every Italy connoisseur's pet town. In my office, whenever Siena is mentioned, someone moans, "Siena? I looove Siena!"

Seven hundred years ago, Siena was a major military power in a class with Florence, Venice, and Genoa. With a population of 60,000, it was even bigger than Paris. In 1348, a disastrous plague weakened Siena. Then, in the 1550s, her bitter rival, Florence, really "salted" her, forever making Siena a nonthreatening backwater. Siena's loss became our sightseeing gain, as its political and economic irrelevance pickled it purely Gothic. Today, Siena's population is still 60,000, compared to Florence's 420,000.

Siena's thriving historic center, with red-brick lanes cascading every which way, offers Italy's best Gothic city experience. Most people do Siena, just 50 kilometers south of Florence, as a day trip, but it's best experienced at twilight. While Florence has the block-buster museums, Siena has an easy-to-enjoy soul: Courtyards sport flower-decked wells, alleys dead-end at rooftop views, and the sky is a rich blue dome. Right off the bat, Siena becomes an old friend.

For those who dream of a Fiat-free Italy, pedestrians rule in the old center of Siena. Sit at a café on the red-brick main square. Take time to savor the first European city to eliminate automobile traffic from its main square (1966) and then, just to be silly, wonder what would happen if they did it in your city.

Planning Your Time

With fine bus and train connections, Siena is a handy day trip
from Florence. With more time, consider spending two nights
and a leisurely day in Siena. I like evenings in Siena even more
than in Florence. After an evening in Siena, its major sights can
be seen in half a day.

Orientation

Siena lounges atop a hill, stretching its three legs out from Il
Campo. This main square, the historic meeting point of Siena's
neighborhoods, is pedestrian-only. And most of those pedestrians
are students from the local university. Everything I mention is
within a 15-minute walk of the square. Navigate by landmarks,
following the excellent system of street-corner signs. The typical
visitor sticks to the San Domenico–Il Campo axis.

Siena is one big sight. Its essential individual sights come in
two little clusters: the square (city hall, museum, tower) and the
cathedral (baptistery, cathedral museum with its surprise viewpoint). Check these sights off, and you're free to wander.

Tourist Information: Pick up a free town map from the main
TI at #56 on Il Campo; look for the yellow "Change" sign—bad
rates, good information (Mon–Sat 8:30–19:30, tel. 0577-280-551,
www.siena.turismo.toscana.it). The little TI at San Domenico is
for hotel promotion only and sells a Siena map for €0.60.

Helpful Hints

Local Guide: Roberto Bechi, a hardworking Sienese guide,
specializes in off-the-beaten-path tours of Siena and the surrounding countryside. Married to an American (Patti) and
having run restaurants in Siena and the United States, Roberto
communicates well with Americans. His passions are Sienese
culture, Tuscan history, and local cuisine. Book well in advance
(full-day tours from $65–95 per person, half-day tours from $30–
50 per person, tel. & fax 0577-704-789, www.toursbyroberto
.com, e-mail: tourrob@tin.it; for U.S. contact, fax Greg Evans
at 540/434-4532).

Internet Access: In this university town, there are lots
of places to get plugged in. **Internet Point** is just off Piazza
Matteotti, on Via Paradiso (across street from McDonald's)
and **Internet Train** is near Il Campo, at Via di Città 121
(tel. 0577-226-366).

Laundromats: Two modern, self-service places are
Lavarapido Wash and Dry (daily 8:00–22:00, Via di Pantaneto 38,
near Logge del Papa) and Onda Blu (daily 8:00–21:00, Via del
Casato di Sotto 17, 50 meters from Il Campo).

Arrival in Siena

By Train: The small train station, located on the edge of town, has a bar and bus office (baggage check and lockers closed indefinitely).

To get from the station to the city center, take a taxi or a city bus. The **taxi stand** is to your far right as you exit the station; allow about €8 to Il Campo, the main square (for taxis at station, call 0577-44504, for taxis at Piazza Matteotti in the center, call 0577-49222). For the **city bus**, buy a €0.75 ticket from the Bus Ticket Office in the station lobby (daily 6:15–19:30, ask for a city map—it's free and just a bus route map but helps get you started). You can also buy a bus ticket from the blue machine in the lobby (touch screen for English and select "urban" for type of ticket). Then cross the parking lot and the street to reach the sheltered bus stop. Catch any orange city bus to get into town (punch ticket in machine on bus to validate it). You'll end up at one of three stops—Piazza Gramsci/Lizza, Piazza Sale, or Stufa Secca—all within several blocks of each other (buses run about every 7 min, fewer on Sun; if you get off at Stufa Secca's tiny square, you're soon faced with two uphill roads—take the one to the right for one block to reach the main drag, Banchi di Sopra.

To get to Siena's train station from the center of Siena, catch the city bus at Piazza del Sale or Stufa Secca; note that bus stops are rarely marked with a "bus stop" sign but instead with a posted schedule and sometimes with yellow lines painted on the pavement, showing a bus-sized rectangle and the word "bus." Confirm with the driver that the bus is going to the *stazione* (stat-zee-OH-nay). Remember to purchase your ticket in advance from a *tabacchi* shop.

By Bus: Some buses arrive in Siena at the train station (see "Arrival by Train," above), others at Piazza Gramsci (a few blocks from city center), and some stop at both. The main bus companies are Sena and Tran. You can store baggage underneath Piazza Gramsci in Sotopassaggio la Lizza (€2.75, daily 7:00–19:30, no overnight).

By Car: Drivers coming from the autostrada take the Porta San Marco exit and follow the *Centro*, then *Stadio*, signs (stadium, soccer ball). The soccer-ball signs take you to the stadium lot (Parcheggio Stadio, €1.50/hr, €12.50/day) at the huge, bare-brick San Domenico Church. The Fortezza lot nearby charges the same. Or park in the lot underneath the railway station. You can drive into the pedestrian zone (a pretty ballsy thing to do) only to drop bags at your hotel. You can park free in the lot below the Albergo Lea, in white-striped spots behind Hotel Villa Liberty, and behind the Fortezza. (The signs showing a street cleaner and a day of the week indicate which day the street is cleaned; there's a €105 tow-fee incentive to learn the days of the week in Italian.)

Sights—Siena's Main Square

▲▲▲**Il Campo**—Siena's great central piazza is urban harmony at its best. Like a people-friendly stage set, its gently tilted floor fans out from the tower and city hall backdrop. It's the perfect invitation to loiter. Think of it as a trip to the beach without sand or water.

Il Campo was located at the historic junction of Siena's various competing districts, or *contrada*, on the old marketplace. The brick surface is divided into nine sections, representing the council of nine merchants and city bigwigs who ruled medieval Siena. At the square's high point, look for the *Fountain of Joy*, the two naked guys about to be tossed in, and the pigeons politely waiting their turn to gingerly tightrope down slippery spouts to slurp a drink. (You can see parts of the original fountain, of which this is a copy, in an interesting exhibit at Siena's Santa Maria della Scala museum, listed below.) At the square's low point is the city hall and tower. The chapel located at the base of the tower was built in 1348 as thanks to God for ending the Black Plague (after it killed more than a third of the population).

To say Siena and Florence have always been competitive is an understatement. In medieval times, a statue of Venus stood on Il Campo (where the *Fountain of Joy* is today). After the plague hit Siena, the monks blamed this pagan statue. The people cut it to pieces and buried it along the walls of Florence.

The market area behind the city hall, a wide-open expanse since the Middle Ages, originated as a farming area within the city walls to feed the city in times of siege. Now the morning produce market is held here Monday through Saturday. (The closest public WCs to Il Campo are each about a block away: at Via Beccheria— a few steps off Via de Città—and on Casato di Sotto; €0.60.)

▲**Museo Civico**—The Palazzo Publico (City Hall), at the base of the tower, has a fine and manageable museum housing a good sample of Sienese art. In order, you'll see the following: the Sala Risorgimento, with dramatic scenes of Victor Emmanuel's unification of Italy (surrounded by statues that don't seem to care); the chapel, with impressive inlaid wood chairs in the choir; and the Sala del Mappamondo, with Simone Martini's *Maesta* (Enthroned Virgin) facing the faded *Guidoriccio da Fogliano* (a mercenary providing a more concrete form of protection). Next is the Sala della Pace—where the city's fat cats met. Looking down on the oligarchy during their meetings were two interesting frescoes showing the effects of good and bad government. Notice the whistle-while-you-work happiness of the utopian community ruled by the utopian government (in the better-preserved fresco) and the fate of a community ruled by politicians with more typical

Siena

1 Piccolo Hotel Etruria
2 Albergo Tre Donzelle
3 To Casa Laura, Hotel Santa Catarina & Palazzo Valli
4 To Hotel Duomo & Pensione Pal. Ravizza
5 Hotel Cannon d'Oro
6 Locanda Garibaldi

7 Albergo Bernini
8 Alma Domus
9 Hotel Chiusarelli
10 To Albergo Lea & Hotel Liberty
11 Jolly Hotel Siena
12 Pizzeria Spadaforte
13 Ristorante Gallo Nero

14 Osteria il Tamburino
15 Osteria Da Divo
16 Il Verrochio
17 Ciao Cafeteria
18 Lavarapido Laundromat
19 Onda Blu Laundromat
20 Sottopassaggio La Lizza

values (in a terrible state of repair). The message: Without justice, there can be no prosperity. The rural view out the window is essentially the view from the top of the big stairs—enjoy it from here (€6.50, combo-ticket with tower €9.50, daily March–Oct 10:00–19:00, July–Sept until 23:00, Nov–Jan 10:00–16:00, last entry 45 min before closing, audioguide €3.75 for 1 person, €5.25 for 2, tel. 0577-292-111).

▲**City Tower (Torre del Mangia)**—Siena gathers around its city hall, not its church. It was a proud republic; its "declaration of independence" is the tallest secular medieval tower in Italy. The 100-meter-tall (330-foot) Torre del Mangia was named after a hedonistic watchman who consumed his earnings like a glutton consumes food (his chewed-up statue is in the courtyard, to the left as you enter). Its 300 steps get pretty skinny at the top, but the reward is one of Italy's best views (€5.50, combo-ticket with Museo Civico €9.50, daily 10:00–19:00, mid-July–mid-Sept until 23:00, Nov–March 10:00–16:00, closed in rain, sometimes long lines, limit of 30 tourists at a time, avoid midday crowd).

▲**Pinacoteca (National Picture Gallery)**—Siena was a power in Gothic art. But the average tourist, wrapped up in a love affair with the Renaissance, hardly notices. This museum takes you on a walk through Siena's art, chronologically from the 12th through the 15th centuries. For the casual sightseer, the Sienese art in the city hall and cathedral museums is adequate. But art fans enjoy this opportunity to trace the evolution of Siena's delicate and elegant art (€4.25, Sun–Mon 8:30–13:15, Tue–Sat 8:15–19:15, plus possibly 20:30–23:30 on Sat in summer, tel. 0577-281-161). From Il Campo, walk out Via di Città to Piazza di Postierla and go left on San Pietro.

Sights—Siena's Cathedral Area

▲▲▲**Duomo**—Siena's cathedral is as Baroque as Gothic gets. The striped facade is piled with statues and ornamentation, and the interior is decorated from top to bottom. The heads of 172 popes peer down from the ceiling, over the fine inlaid art on the floor. This is one busy interior.

To orient yourself in this *panforte* of Italian churches, stand under the dome and think of the church floor as a big clock. You're the middle, and the altar is high noon: You'll find the *Slaughter of the Innocents* roped off on the floor at 10:00, Pisano's pulpit between two pillars at 11:00, Bernini's chapel at 3:00, two Michelangelo statues (next to doorway leading to a shop, snacks, and WC) at 7:00, the library at 8:00, and a Donatello statue at 9:00. Take some time with the floor mosaics in the front. Nicola Pisano's wonderful pulpit is crowded with delicate Gothic storytelling from 1268. To understand why Bernini is considered the greatest Baroque sculptor, step into his sumptuous Cappella della Madonna del Voto. This last work in the cathedral, from 1659, is enough to make a Lutheran light a candle. Move up to the altar and look back at the two Bernini statues: Mary Magdalene in a state of spiritual ecstasy, and St. Jerome playing the crucifix like a violinist lost in beautiful music.

The Piccolomini altar is most interesting for its two Michelangelo statues (the lower big ones). Paul, on the left, may be a self-portrait. Peter, on the right, resembles Michelangelo's more famous statue of Moses. Originally contracted to do 15 statues, Michelangelo left the project early (1504) to do his great *David* in Florence.

The Piccolomini Library—worth the €1.50 entry—is brilliantly frescoed with scenes glorifying the works of a pope from 500 years ago. It contains intricately decorated, illuminated music scores and a statue (a Roman copy of a Greek original) of the Three Graces (library open Sun 13:30–19:30, Tue–Sat same as church hours, below). Donatello's bronze statue of St. John the Baptist, in his famous rags, is in a chapel to the right of the library.

Hours: The church is open mid-March–Oct daily 7:30–19:30 but Sun 10:15–14:00 is reserved for worship only; Nov–mid-March Mon–Sat 7:30–17:00, Sun 14:30–17:30 (modest dress required). In September, when much of the elaborate mosaic floor is uncovered, you'll pay a fee to enter the church (€2.75 for *pavimento Cattedrale*).

Audioguides: There's a daunting number of audioguides. An audioguide for just the church costs €3.10; add the library, and it's €3.60; add the Cathedral Museum (Museo dell' Opera de Panorama), and pay €5.25. For the church and museum only, it's €4.25. Two headphones are available at a price break.

▲**Santa Maria della Scala**—This renovated old hospital-turned-museum (opposite the Duomo entrance) was used as a hospital as recently as the 1980s. Now it displays a lavishly frescoed hall, a worthwhile exhibit on Quercia's *Fountain of Joy* (downstairs), and a so-so archaeological museum (subterranean, in labyrinthine tunnels). The entire museum is a maze, with various exhibitions and paintings plugged in to fill the gaps.

The frescoes in the **Pellegrinaio Hall** show medieval Siena's innovative health care and social welfare system in action (c. 1442, wonderfully described in English). The hospital was functioning as early as the 11th century, nursing the sick and caring for abandoned children (see frescoes). The good work paid off, as bequests and donations poured in, creating the wealth that's evident in the chapels elsewhere on this floor. The Old Sacristy was built to house precious relics, including a Holy Nail thought to be from Jesus' cross.

Downstairs, the engaging exhibit on Jacopo della Quercia's early 15th-century *Fountain of Joy* doesn't need much English description, fortunately, because there isn't much. In the 19th century, the *Fountain of Joy* in Il Campo was deteriorating. It was dismantled and plaster casts were made of the originals. Then replicas were made, restoring the pieces as if brand-new. The *Fountain of Joy* that stands in Il Campo today is a replica. In this exhibit, you'll see the plaster casts of the original, eroded panels paired with their restored twins. Statues originally stood on the edges of the fountain (see the statues and drawings). In general, the pieces at the beginning and end of the exhibit are original. If there's a piece in a dim room near the exit of the exhibit, it's likely an original chunk awaiting cleaning.

The **Archaeological Museum,** way downstairs, consists mainly of pottery fragments in cases lining tunnel after tunnel. It's like being lost in a wine cellar without the wine. Unless there's an exhibition, it's not worth the trip.

Cost and Hours: €5.25, daily 10:00–18:00, Fri–Sat in summer until 23:00, off-season 11:30–16:30, closed some Sundays. The chapel just inside the door to your left is free (English description inside chapel entrance).

▲**Baptistery**—Siena is so hilly that there wasn't enough flat ground on which to build a big church. What to do? Build a big church and prop up the overhanging edge with the baptistery. This dark and quietly tucked-away cave of art is worth a look (and €2.50) for its cool tranquility and the bronze panels and angels—by Ghiberti, Donatello, and others—adorning the pedestal of the baptismal font (daily mid-March–Sept 9:00–19:30, Oct 9:00–18:00, Nov–mid-March 10:00–13:00 & 14:30–17:00).

▲▲**Cathedral Museum (Museo dell' Opera e Panorama)**—Siena's most enjoyable museum, on the Campo side of the church (look for the yellow signs), was built to house the cathedral's art. The ground floor is filled with the cathedral's original Gothic sculpture by Giovanni Pisano (who spent 10 years in the late 1200s carving and orchestrating the decoration of the cathedral) and a fine Donatello *Madonna and Child.* Upstairs to the left awaits a private audience with Duccio's *Maesta* (*Enthroned Virgin*). Pull up a chair and study one of the great pieces of medieval art. The flip side of the *Maesta* (displayed on the opposite wall), with 26 panels—the medieval equivalent of pages—shows scenes from the Passion of Christ. Climb onto the "Panorama dal Facciatone." From the first landing, take the skinnier second spiral for Siena's surprise view. Look back over the Duomo and consider this:

When rival republic Florence began its grand cathedral, proud Siena decided to build the biggest church in all Christendom. The existing cathedral would be used as a transept. You're atop what would have been the entry. The wall below you, connecting the Duomo with the museum of the cathedral, was as far as Siena got before a plague killed the city's ability to finish the project. Had it been completed, you'd be looking straight down the nave—white stones mark where columns would have stood (€5.50, worthwhile €2.60 40-minute audioguide, daily mid-March–Sept 9:00–19:30, Oct 9:00–18:00, Nov–mid-March 9:00–13:30, tel. 0577-283-048).

Sights—Siena's San Domenico Area

Church of San Domenico—This huge brick church is worth a quick look. The bland interior fits the austere philosophy of the Dominicans. Walk up the steps in the rear for a look at various paintings from the life of Saint Catherine, patron saint of Siena. Halfway up the church on the right, you'll see a metal bust of Saint Catherine and a small case containing her finger. In the adjacent chapel (to the left), you'll see her actual head (free, daily March–Oct 7:00–13:00 & 14:30–18:30, Nov–Feb 9:00–13:00 & 15:00–18:00; WC for €0.60 at far end of parking lot—facing church entrance, it's to your right).

Sanctuary of Saint Catherine—Step into Catherine's cool and peaceful home. Siena remembers its favorite hometown girl, a simple, unschooled, but mystically devout girl who, in the mid-1300s, helped convince the pope to return from France to Rome. Pilgrims have come here since 1464. Since then, architects and artists have greatly embellished what was probably a humble home (her family worked as wool-dyers). Enter through the courtyard and walk to the far end. The chapel on your right was built over the spot where Saint Catherine received the stigmata while praying. The chapel on your left used to be the kitchen. Go down the stairs to the left of the chapel/kitchen to reach the saint's room. The saint's bare cell is behind see-through doors. Much of the art throughout the sanctuary depicts scenes from the saint's life (free, daily 9:30–18:00, winter 9:30–13:30 & 15:00–18:30, Via Tiratoio). It's a few downhill blocks toward the center from San Domenico (follow signs to the Santuario di Santa Caterina).

Nightlife—Join the evening *passeggiata* (peak strolling time is 19:00) along Via Banchi di Sopra with gelato in hand. **Nannini's** at Piazza Salimbeni has fine gelato (daily 11:00–24:00).

The **Enoteca Italiana** is a good wine bar in a cellar in the Fortezza/Fortress (Mon 12:00–20:00, Tue–Sat 12:00–1:00, closed Sun, sample glasses in 3 different price ranges: €1.55, €2.75,

€5.25, bottles and snacks available, CC, cross bridge and enter fortress, go left down ramp, tel. 0577-288-497).

Shopping—Shops line Via Banchi di Sopra, the *passeggiata* route. For a department store, try Upim on Piazza Matteotti (Mon–Sat 9:30–19:50, closed Sun). The large, colorful scarves/flags, each depicting the symbol of one of Siena's 17 different neighborhoods (such as the wolf, the turtle, and the snail), are easy-to-pack souvenirs, fun for decorating your home (€7.25 apiece for large size, sold at souvenir stands).

Siena's Palio

In the Palio, the feisty spirit of Siena's 17 *contrada* (neighborhoods) lives on. These neighborhoods celebrate, worship, and compete together. Each even has its own historical museum. *Contrada* pride is evident any time of year in the colorful neighborhood banners and parades. (If you hear distant drumming, run to it for some medieval action.) But *contrada* pride is most visible twice a year—on July 2 and August 16—when they have their world-famous horse race, the Palio di Siena. Ten of the 17 neighborhoods compete (chosen by lot), hurling themselves with medieval abandon into several days of trial races and traditional revelry. On the big day, jockeys and horses go into their *contrada*'s church to be blessed ("Go and win," says the priest). It's considered a sign of luck if a horse leaves droppings in the church.

On the evening of the big day, Il Campo is stuffed to the brim

with locals and tourists, as the horses charge wildly around the square in this literally no-holds-barred race. A horse can win even if its rider has fallen off. Of course, the winning neighborhood is the scene of grand celebrations afterward. The grand prize: simply proving your *contrada* is numero uno. All over town, sketches and posters depict the Palio. This is not some folkloristic event. It's a real medieval moment. If you're packed onto the square with 15,000 people who each really want to win, you won't see much, but you'll feel it. While the actual Palio packs the city, you could side-trip in from Florence to see horse-race trials each of the three days before the big day (usually at 9:00 and around 19:30).

▲**Palio al Cinema**—This 20-minute film, *Siena, the Palio, and its History*, helps recreate the craziness of the Palio. See it at the Cinema Moderno in Piazza Tolomei, two blocks from Il Campo (runs May–Sept only, €5.25, with this book pay €4.25, or €7.75 for 2; Mon–Sat 9:30–17:30, English showings generally hourly at :30 past the hour, schedule posted on door, closed Sun, air-con, tel. 0577-289-201). Call or drop by to confirm when the next English showing is scheduled—there are usually seven a day. At the ticket desk, you can buy the same show on video (discounted from €13 to €10.50 with this book, video must be labeled "NTSC American System" or it'll be a doorstop at your home).

Sleeping in Siena
(€1 = about $1, country code: 39, zip code: 53100)

Sleep Code: **S** = Single, **D** = Double/Twin, **T** = Triple, **Q** = Quad, **b** = bathroom, **s** = shower only, **CC** = Credit Cards accepted, **no CC** = Credit Cards not accepted, **SE** = Speaks English, **NSE** = No English. Breakfast is generally not included. Have breakfast on Il Campo or in a nearby bar.

To help you easily sort through these listings, I've divided the rooms into three categories based on the price for a standard double room with bath:

Higher Priced—most rooms more than €110
Moderately Priced—most rooms €110 or less
Lower Priced—most rooms €80 or less

Finding a room is tough during Easter or the Palio in early July and mid-August. Call ahead any time of year, as Siena's few budget places are listed in all the budget guidebooks. While day-tripping tour groups turn the town into a Gothic amusement park in mid-summer, Siena is basically yours in the evenings and off-season.

Nearly all listed hotels lie between Il Campo and the Church of San Domenico. About a third of the listings don't take credit cards, no matter how earnestly you ask. Cash machines are plentiful on the main streets.

Sleeping near Il Campo

Each of these listings is forgettable but inexpensive, and just a horse wreck away from one of Italy's most wonderful civic spaces.

HIGHER PRICED

These two places are a 10-minute walk from Il Campo.

Hotel Duomo is a classy place with 23 spacious rooms

(Sb-€110, Db-€150, Tb-€175, Qb-€200, includes breakfast, CC, air-con, picnic-friendly roof terrace, free parking, follow Via di Città, which becomes Via Stalloreggi, to Via Stalloreggi 38, tel. 0577-289-088, fax 0577-43043, www.hotelduomo.it, e-mail: booking@hotelduomo.it, Stefania SE). If you arrive by train, take a taxi (€8); if you drive, go to Porta San Marco and follow the signs to the hotel, drop off your bags, and then park in nearby "Il Campo" lot.

Pensione Palazzo Ravizza, elegant and friendly, has an aristocratic feel and a peaceful garden (Db-€148–255, suites available, includes breakfast and dinner, cheaper mid-Nov–Feb, CC, elevator, back rooms face open country, good restaurant, half-pension required in summer, free parking, Via Pian dei Mantellini 34, tel. 0577-280-462, fax 0577-221-597, www.palazzoravizza.it, e-mail: bureau@palazzoravizza.it, SE).

LOWER PRICED
Piccolo Hotel Etruria, a good bet for a hotel with 19 decent rooms but not much soul, is just off the square (S-€39, Sb-€44, Db-€73, Tb-€91, Qb-€114, breakfast-€4.75, CC, with your back to the tower, leave Il Campo to the right at 2:00, Via Donzelle 1-3, curfew at 00:30, tel. 0577-288-088, fax 0577-288-461, e-mail: hetruria@tin.it, Fattorini family SE).

Albergo Tre Donzelle has 27 plain, institutional rooms next door to Piccolo Hotel Etruria that make sense only if you think of Il Campo as your terrace (S-€34, D-€47, Db-€60, CC, Via Donzelle 5, tel. 0577-280-358, fax 0577-223-933, Signora Iannini SE).

Locanda Garibaldi is a modest, very Sienese restaurant/ *albergo.* Gentle Marcello wears two hats, as he runs a fine, busy restaurant downstairs and seven pleasant rooms up a funky, artsy staircase (Db-€70, Tb-€89, family deals, no CC, takes reservations only a week in advance, half a block downhill off the square at Via Giovanni Dupre 18, tel. 0577-284-204, NSE).

Hotel Cannon d'Oro, a few blocks up Via Banchi di Sopra, is spacious and group-friendly (30 rooms, Sb-€66, Db-€82, Tb-€104, Qb-€122, these discounted prices promised through 2003 with this book, family deals, breakfast-€6, CC, Via Montanini 28, tel. 0577-44321, fax 0577-280-868, e-mail: cannondoro @libero.it, Maurizio and Debora SE).

Sleeping near San Domenico Church
These hotels are also within a 10-minute walk of Il Campo. Albergo Bernini and Alma Domus, which enjoy views of the old town and cathedral, are the best values in town.

HIGHER PRICED

Hotel Villa Liberty has 18 big, bright, comfortable rooms (S-€75, Db-€130, includes breakfast, CC, only one room with twin beds; elevator, bar, air-con, TVs, courtyard, facing fortress at Viale V. Veneto 11, tel. 0577-44966, fax 0577-44770, www .villaliberty.it, e-mail: info@villaliberty.it, SE).

Jolly Hotel Siena, for people who want a four-star hotel, has 126 rooms that are clean but dated. Across the street from Piazza Gramsci, it's convenient if you're arriving by bus and if you have lots of luggage—and money (Sb-€124–160, Db-€170–233, includes breakfast, CC, non-smoking floor, Piazza La Lizza, tel. 0577-288-448, fax 0577-41272, e-mail: siena@jollyhotels.it).

MODERATELY PRICED

Albergo Bernini makes you part of a Sienese family in a modest, clean home with nine fine rooms. Friendly Nadia and Mauro welcome you to their spectacular view terrace for breakfast and picnic lunches and dinners. Outside of breakfast and checkout time, Mauro, an accomplished accordionist, might play a song for you if you ask (Sb-€77, D-€62, Db-€82, breakfast-€7, less in winter, no CC, midnight curfew, on the main San Domenico–Il Campo drag at Via Sapienza 15, tel. & fax 0577-289-047, www .albergobernini.com, e-mail: hbernin@tin.it, son Alessandro SE).

Hotel Chiusarelli, a proper hotel in a beautiful building with a handy location, comes with traffic noise at night—ask for a quieter room in the back (49 rooms, S-€57, Sb-€72, Db-€108, Tb-€146, includes big buffet breakfast, CC, suites available, air-con, pleasant garden terrace, across from San Domenico at Viale Curtatone 15, tel. 0577-280-562, fax 0577-271-177, www.chiusarelli.com, e-mail: info@chiusarelli.com, SE).

Albergo Lea is a sleepable place in a residential neighborhood a few blocks away from the center (past San Domenico) with 11 rooms and easy parking (S-€52, Db-€93, Tb-€120, cheaper in winter, includes breakfast, CC, rooftop terrace, Viale XXIV Maggio 10, tel. & fax 0577-283-207, SE).

LOWER PRICED

Alma Domus is ideal—unless nuns make you nervous, you need a double bed, or you plan on staying out past the 23:30 curfew (no mercy given). This quasi-hotel (not a convent) is run with firm but angelic smiles by sisters who offer clean and quiet rooms for a steal and save the best views for foreigners. Bright lamps, quaint balconies, fine views, grand public rooms, top security, and a friendly atmosphere make this a great value. The checkout time is strictly 10:00, but they will store your luggage in their secure courtyard (Db-€59, Tb-€72, Qb-€90, no CC, ask for view room—*con vista*, elevator, from San Domenico walk downhill with the church on your right toward the view, turn left down Via Camporegio, make a U-turn at the little chapel down the brick steps to Via Camporegio 37, tel. 0577-44177 and 0577-44487, fax 0577-47601, NSE).

Sleeping Farther from the Center

The first two listings are near Porta Romana.

HIGHER PRICED

Hotel Santa Caterina is a three-star, 18th-century place, best for drivers who need air-conditioning. Professionally run with real attention to quality, it has 22 comfortable rooms with a delightful garden (Sb-€98, small Db-€98, Db-€133, Tb-€179, mention this book to get these prices, includes buffet breakfast, elevator, CC, garden side is quieter but street side—with multi-paned windows—isn't bad, fridge in room, parking-€12/day—request when you reserve, 100 meters outside Porta Romana at Via E.S. Piccolomini 7, tel. 0577-221-105, fax 0577-271-087, www.hscsiena.it, e-mail: info@hscsiena.it, SE). A city bus runs frequently (Mon–Sat 4/hr, Sun 2/hr) to the town center. A taxi to/from the station runs around €8.

Palazzo di Valli, with 11 spacious rooms and a garden, is 800 meters beyond Porta Romana (the Roman gate) and feels like it's in the country. Catch the city bus into town (Db-€140, Tb-€170, includes breakfast, CC, parking, Via E.S. Piccolomini, bus to center Mon–Sat 4/hr, Sun 2/hr; tel. 0577-226-102, fax 0577-222-255, Camarda family SE). From the autostrada, exit at Siena Sud in the direction of Porta Romana.

Frances' Lodge is a small farmhouse B&B 1.5 kilometers out of Siena. English-speaking Franca and Franco rent four modern rooms in a rustic yet elegant old place with a swimming pool, peaceful garden, eight acres of olive trees and vineyards, and great Siena views (Db-€150–180, Tb-€210, easy parking, near shuttle bus into town, Strada di Valdipugna 2, tel. 0577-281-061, fax 0577-222-224, www.franceslodge.it).

MODERATELY PRICED

Casa Laura has five clean, well-maintained rooms, some of which have brick-and-beam ceilings (Db-€83 with breakfast, €73 without, cheaper off-season or for 3 nights or more, CC, Via Roma 3, about a 10-min walk from Il Campo toward Porta Romana, closed Nov-March, tel. 0577-226-061, fax 0577-225-240, e-mail: labenci@tin.it, NSE).

LOWER PRICED

Siena's **Guidoriccio Youth Hostel** has 120 cheap beds, but, given the hassle of the bus ride and the charm of downtown Siena at night, I'd skip it (office open 15:00–1:00, €13 beds in doubles, triples, and dorms with sheets and breakfast, CC, bus #10 from train station or bus #15 from Piazza Gramsci, Via Fiorentina 89 in Stellino neighborhood, tel. 0577-52212, SE).

Eating in Siena

Sienese restaurants are reasonable by Florentine and Venetian standards. Even with higher prices, lousy service, and lower-quality food, consider eating on Il Campo—a classic European experience.

Pizzeria Spadaforte, at the edge of Il Campo, has a decent setting, mediocre pizza, and tables steeper than its prices (daily 12:00–16:00 & 19:30–22:30, CC, to far right of city tower as you face it, tel. 0577-281-123).

For authentic Sienese dining at a fair price, eat at **Locanda Garibaldi,** down Via Giovanni Dupre at #18, within a block of Il Campo (€15 menu, Sun–Fri opens at 12:00-14:00 for lunch and 19:00-21:00 for dinner, arrive early to get a table, closed Sat). Marcello does a nice little *piatto misto dolce* for €2.75, featuring several local desserts with sweet wine.

Osteria il Tamburino is friendly, small, and intimate and serves up tasty meals (Mon–Sat 12:00–14:30 & 19:00–20:30, closed Sun, CC, follow Via di Città off Il Campo, becomes Stalloreggi, Via Stalloreggi 11, tel. 0577-280-306).

Taverna San Giuseppe, a local favorite, offers traditional food with a creative flair. Reserve or arrive early (Mon–Sat 12:15–14:15 & 17:15–21:45, closed Sun, Via Giovanni Dupre 132, tel. 0577-42286).

Antica Osteria Da Divo is the place for a fine €40 meal. The kitchen is creative, the food is fresh and top notch, and the ambience is candlelit. You'll get a basket of exotic fresh breads. They offer excellent seasonal dishes. The lamb goes baaa in your mouth. And the chef is understandably proud of his desserts (daily 12:00–14:30 & 19:00–22:00, CC, Via Franciosa 29, facing baptistery door, take the far right and walk one long curving block, reserve for summer eves, tel. 0577-286-054).

Trattoria La Tellina has patient waiters and great food, including homemade tiramisu. Arrive early to get a seat (Via dell Terme 52, between St. Catherine's House and Piazza Tolomei—where Palio film is shown, tel. 0577-283-133).

Osteria Nonna Gina wins praise from locals for its good quality and prices (Tue–Sun 12:30–14:30 & 19:30–20:30, closed

Mon, CC, Piano dei Mantellini 2, 10-min walk from Il Campo, near Hotel Duomo, tel. 0577-287-247).

Ristorante Gallo Nero is a friendly "grotto" for Tuscan cuisine. Popular with groups, this "black rooster" serves *ribollita* (hearty Tuscan bean soup) and offers a €23 "medieval menu," as well as several Tuscan menus, starting at €16 (daily 12:00–15:30 & 19:00–24:00, CC, 3 blocks down Via del Porrione from Il Campo at #65, tel. 0577-284-356).

Il Verrochio, a block away—tucked between a church and loggia—serves a decent €13 menu in a cozy, wood-beamed setting (daily 12:00–14:30 & 19:00–22:00, closed Wed in winter, CC, Logge del Papa 1, tel. 0577-284-062).

Le Campane, two blocks off Il Campo, is classy and a little pricey (daily 12:15–14:30 & 19:15–22:00, closed Mon in winter, CC, indoor/outdoor seating, a few steps off Via di Città at Via delle Campane 6, tel. 0577-284-035).

Osteria la Chiacchera, while touristy, is an atmospheric, tasty, and affordable hole-in-the-brick-wall (daily 11:00–24:00, CC, 2 rooms, below Pension Bernini at Costa di San Antonio 4, reservations wise, skip the *trippa*—tripe, tel. 0577-280-631).

Cheap Meals, Snacks, and Picnics

Snack with a view from a small balcony overlooking Il Campo. Survey these three places from Il Campo to see which has a free table. On Via di Città, you'll find **Gelateria Artigiana,** which has perhaps Siena's best ice cream, and **Barbero d'Oro,** which serves cappuccino and *panforte* (€1.75/100 grams; balcony with 2 tables, closed Sun). **Bar Paninoteca** is on Vicolo di S. Paolo, on the stairs leading down to Il Campo (sandwiches, has a row of chairs on balcony, closed Mon).

At the bottom of Il Campo, a **Ciao** cafeteria offers easy self-service meals, no ambience, and no views. The crowded **Spizzico,** a pizza counter in the front half of Ciao, serves huge, inexpensive quarter pizzas; on sunny days, people take the pizza, trays and all, out on Il Campo for a picnic (daily 11:00–22:00, non-smoking section—*non fumatori*—in back, CC only in cafeteria, to left of city tower as you face it).

Budget eaters look for *pizza al taglio* shops, scattered throughout Siena, selling pizza by the slice. Picnickers enjoy the market held mornings (except Sun) behind Il Campo, on Piazza del Mercato. Of the grocery shops scattered throughout town, the biggest is called simply **Alimentari;** it's one block off Piazza Matteotti, toward Il Campo. Their pesto is the besto (Mon–Sat 8:00–19:30, Via Pianigiani 5, no sign).

Sienese Sweets

All over town, **Prodotti Tipici** shops sell Sienese specialties. Siena's claim to caloric fame is its *panforte*, a rich, chewy concoction of nuts, honey, and candied fruits that impresses even fruitcake-haters (although locals prefer a white macaroon-and-almond cookie called *ricciarelli*).

Transportation Connections—Siena

By train to Florence (9/day, 1.75 hrs, last one at 21:00).

By bus to: Florence (2/hr, 1.25–2 hrs, by Tran bus), **San Gimignano** (6/day, 1.25 hrs, by Tran bus, more frequent with transfer in Poggibonsi), **Assisi** (2/day, 2 hrs, by Sena bus; the morning bus goes direct to Assisi, the afternoon bus might terminate at Santa Maria Angeli, from here catch a local bus to Assisi, 2/hr, 20 min), **Rome** (7/day, 3 hrs, by Sena bus, arrives at Rome's Tiburtina station), **Milan** (4/day, 14 hr). Schedules get sparse on Sunday.

Buses depart Siena from Piazza Gramsci, the train station, or both; confirm when you purchase your ticket. You can get tickets for Tran buses or Sena buses at the train station (Tran bus office: Mon–Sat 5:50–20:00; for Sena, buy tickets at *tabacchi* shop unless they've opened a separate office in the station), or easier and more central, under Piazza Gramsci at Sottopassaggio La Lizza (Tran bus office: daily 5:50–20:00, tel. 0577-204-225, toll-free tel. 800-373-760; Sena bus office: Mon–Sat 7:45–19:45, Sun 15:30–19:30, tel. 0577-283-203, www.senabus.it).

Sottopassaggio La Lizza, under Piazza Gramsci, has a cash machine (neither bus office accepts credit cards), luggage storage (€2.75/day, €1.50/half day, daily 7:00–19:30, no overnight storage), posted bus schedules, TV monitors (listing imminent departures), an elevator, and expensive WCs (€0.55). If you decide to depart Siena after the bus offices close, you can buy the ticket directly from the driver (and get charged a supplement).

On schedules, the fastest buses are marked *corse rapide*. Note that if a schedule lists your departure point as Via Tozzi or La Lizza, you catch the bus at Piazza Gramsci (Via Tozzi is the street that runs alongside Piazza Gramsci and La Lizza is the name of the bus station).

SLEEPING

For hassle-free efficiency, we favor hotels and restaurants handy to your sightseeing activities. Our recommended accommodations are located in Florence's downtown core and just across the river.

The accommodations scene varies wildly with the season. Spring and fall are very tight and expensive, while mid-July through August is wide open and discounted. November through February is also generally empty. I've listed prices for peak season: April, May, June, September, and October. If a price range is listed, the lower end reflects off-season and the higher end, peak season.

With good information and a phone call ahead, you can find a stark, clean, and comfortable double with breakfast for about €65 (for the room, not per person), with a private shower for €100 (less at the smaller places, such as the *soggiornos*). You get elegance for €140. Some places listed are old and rickety; I can't imagine Florence any other way. Rooms with air-conditioning cost around €100—worth the extra money in the summer. Virtually all of the places are central, within minutes of the great sights. Few hotels escape Vespa noise at night.

Call ahead. I repeat, call ahead. Places will hold a room until early afternoon. If they say they're full, mention that you're using this book.

Book direct—not through any tourist agency. Tourist information room-finding services cannot give opinions on quality. A major advantage of this book is its extensive listing of good-value rooms. I like places that are clean, small, central, relatively quiet at night, traditional, inexpensive, and friendly, with firm beds—and not listed in other guidebooks. (In Florence, 6 out of 9 means it's a keeper.)

Hotels

Most rooms cluster around €110–140 (with private bathrooms). Three or four people economize by sharing larger rooms. Solo travelers find that the cost of a *camera singola* is often only 25 percent less than a *camera doppia*. Most listed hotels have rooms for anywhere from one to five people. If there's room for an extra cot, they'll cram it in for you.

You normally get close to what you pay for. Prices are fairly standard. Shopping around earns you a better location and more character, but rarely a cheaper price.

However, prices at nearly any hotel can get soft if you do any of the following: arrive direct (without using a pricey middleman like the TI), offer to pay cash, stay at least three nights, mention this book, or visit off-season. Breakfasts are legally optional (though some hotels insist they're not). Initial prices quoted often include a small breakfast and a private bathroom. Offer to skip breakfast for a better price. If you're on a budget, ask for a cheaper room or a discount. Always ask.

You'll save €20–30 if you request a room without a shower and just use the shower down the hall. Generally rooms with a bath or shower also have a toilet and a bidet (which Italians use for quick sponge baths). Tubs usually come with a frustrating "telephone shower" (hand-held nozzle). If a shower has no curtain, the entire bathroom showers with you. The cord that dangles over the tub or shower is not a clothesline. You pull it when you've fallen and can't get up.

Double beds are called *matrimoniale*, even though hotels aren't interested in your marital status. Twins are *due letti singoli*.

Many hotel rooms have a TV and phone. Rooms in fancier hotels usually come with air-conditioning (some-times you pay an extra per-day charge for this), a small safe, and a small stocked fridge called a *frigo bar* (pron. FREE-goh bar).

If you arrive on an overnight train, your room may not be ready. Drop your bag at the hotel and dive right into Florence.

When you check in, the receptionist will normally ask for your passport and keep it for a couple of hours. Hotels are legally required to register each guest with the local police. Relax. Americans are notorious for making this chore more difficult than it needs to be.

The hotel breakfast, while convenient, is often a bad value— €9 for a roll, jelly, and usually unlimited *caffè latte*. You can request cheese or salami (€3 extra). I enjoy taking breakfast at the corner café. It's OK to supplement what you order with a few picnic goodies.

Rooms are safe. Still, zip cameras and keep money out of

Sleep Code

To help you easily sort through these listings, I've divided the rooms into three categories based on the price for a standard double room with bath:

Higher Priced—Most rooms more than €160.
Moderately Priced—Most rooms €160 or less.
Lower Priced—Most rooms €110 or less.

To give maximum information in a minimum of space, I use the following code to describe the accommodations listed in this book. Prices listed are per room, not per person.

S = Single room (or price for one person in a double).

D = Double or Twin room. "Double beds" are often two twins sheeted together and are usually big enough for nonromantic couples.

T = Triple (generally a double bed with a single).

Q = Quad (usually two double beds).

b = Private bathroom with toilet and shower or tub.

s = Private shower or tub only (the toilet is down the hall).

CC = Accepts credit cards (Visa and MasterCard, rarely American Express).

no CC = Doesn't accept credit cards; pay in local cash.

SE = Speaks English. This code is used only when it seems predictable that you'll encounter English-speaking staff.

NSE = Does not speak English. Used only when it's unlikely you'll encounter English-speaking staff.

According to this code, a couple staying at a "Db-€140, CC, SE" hotel would pay a total of €140 (about $140) for a double room with a private bathroom. The hotel accepts credit cards or Italian cash (euros). The staff speaks English.

sight. More pillows and blankets are usually in the closet or available on request. In Italy, towels and linen aren't always replaced every day. Hang your towel up to dry.

To avoid the time-wasting line at the reception desk in the morning, settle up your bill the evening before you leave.

Country Code and Exchange Rate

If you're phoning Italy, you'll need to know its country code: 39. To call Italy from the United States or Canada, dial 011-39-local number. If calling Italy from another European country, dial 00-39-local number.

The exchange rate: €1 = about $1.

Making Reservations

To reserve from home, telephone first to confirm availability, then fax or e-mail your formal request. It's easy to reserve by phone. (For detailed instructions on making calls, see "Telephones" in this book's introduction.) Most hotels listed are accustomed to English-only speakers. Fax costs are reasonable, e-mail's a steal, and simple English is usually fine. To fax, use the handy form in the appendix; for e-mailers, the form's online at www.ricksteves.com/reservation. If you don't get an answer to your fax request, consider that a "no." (Many little places get 20 faxes a day after they're full and can't afford to respond.)

A two-night stay for the nights of August 16 and 17 would be "2 nights, 16/8/03 to 18/8/03" (Europeans write the date day/month/year and hotel jargon uses your day of departure). You'll often receive a response back requesting one night's deposit. If your credit-card number is accepted as the deposit (which is usually the case), you can pay with your card or cash when you arrive; if you don't show up, you'll be billed for one night. Always reconfirm your reservations a day or two in advance by phone.

Honor (or cancel by phone) your reservations. Long distance is cheap from public phone booths. Don't let these people down—I promised you'd call and cancel if for some reason you can't show up.

Sleeping between the Station and Duomo
(zip code: 50123)

HIGHER PRICED

Palazzo Castiglioni offers sixteen grand rooms with all the conveniences in a peaceful, 19th-century *palazzo* package. Most rooms are spacious, several have frescoes, and all make a fine splurge (Db-€165, Db suite-€207, Tb-€207, air-con, elevator, Via del Giglio 8, tel. 055-214-886, fax 055-274-0521, e-mail: pal.cast@flashnet.it, Laura SE).

MODERATELY PRICED

Hotel Accademia is an elegant two-star hotel with marble stairs, parquet floors, attractive public areas, 22 pleasant rooms, and a floor plan that defies logic (Sb-€87, Db-€140, Tb-€170, these discounted prices are promised through 2003 only with this book, CC, air-con, TV, tiny courtyard, Via Faenza 7, tel. 055-293-451, fax 055-219-771, www.accademiahotel.net, e-mail: info@accademiahotel.net, SE).

Residenza dei Pucci, a block north of the Duomo, has 12 tastefully decorated rooms—in soothing earth tones—with aristocratic furniture and tweed carpeting. It's fresh and bright (Sb-€130, Db-€145, Tb-€165, suite with grand Duomo view-€207 for 2 people, €233 for 4, claim a 10 percent discount through 2003 with this book and payment in cash, breakfast served in room, CC, Via dei Pucci 9, tel. 055-281-886, fax 055-264-314, http://residenzapucci .interfree.it, e-mail: residenzapucci@interfree.it, SE).

LOWER PRICED

Hotel Bellettini rents 34 bright, cool, well-cared-for rooms with inviting lounges and a touch of class. Its five rooms in an annex two blocks away are of higher quality with all the comforts, but you need to come to the main hotel for breakfast (main building: S-€75, Sb-€95, D-€100, Db-€130, Tb-€170, Qb-€210; annex: Sb-€110, Db-€155, Tb-€209, CC, 5 percent discount with this book only if you claim it upon arrival, air-con, free Internet access, Via de' Conti 7, tel. 055-213-561, fax 055-283-551, www.firenze.net/hotelbellettini, e-mail: hotel.bellettini @dada.it, frisky Gina SE).

Hotel Aldobrandini, a good budget choice, has 15 decent, clean, affordable rooms, with the San Lorenzo market at its doorstep and the entrance to the Medici Chapel a few steps away (Ss-€42, Sb-€52, D-€67, Db-€83, CC, lots of night noise but has double-paned windows, fans, Piazza Madonna Degli Aldobrandini 8, tel. 055-211-866, fax 055-267-6281, Ignazio SE).

Pensione Centrale, a traditional-feeling place with 18 spacious rooms, is indeed central, though run without warmth (D-€93, Db-€109, CC, quiet, some air-con rooms, often filled with American students, elevator, Via de' Conti 3, tel. 055-215-761, fax 055-215-216, www.pensionecentrale.it, e-mail: info @pensionecentrale.it). They sometimes send people to a nearby, noisier pension; confirm that your reservation is for this place.

Sleeping near the Central Market
(zip code: 50129)

MODERATELY PRICED

Hotel Basilea offers predictable three-star, air-conditioned comfort in its 38 modern rooms (Db-€110–160 depending on season, CC, elevator, terrace, free e-mail service, Via Guelfa 41,

Florence Hotels

1. HOTEL ACCADEMIA
2. HOTEL MORANDI ALLA CROCETTA
3. CASA RABATTI
4. SOGGIORNO PEZZATI
5. PENSIONE BRETAGNA
6. SOGGIORNO MAGLIANI
7. HOTEL LOGGIATO DEI SERVITI
8. DUE FONTANE HOTEL
9. OBLATE SISTERS OF THE ASSUMPTION
10. RESIDENZA DEI PUCCI
11. PALAZZO CASTIGLIONI & HOTEL ALDOBRANDINI
12. HOTEL BELLETTINI
13. HOTEL BASILEA
14. PENSIONE CENTRALE
15. HOTEL SOLE
16. SOGGIORNO BATTISTERO
17. HOTEL PENDINI
18. PENSIONE MAXIM
19. ALBERGO FIRENZE
20. HOTEL ELITE
21. TORRE GUELFA, APOSTOLI & ALESSANDRA HOTELS
22. FLORENCE WALKING TOURS

at intersection with Nazionale—a busy street, ask for rooms in the back, tel. 055-214-587, fax 055-268-350, www.florenceitaly.net, e-mail: basilea@dada.it).

LOWER PRICED
Casa Rabatti is the ultimate if you always wanted to be a part of a Florentine family. Its four simple, clean rooms are run with motherly warmth by Marcella and her husband Celestino, who speak minimal English (D-€50, Db-€60, €25 per bed in shared quad or quint, prices good with this book, no breakfast, no CC, fans, no sign other than on doorbell, 5 blocks from station, Via San Zanobi 48 black, tel. 055-212-393, e-mail: casarabatti@inwind.it).

Soggiorno Pezzati Daniela is another little place with six homey rooms (Sb-€45, Db-€62, Tb-€86, cheaper off-season, no breakfast, no CC, all rooms have a fridge, air-con extra; marked only by small sign near door, Via San Zanobi 22, tel. 055-291-660, fax 055-287-145, www.soggiornopezzati.it, e-mail: 055291660@iol.it, Daniela SE). If you get an Italian recording when you call, hang on—your call is being transferred to a cell phone.

Central and humble, with seven rooms, **Soggiorno Magliani** feels and smells like a great-grandmother's place (S-€33, D-€43, cash only but secure reservation with CC, no breakfast, double-paned windows, near Via Guelfa at Via Reparata 1, tel. 055-287-378, e-mail: hotel-magliani@libero.it, run by a friendly family duo, Vincenza and English-speaking daughter Cristina).

Sleeping East of the Duomo
(zip code: 50122)
The first two listings are near the Accademia, on Piazza S.S. Annunziata. The third is just off the square.

HIGHER PRICED
Hotel Loggiato dei Serviti, at the most prestigious address in Florence on the most Renaissance square in town, gives you Renaissance romance with hair dryers. Stone stairways lead you under open-beam ceilings through this 16th-century monastery's elegant public rooms. The 34 cells, with air-conditioning, TVs, mini-bars, and telephones, wouldn't be recognized by their original inhabitants. The hotel staff is both professional and friendly (Sb-€146, Db-€210, family suites from €263, book a month ahead during peak season, discounts in Aug and winter, 5 elegant rooms in 17th-century annex, CC, elevator, Piazza S.S. Annuziata 3, tel. 055-289-592, fax 055-289-595, www .loggiatodeiservitihotel.it, e-mail: info@loggiatodeiservitihotel.it, Simonetta, Francesca, and Andrea SE).

MODERATELY PRICED

Le Due Fontane Hotel faces the same great square but fills its old building with a smoky, 1970s, business-class ambience. Its 57 air-conditioned rooms are big and comfortable (Sb-€103, Db-€140, Tb-€196, these discounted prices are promised through 2003 but only if you claim them upon reserving, CC, elevator, Piazza S.S. Annunziata 14, tel. 055-210-185, fax 055-294-461, www.leduefontane.it, e-mail: leduefontane@dada.it, SE).

At **Hotel Morandi alla Crocetta,** a former convent, you're enveloped in a 16th-century cocoon. Located on a quiet street, with period furnishings, parquet floors, and wood-beamed ceilings, it draws you in (Sb-€100, Db-€160, breakfast-€11, CC, Via Laura 50, a block off Piazza S.S. Annunziata, tel. 055-234-4747, fax 055-248-0954, www.hotelmorandi.it, e-mail: welcome@hotelmorandi.it, SE).

LOWER PRICED

The **Oblate Sisters of the Assumption** run a 20-room hotel in a Renaissance building with a dreamy garden and a quiet, institutional feel (S-€34, D-€62, Db-€67, elevator, no CC, Borgo Pinti 15, 50121 Firenze, tel. 055-248-0582, fax 055-234-6291, NSE).

Sleeping on or near Piazza Repubblica
(zip code: 50123)

These are the most central of my accommodations recommendations, though given Florence's walkable core, nearly every hotel can be considered central.

MODERATELY PRICED

Hotel Pendini, a well-run three-star hotel with 42 old-time rooms (8 with views of the square), is popular and central, overlooking Piazza Repubblica (Sb-€86–110, Db-€110–150 depending on season, CC, elevator, fine lounge and breakfast room, air-con, Via Strozzi 2, reserve ASAP, tel. 055-211-170, fax 055-281-807, www.florenceitaly.net, e-mail: pendini@dada.it, SE).

Residenza Giotto has six bright and modern rooms, and a terrace so close to the Duomo you can almost touch it (Sb-€120, Db-€130, Tb-€145, 10 percent discount through 2003 with this book and payment in cash, breakfast served in room, CC, Via Roma 6, 4th floor, tel. 055-214-593, fax 055-264-8568, www .residenzagiotto.it, e-mail: residenzagiotto@tin.it, SE).

Pensione Maxim, right on Via Calz, is a big, institutional-feeling place as close to the sights as possible. Its halls are narrow, but the 29 rooms are comfortable and well-maintained (Sb-€83, Db-€113, Tb-€148, Qb-€173, CC but pay first night in cash, Internet access, elevator, Via dei Calzaiuoli 11,

tel. 055-217-474, fax 055-283-729, www.hotelmaximfirenze.it
e-mail: hotmaxim@tin.it, Paolo and Nicola Maioli SE).

LOWER PRICED
Soggiorno Battistero, next door to the Baptistery, has seven
simple, airy rooms, most with urban noise but also great views,
overlooking the Baptistery and square. You're in the heart of
Florence (S-€73, Db-€95, Tb-€130, Qb-€140, these prices
good with this book, 5 percent additional discount with cash,
breakfast served in room, Internet access, CC, Piazza San
Giovanni 1, 3rd floor, no elevator, tel. 055-295-143, fax 055-268-
189, www.soggiornobattistero.it, e-mail: battistero@dada.it,
lovingly run by Italian Luca and his American wife, Kelly).

Albergo Firenze, a big, efficient place, offers good, basic,
and spacious rooms in a wonderfully central, reasonably quiet
locale two blocks behind the Duomo (Sb-€67, Db-€88, Tb-€126,
Qb-€156, cash only, must prepay first night with a bank draft or
traveler's check, elevator, off Via del Corso at Piazza Donati 4,
tel. 055-214-203, fax 055-212-370, SE).

Sleeping North of the Train Station
(zip code: 50123)

MODERATELY PRICED
Hotel Beatrice, a three-star hotel popular with tour groups, is
well-located if you've packed heavy—it's just a block north of the
train and bus stations (Sb-€75–90, Db-€95–142, CC, most rooms
air-con, elevator, Via Fiume 11, tel. 055-216-790, fax 055-280-711,
www.hotelbeatrice.it, e-mail: info@hotelbeatrice.it).

Sleeping South of the Train Station
near Piazza Santa Maria Novella
(zip code: 50123)
From the station (with your back to the tracks), cross the wide
square to reach the Santa Maria Novella church and continue
to the piazza in front of the church (avoid the underground
Galleria S. M. Novella tunnel—popular with thieves—that leads
from the station under the square to the church). Piazza Santa
Maria Novella is a pleasant square by day that becomes a little
sleazy after dark.

LOWER PRICED
Hotel Pensione Elite, run warmly by Maurizio and Nadia,
is a fine basic value, with 10 comfortable rooms and a charm
rare in this price range (Ss-€52, Sb-€72, Ds-€67, Db-€83,

breakfast-€6, maybe CC, fans, at south end of square with back to church, go right to Via della Scala 12, 2nd floor, tel. & fax 055-215-395, SE).

Hotel Sole, a clean, cozy, family-run place with eight bright, modern rooms, is just off Santa Maria Novella toward the river (Sb-€47, Db-€78, Tb-€104, no breakfast, no CC, air-con, elevator, curfew at 01:00, Via del Sole 8, 3rd floor, tel. & fax 055-239-6094, friendly Anna NSE, but daughter SE).

Sleeping near Arno River and Ponte Vecchio
(zip code: 50123)

HIGHER PRICED

Hotel Torre Guelfa is topped with a fun medieval tower with a panoramic rooftop terrace and a huge living room. Its 29 rooms vary wildly in size (small Db-from €145, standard Db-€170, Db junior suite-€220, 5 percent discount with cash). Room #15, with a private terrace—€210—is worth reserving several months in advance (CC, elevator, air-con, a couple blocks northwest of Ponte Vecchio, Borgo S.S. Apostoli 8, tel. 055-239-6338, fax 055-239-8577, www.hoteltorreguelfa.com, e-mail: torreguelfa@flashnet.it, Giancarlo, Carlo, and Sandro all SE).

MODERATELY PRICED

Hotel Pensione Alessandra is an old, 16th-century, peaceful place with 27 big, modern rooms (S-€82, Sb-€109, D-€119, Db-€150, T-€140, Tb-€181, Q-€155, Qb-€202, CC but 5 percent discount with cash, air-con, Internet access, Borgo S.S. Apostoli 17, tel. 055-283-438, fax 055-210-619, www .hotelalessandra.com, e-mail: info@hotelalessandra.com, SE).

LOWER PRICED

Pensione Bretagna is an Old World–ramshackle place run by helpful Antonio and Maura. Imagine eating breakfast under a painted, chandeliered ceiling overlooking the Arno River (S-€50, Sb-€59, small Db-€95, big Db-€105, Tb-€129, Qb-€150, family deals, prices special with this book through 2003, CC, air-con, Internet access, just past Ponte San Trinita, Lungarno Corsini 6, tel. 055-289-618, fax 055-289-619, www.bretagna.it, e-mail: hotel@bretagna.it). They also run **Soggiorno Althea,** a cheaper place with nicer rooms, near Piazza San Spirito in the Oltrarno neighborhood (6 rooms, Db-€71, air-con, no breakfast, no reception desk, call Bretagna to book, www.florencealthea.it).

Sleeping in Oltrarno, South of the River
(zip code: 50125)

Across the river in the Oltrarno area, between the Pitti Palace and Ponte Vecchio, you'll still find small traditional crafts shops, neighborly piazzas, and family eateries. The following places are a few minutes' walk from the Ponte Vecchio.

HIGHER PRICED

Hotel Lungarno is the place to stay if money is no object. This deluxe, four-star hotel with 70 rooms strains anything stressful or rough out of Italy, and gives you only service with a salute, physical elegance everywhere you look, plus fine views over the Arno and Ponte Vecchio (Sb-€225, Db-€360, Db facing river-€460, fancier suites, great riverside public spaces, CC, 100 meters from Ponte Vecchio at Borgo San Jacopo 14, tel. 055-27261, fax 055-268-437, www.lungarnohotels.com, e-mail: bookings @lungarnohotels.com, SE).

MODERATELY PRICED

Hotel La Scaletta, an elegant, dark, cool place with 13 rooms, a labyrinthine floor plan, lots of Old World lounges, and a romantic and panoramic roof terrace, is run by Barbara, her son Manfredo, and daughters Bianca and Diana (S-€52, Sb-€95, D-€105, Db-€113–130, Tb-€115–150, Qb-€130–170, higher price is for quieter rooms in back, €5–10 discount if you pay cash, CC, air-con in 10 rooms and fans in others, elevator, bar with fine wine at good prices, Via Guicciardini 13 black, 150 meters south of Ponte Vecchio, tel. 055-283-028, fax 055-289-562, www.lascaletta.com, e-mail: info@lascaletta.com, SE). Secure your reservation with a personal check or traveler's check. Manfredo loves to cook. If he's cooking dinner, eat here. He serves a €10 "Taste of Tuscany" deal (plate of quality Tuscan meats and cheeses with bread and 2 glasses of robust Chianti)—ideal for a light lunch on the terrace.

    Hotel Silla, a classic three-star hotel with 36 cheery, spacious, pastel, and modern rooms, is a fine value. It faces the river and overlooks a park opposite the Santa Croce Church (Db-€170, Tb-€210, mention this book for a discount, CC, elevator, air-con, Via dei Renai 5, 50125 Florence, tel. 055-234-2888, fax 055-234-1437, www.hotelsilla.it, e-mail: hotelsilla@tin.it, Laura SE).

    Pensione Sorelle Bandini is a ramshackle, 500-year-old palace on a perfectly Florentine square, with cavernous rooms, museum-warehouse interiors, a musty youthfulness, cats, a balcony lounge-loggia with a view, and an ambience that, for romantic bohemians, can be a highlight of Florence. Mimmo or

Oltrarno Neighborhood Hotels

1. HOTEL LA SCALETTA
2. TO HOTEL SILLA
3. PENSIONE SORELLE BANDINI
4. HOTEL LUNGARNO
5. SOGGIORNO PEZZATI ALESSANDRA
6. ISTITUTO GOULD
7. OSTELLO SANTA MONACA
8. TRATTORIA BORDINO
9. RISTORANTE BIBO
10. BORGO ANTICO REST., OSTERIA SANTO SPIRITO, & RICCHI CAFFÈ
11. TRATTORIA CASALINGA
12. CAMMILLO TRATTORIA
13. OSTERIA DEL CINGHIALE BIANCO
14. TRATTORIA ANGIOLINO
15. TO TRATTORIA SABATINO

Sr. Romeo will hold a room until 16:00 with a phone call (D-€103, Db-€125, T-€141, Tb-€171, includes breakfast—which during low times is optional, saving €9 per person—no CC, elevator, Piazza Santo Spirito 9, tel. 055-215-308, fax 055-282-761, SE).

LOWER PRICED

Soggiorno Pezzati Alessandra is a warm and friendly place renting five great rooms in the Oltrarno neighborhood (Sb-€45, Db-€62, Tb-€86, Qb-€108, cheaper off-season, no breakfast, no CC, all rooms have a fridge, air-con extra, Via Borgo San Frediano 6, tel. 055-290-424, fax 055-218-464, e-mail: alex170169

@libero.it, Alessandra). If you get an Italian recording when you call, hang on—your call is being transferred to a cellular phone.

Istituto Gould is a Protestant Church–run place with 33 clean but drab rooms with twin beds and modern facilities (S-€30, Sb-€35, D-€44, Db-€52, Tb-€63, €20 per person in quads, no breakfast, no CC, quieter rooms in back, Via dei Serragli 49, tel. 055-212-576, fax 055-280-274, e-mail: gould.reception@dada.it). You must arrive when the office is open (Mon–Fri 9:00–13:00 & 15:00–19:00, Sat 9:00–13:00, no check-in Sun, SE).

Ostello Santa Monaca, a cheap hostel, is a few blocks south of Ponte Alla Carraia, one of the bridges over the Arno (€15.50 beds, 4- to 20-bed rooms, breakfast extra, CC, 1:00 curfew, Via Santa Monaca 6, tel. 055-268-338, fax 055-280-185).

Sleeping Away from the Center

MODERATELY PRICED

Hotel Ungherese is good for drivers. It's northeast of the city center (near *stadio*, en route to Fiesole), with easy, free street parking and quick bus access (#11 and #17) into central Florence (Sb-€72, Db-€123, extra bed-€30, these discounted prices available with this book, pay cash to get additional 7 percent discount, rooms are 20 percent less off-season, includes breakfast, CC, air-con, Via G. B. Amici 8, tel. & fax 055-573-474, www .hotelungherese.it, e-mail: hotel.ungherese@dada.it, Giovanni, Francesca SE). It has great singles and a backyard garden terrace (ask for a room on the garden). They can recommend good eateries nearby.

LOWER PRICED

Villa Camerata, classy for an IYHF hostel, is on the outskirts of Florence (€14.50 per bed with breakfast, 4- to 12-bed rooms, must have IYHF card, no CC, ride bus #17 to Salviatino stop, Via Righi 2, tel. 055-601-451).

EATING

The Italians are masters of the art of fine living. That means eating…long and well. Lengthy, multicourse lunches and dinners and endless hours sitting in outdoor cafés are the norm. Americans eat on their way to an evening event and complain if the check is slow in coming. For Italians, the meal is an end in itself, and only rude waiters rush you. When you want the bill, mime-scribble on your raised palm or ask for it: *"Il conto?"*

Even those of us who liked dorm food will find that the local cafés, cuisine, and wines become a highlight of our Italian adventure. This is sightseeing for your palate, and even if the rest of you is sleeping in cheap hotels, your taste buds will relish an occasional first-class splurge. You can eat well without going broke. But be careful; you're just as likely to blow a small fortune on a disappointing meal as you are to dine wonderfully for $20.

TYPES OF EATERIES

To save money and time for sights, you can keep lunches fast and simple, eating in one of the countless pizzerias and self-service cafeterias (or picnicking—try juice, yogurt, cheese, and a roll for €5). For dessert, it's gelato (see page 216).

Restaurants

Restaurants rarely open before 19:00 for dinner. When restaurant-hunting, choose places filled with locals, not the place with the big neon signs boasting, "We speak English and accept credit cards." Restaurants parked on famous squares generally serve bad food at high prices to tourists. Locals eat better at lower-rent locales. Family-run places operate without hired help and can offer cheaper meals. The word *osteria* (normally a simple local-style restaurant) makes me salivate. For unexciting but basic values, look for a *menù*

Tipping

Tipping is an issue only at restaurants that have waiters and waitresses. If you order your food at a counter, don't tip.

If the menu states that service is included (*servizio incluso*), there's no need to tip beyond that, but if you like to tip and you're pleased with the service, throw in €1 to €2 euros per person.

If service is not included, tip 5 to 10 percent by rounding up or leaving the change from your bill. Leave the tip on the table or hand it to your server. It's best to tip in cash even if you pay with your credit card. Otherwise the tip may never reach your waiter.

turistico, a three- or four-course, set-price menu. Galloping gourmets order à la carte with the help of a menu translator. (The *Marling Italian Menu Master* is excellent. *Rick Steves' Italian Phrase Book* has enough phrases for intermediate eaters.)

A full meal consists of an appetizer (*antipasto*, €3–6), a first course (*primo piatto*, pasta or soup, €4.50–7.50), and a second course (*secondo piatto*, expensive meat and fish dishes, €5.50–11). Vegetables (*contorni, verdure*) may come with the *secondo* or cost extra (€3.50) as a side dish. Restaurants normally pad the bill with a cover charge (*pane e coperto*—"bread and cover charge," around €2–3) and a service charge (*servizio*, 15 percent); these charges are listed on the menu (see "Tipping" above).

The euros can add up in a hurry. Light and budget eaters get by with a *primo piatto* each and sharing an *antipasto*. Italians admit that the *secondo* is the least interesting aspect of the local cuisine.

Delis, Cafeterias, Pizza Shops, and *Tavola Calda* (Hot Table) Bars

Florence offers many cheap alternatives to restaurants. Stop by a *rosticceria* for great cooked deli food; a self-service cafeteria (called "free flow" in Italian) that feeds you without the add-ons; a *tavola calda* bar for an assortment of veggies; or a Pizza Rustica shop for stand-up or take-out pizza.

Pizza is cheap and everywhere. Key pizza vocabulary: *capricciosa* (generally ham, mushrooms, olives, and artichokes), *funghi* (mushrooms), *marinara* (tomato sauce, oregano, garlic, no cheese), *quattro formaggi* (4 different cheeses), and *quattro stagioni* (different toppings on each of the four quarters for those who can't choose

Ordering Food at Tavola Caldas

plate of mixed veggies	*piatto misto di verdure*	pee-AH-toh MEES-toh dee vehr-DOO-ray
"Heated, please."	*"Scaldare, per favore."*	skahl-DAH-ray, pehr fah-VOH-ray
"A taste, please."	*"Un assaggio, per favore"*	oon ah-SAH-joh, pehr fah-VOH-ray
artichoke	*carciofo*	kar-CHOH-foh
asparagus	*asparagi*	ah-spah-RAH-jee
beans	*fagioli*	fah-JOH-lee
green beans	*fagiolini*	fah-joh-LEE-nee
broccoli	*broccoli*	BROK-oh-lee
canteloupe	*melone*	May–LOH-nay
carrots	*carote*	kah-ROT-ay
ham	*prosciutto*	proh-SHOO-toh
mushrooms	*funghi*	FOONG-ghee
potatoes	*patate*	pah-TAH-tay
rice	*riso*	REE-zoh
spinach	*spinaci*	speen-AH-chee
tomatoes	*pomodori*	poh-moh-DOH-ree
zucchini	*zucchine*	zoo-KEE-nay
breadsticks	*grissini*	gree-SEE-nee

(Excerpted from *Rick Steves' Italian Phrase Book*)

just one menu item). If you ask for *peperoni* on your pizza, you'll get green or red peppers, not sausage. Kids like *diavola* (closest thing in Italy to American "pepperoni") and *margherita* (tomato and cheese) pizzas. At Pizza Rustica take-out shops, slices are sold by weight (100 grams, or *un etto*, is a hot, cheap snack; 200 grams, or *due etti*, makes a light meal).

For a fast, cheap, and healthy lunch, find a *tavola calda* bar with a buffet spread of meat and vegetables and ask for a mixed plate of vegetables with a hunk of mozzarella (*piatto misto di verdure con mozzarella*). Don't be limited by what you can see. If you'd like a salad with a slice of cantaloupe and a hunk of cheese, they'll whip that up for you in a snap. Step up to the bar and, with a pointing finger and key words from the chart in this chapter, you can get a fine mixed plate of vegetables. If something's a mystery, ask for *un assaggio* (a little taste).

Italian Bars/Cafés

Italian "bars" are not taverns but cafés. These local hangouts serve coffee, minipizzas, sandwiches, and cartons of milk from the cooler. Many dish up plates of fried cheese and vegetables from under the glass counter, ready to reheat. This is our budget choice, Italian pub grub.

For quick meals, bars usually have trays of cheap ready-made sandwiches (*panini* or *tramezzini*)—some kinds are delightful grilled. To save time for sightseeing and room for dinner, my favorite lunch is a ham and cheese *panini* at a bar (called *tost*, grilled twice to get really hot). To get food "to go," say, "*Da portar via*" (for the road). All bars have a WC (*toilette, bagno*) in the back, and the public is entitled to use it.

Bars serve great drinks—hot, cold, sweet, or alcoholic. Chilled bottled water (*natural* or *frizzante*) is sold cheap to go.

Coffee: If you ask for "*un caffè*," you'll get espresso. Cappuccino is served to locals before noon and tourists any time of day. (To an Italian, cappuccino is a breakfast drink and a travesty after anything with tomatoes.) Italians like it only warm. To get it hot, request "*Molto caldo*" (very hot) or "*Più caldo, per favore*" ("Hotter, please"; pron. pew KAHL-doh, pehr fah-VOH-ray).

Experiment with a few of the options...

- *caffè freddo:* sweet and iced espresso
- *cappuccino freddo:* iced cappuccino
- *caffè hag:* espresso decaf (decaf is easily available for any coffee drink)
- *macchiato:* with only a little milk
- *caffè latte:* coffee with lots of hot milk, no foam. Note that ordering a *latte* gets you only milk.
- *caffè Americano:* espresso diluted with water
- *caffè corretto:* espresso with a shot of liqueur

Beer: Beer on tap is "*alla spina.*" Get it *piccola* (33 cl), *media* (50 cl), or *grande* (a liter).

Wine: To order a glass (*bicchiere*; pron. bee-kee-AY-ree) of red (*rosso*) or white (*bianco*) wine, say, "*Un bicchiere di vino rosso/bianco.*" *Corposo* means full-bodied. House wine often comes in a quarter-liter carafe (*un quarto*).

Prices: You'll notice a two-tiered price system. Drinking a cup of coffee while standing at the bar is cheaper than drinking it at a table. If you're on a budget, don't sit without first checking out the financial consequences.

If the bar isn't busy, you'll often just order and pay when you leave. Otherwise, (1) decide what you want; (2) find out the price by checking the price list on the wall, the prices posted near the food, or by asking the barman; (3) pay the cashier; and (4) give the receipt to the barman (whose clean fingers handle no dirty euros) and tell him what you want.

Picnics

In Florence, picnicking saves lots of euros and is a great way to sample local specialties. For a colorful experience, gather your ingredients in the morning at Florence's Mercato Centrale (Central Market, near Church of San Lorenzo); you'll probably visit several market stalls to put together a complete meal. A local *alimentari* is your one-stop corner grocery store (most will slice and stuff your sandwich for you if you buy the ingredients there). The rare *supermercato* gives you more efficiency with less color for less cost.

Juice-lovers can get a liter of O.J. for the price of a Coke or coffee. Look for "100% *succo*" (juice) on the label. Hang onto the half-liter mineral-water bottles (sold everywhere for about €0.50). Buy juice in cheap liter boxes, drink some, and store the extra in your water bottle. (I drink tap water—*acqua del rubinetto.*)

Picnics can be an adventure in high cuisine. Be daring. Try the fresh mozzarella, *presto* pesto, shriveled olives, and any UFOs the locals are excited about. Shopkeepers are happy to sell small quantities of produce. But in a busy market, a merchant may not want to weigh and sell small, three-carrot-type quantities. In this case, estimate generously what you think it should cost, and hold out the coins in one hand and the produce in the other. Wear a smile that says, "If you take the money, I'll go." He'll grab the money. A typical picnic for two might be fresh rolls, 100 grams of cheese, 100 grams of meat (100 grams = about a quarter pound, called *un etto* in Italy), two tomatoes, three carrots, two apples, yogurt, and a liter box of juice. Total cost—about $10.

FLORENTINE CUISINE

While many Florentine restaurants serve your basic Italian fare—pasta and pizza, veal cutlets, and mixed salad—there are a few local specialties you'll find without looking too hard. In general, Florentine cuisine is hearty, simple, farmers' food: grilled meats, high-quality seasonal vegetables, fresh herbs, prized olive oil, and rustic bread. Tuscans are known as very thrifty, not wasting a single breadcrumb. They are also known as *mangiafagioli* (bean-eaters)—and sorting through the many beans on Florentine menus you'll learn why.

Note that steak and seafood are often sold by weight (if you see "100 g" or "l *etto*" by the price on the menu, you'll pay that price per 100 grams—about a quarter pound). Sometimes, especially for steak, restaurants require a minimum order of four or five *etti.*

Here are some typical foods you'll encounter in Florence:

Appetizers *(Antipasti)*

Tuscan bread: Rustic-style breads (not baguettes) with a thick crust and chewy interior. It's a type of sourdough bread, unsalted and nearly flavorless, to accompany the heartier-flavored cuisine. Slathered with olive oil and salt, it is a popular afternoon snack.

Bruschetta: Toasted bread slices brushed with olive oil and topped with garlic, chopped tomato, or a variety of spreads.

Crostini: Small toasted bread rounds topped with meat or vegetable pastes. *Lardo* (animal fat) is also a favorite traditional spread.

Panzanella: A simple Tuscan salad made of chunks of day-old bread and chopped tomatoes, onion, and basil, tossed in a light vinaigrette.

Pecorino cheese: Fresh or aged, from ewe's milk.

Porcini mushrooms: Harvested in the fall and used in pasta and soups.

Finocchiona sbriciolona: A soft salami flavored with fennel seed.

First Course *(Primo Piatto)*

Ribollita: Literally "reboiled," this soup consists of white beans *(fagioli)*, seasonal vegetables, and olive oil layered with day-old Tuscan bread slices.

Pappardelle sulla lepre: This broad noodle is served with a rich sauce made from wild hare.

Pici al ragu: A fat, spaghetti-like pasta served most often with a meat-tomato sauce.

Main Course *(Secondo Piatto)*

Bistecca alla fiorentina: A thick T-bone steak, grilled and lightly seasoned. (The best is from the white Chiana breed of cattle you'll see grazing throughout Tuscany.) This dish is often sold by weight (per *etto*, or 100 grams), not per portion.

Cinghiale: Wild boar, served grilled or in soups, stews, and pasta. It is also made into many varieties of sausage.

Arrosto misto or *Spiedino:* Mixed roast meats or meats on a skewer.

Various game birds: Squab, pheasant, and guinea hen.

Trippa alla fiorentina: Tripe (intestines) and vegetables sautéed in a tomato sauce, baked with parmesan cheese.

...alla fiorentina: Anything cooked "in the Florentine style." Can mean almost anything, but often means it's cooked with vegetables, especially spinach.

Eating with the Seasons

Italian cooks love to serve you fresh produce and seafood at its tastiest. If you must have porcini mushrooms outside of October and November, they'll be frozen. To get the freshest veggies at a fine restaurant, request *"Il piatto del la stagioni, per favore"* (a plate of what's seasonal, please).

Here are a few examples of what's fresh when:

April–May:	Calamari, squid, green beans, and zucchini flowers
April, May, Sept, Oct:	Black truffles
May–June:	Mussels, asparagus, zucchini, cantaloupe, and strawberries
May–Aug:	Eggplant
Oct–Nov:	Mushrooms and white truffles
Fresh year-round:	Clams, meats, and cheese

Dessert *(Dolci)*

Panforte: Dense, dark, clove-and-cinnamon-spiced cake from Siena. *Panforte* makes a good, enduring gift.

Gelato: The Florentines claim they invented Italian-style ice cream. Many think they serve some of the world's best. Consider skipping dessert at the restaurant and stretching your legs before finding a good *gelateria.*

Cantucci and *Vin Santo:* Florentines love this simple way to end a meal, by dipping the crunchy almond *biscotti* in *Vin Santo* (literally "holy wine"), a sweet, golden dessert wine.

Wines *(Vini)*

Chianti: The hearty red from the Chianti region (30 km south of Florence), made mostly from the Sangiovese grape, is world-famous. "Chianti Classico," with a black rooster symbol on the bottle neck, is from a subregion and generally denotes higher quality.

Brunello di Montalcino: One of Italy's greatest red wines, made from Sangiovese *grosso* grapes, is from the commune of Montalcino, south of Siena. This full-bodied wine is aged at least four years in wooden casks, resulting in a bold, smooth character.

Rosso di Montalcino: A lower-priced, younger version of Brunello.

Montepulciano: Hearty red, about midway in strength and flavor between a mellow Chianti and a strong Brunello di Montalcino. It's from the region 90 kilometers southwest of Florence.

Super Tuscans: This newer breed of Italian wine is made from non-Italian grapes. These ultra-expensive, high-quality reds are often made from French grapes like Cabernet and Merlot. A couple of names to look for are Sassicia and Tignanello.
White Wines: Tuscany produces less distinctive whites. Try Vernaccia di San Gimignano, a light-medium dry white.

RESTAURANTS IN FLORENCE
Eating in Oltrarno, South of the River
For a change of scene, eat across the river in Oltrarno. Here are a few good places just over the Ponte Vecchio.

At Piazza San Felicita: A block south of the Ponte Vecchio is the unpretentious and happy Piazza San Felicita, with two good restaurants. The cozy and candlelit **Trattoria Bordino,** just up the street and actually built into the old town wall (c. 1170), serves tasty and beautifully presented Florentine cuisine "with international influence" (a little pricey, Mon–Sat 12:00–14:30 & 19:30–22:30, closed Sun, Via Stracciatella 9 red, tel. 055-213-048). Right on the square, the more touristy **Ristorante Bibo** serves *"cucina tipica Fiorentina"* with a pink-tablecloth-and-black-bowties dressiness and leafy, candlelit outdoor seating (good €15 3-course meal, CC, reserve for outdoor seating, Wed–Mon 12:00–14:30 & 19:00–22:30, closed Tue, Piazza San Felicita 6 red, tel. 055-239-8554).

On Via di Santo Spirito/Borgo San Jacopo: Several good and colorful restaurants line this multinamed street a block off the river in Oltrarno. I'd survey the scene (perhaps following the self-guided Oltrarno walk described on page 34) before making a choice.

At **Cammillo Trattoria,** while Cammillo is slurping spaghetti in heaven, his granddaughter Chiara carries on the tradition, mixing traditional Tuscan with "creative" modern cuisine. With a charcoal grill and a team of white-aproned waiters cranking out wonderful food in a fun, dressy-but-down-to-earth ambience, this place is a hit (full dinners about €36 plus wine, Thu–Tue 12:00–14:30 & 19:30–22:30, closed Wed, CC, Borgo San Jacopo 57 red, reservations smart, tel. 055-212-427).

Other inviting places along this street: **Osteria del Cinghiale Bianco** is popular but cramped (around €30 for dinner plus wine, Borgo San Jacopo 43 red, air-con, Thu–Tue 12:00–15:00 & 18:30–23:30, closed Wed, reservations wise, tel. 055-215-706). The more relaxed **Trattoria Angiolino** serves good, old-fashioned local cuisine (about €20 for dinner plus wine, Tue–Sun 12:00–14:30 & 19:30–22:30, closed Mon, Via di Santo Spirito 36 red, tel. 055-239-8976). **Trattoria Sabatino** is spacious and disturbingly cheap, with family character, red-checkered tablecloths, a simple menu,

Florence Restaurants

1. OSTERIA BELLEDONNE
2. RIST. LA SPADA
3. TRATTORIA MARIONE
4. TRATTORIA SOSTANZA-TROIA
5. TRATTORIA IL CONTADINO
6. TRATTORIA DA GIORGIO
7. LA GROTTA DI LEO
8. MERCATO CENTRALE
9. TRATTORIA LA BURRASCA & OSTERIA LA CONGREGA

10. SELF-SERVICE REST. LEONARDO
11. RIST. IL CAVALLINO
12. OSTERIA VINI E VECCHI SAPORI
13. CANTINETTA DEI VERRAZZANO & RIST. PAOLI
14. I FRATELLINI WINE & SANDWICH SHOP
15. TRATTORIA ICCHE C'E C'E
16. PICNIC SPOT IF IT'S NOT TOO HOT

and the fewest tourists of all. A wonderful place to watch locals munch, it's just outside the Porta San Frediano (medieval gate), a 15-minute walk from the Ponte Vecchio (Mon–Fri 12:00–14:30 & 19:20–22:00, closed Sat–Sun, Via Pisana 2 red, tel. 055-225-955, NSE). If you eat here, read my self-guided Oltrarno walk (on page 34) before hiking out to the gate.

At Piazza Santo Spirito: This classic Florentine square (lately a hangout for drug pushers, therefore a bit seedy-feeling and plagued by Vespa bag-snatchings) has two popular little restaurants. Both offer good local cuisine every night of the week, indoor and on-the-square seating (reserve for on-the-square), moderate prices, and impersonal service: **Borgo Antico** (Piazza Santo Spirito 6 red, tel. 055-210-437) and **Osteria Santo Spirito** (pricier, more peaceful outdoor seating, Piazza Santo Spirito 16 red, tel. 055-238-2383).

Ricchi Caffè, next to Borgo Antico, has fine *gelato* and shaded outdoor tables. After noting the plain facade of the Brunelleschi church facing the square, step inside the café, and pick your favorite of the many ways it might be finished. **Café Cabiria,** next door, is a great local hangout with good light meals and a cozy Florentine funky room in back.

Trattoria Casalinga is an inexpensive standby. Famous for its home cooking, it's now filled with tourists rather than locals. But it sends them away full, happy, and with euros left for gelato (Mon–Sat 12:00–14:30 & 19:00–21:45, closed Sun and all of Aug, CC, just off Piazza Santo Spirito, near the church at Via dei Michelozzi 9 red, after 20:00 reserve or wait, tel. 055-218-624).

Eating North of the River

Eating near Santa Maria Novella and the Train Station

Osteria Belledonne is a crowded and cheery bohemian hole-in-the-wall serving great food at good prices. I loved the meal but had to correct the bill—read it carefully. They take only a few reservations. Arrive early or wait (Mon–Fri 12:00–14:30 & 19:00–22:30, closed Sat–Sun, Via delle Belledonne 16 red, tel. 055-238-2609).

Ristorante La Spada, nearby, is another fine local favorite serving typical Tuscan cuisine with less atmosphere and more menu (€11 lunch special, about €20 for dinner plus wine, daily 12:00–15:00 & 19:00–22:30, air-con, near Via della Spada at Via del Moro 66 red, evening reservations smart, tel. 055-218-757).

Trattoria Marione serves good home-cooked-style meals to a local crowd in a happy, food-loving ambience (closed Sun, dinners run about €15 plus wine, pretty smoky, Via della Spada 27 red, tel. 055-214-756).

Trattoria Sostanza-Troia is a characteristic and also a

well-established place with shared tables and a loyal local following. Whirling ceiling fans and walls strewn with old photos create a time-warp ambience. They offer two seatings, requiring reservations: one at 19:30 and one at 21:00 (dinners for about €15 plus wine, great steaks, lunch 12:00–14:00, closed Sat, Via del Porcellana 25 red, tel. 055-212-691).

Two smoky chow houses for local workers offer a €9, hearty, family-style, fixed-price menu with a bustling working class/ budget-Yankee-traveler atmosphere (Mon–Sat 12:00–14:30 & 18:15–21:30, closed Sun, 2 blocks south of train station): **Trattoria il Contadino** (Via Palazzuolo 69 red, tel. 055-238-2673) and **Trattoria da Giorgio** (across the street at Via Palazzuolo 100 red). Arrive early or wait. The touristy **La Grotta di Leo** (a block away) has a cheap, straightforward menu and edible food and pizza (daily 11:00–1:00, Via della Scala 41 red, tel. 055-219-265). Because these places are a block from the station, they are handy, but the street scene is grotty.

Eating near the Central and San Lorenzo Markets

For piles of picnic produce, people-watching, or just a sandwich, try the huge Central Market—**Mercato Centrale** (Mon–Sat 7:00–14:00, a block north of San Lorenzo street market).

Trattoria la Burrasca is a funky, family-run place ideal for Tuscan home cooking. It's small—10 tables—and inexpensive— pasta for €4. Anna and Antonio Genzano have cooked and served here with passion since 1982. If Andy Capp were Italian, he'd eat here for special nights out. Everything is homemade except the desserts. And, if you want good wine cheap, order it here (Fri–Wed 12:00–15:00 & 19:00–22:00, closed Thu, Via Panicale 6b, at north corner of Central Market, tel. 055-215-827, NSE).

Osteria la Congrega brags it's a Tuscan wine bar designed to help you lose track of time. In a fresh and romantic two-level setting, creative chef/owner Mahyar has designed a fun, easy menu featuring modern Tuscan cuisine, with top-notch local meat and produce. He offers fine vegetarian dishes. With just 10 uncrowded tables, reservations are required for dinner (moderate with €13 dinner plates, CC, daily 12:00–15:00 & 19:00–23:00, Via Panicale 43 red, tel. 055-264-5027).

For a cheap lunch, try **Trattoria San Zanobi's** Pasta Break Lunch (most pastas around €5, Via San Zanobi 33 red, a couple blocks northeast of the Central Market, tel. 055-475-286).

Eating near the Accademia and Museum of San Marco

Gran Caffè San Marco, conveniently located on Piazza San Marco, offers reasonably priced pizzas, sandwiches, and desserts (no cover charge, self-service and restaurant, Piazza San Marco 11 red, across square from Museum of San Marco entrance, tel. 055-215-833).

Eating near the Cathedral (Duomo)

Self-Service Restaurant Leonardo is fast, cheap, air-conditioned, and very handy, just a block from the Duomo, southwest of the Baptistery (€3 pastas, €4 main courses, Sun–Fri 11:45–14:45 & 18:45–21:45, closed Sat, upstairs at Via Pecori 5, tel. 055-284-446). Luciano (like Pavarotti) runs the place with enthusiasm.

Eating near Palazzo Vecchio

Piazza Signoria, the square facing the old city hall, is ringed by beautifully situated yet touristic eateries. Any will do for a reasonably priced pizza. Perhaps the best value is **Ristorante il Cavallino** (€10 fixed-price lunch menu, €16 fixed-price dinner menu, great outdoor seating in shadow of palace, tel. 055-215-818).

Osteria Vini e Vecchi Sapori is a colorful hole-in-the-wall serving traditional food, including plates of mixed *crostini* (€0.75 each—you choose), half a block north of Palazzo Vecchio (Tue–Sun 10:00–23:00, closed Mon, Via dei Magazzini 3 red, facing the bronze equestrian statue in Piazza della Signoria, go behind its tail into the corner and to your left, NSE).

Cantinetta dei Verrazzano is a long-established bakery/café/wine bar, serving delightful sandwich plates in an elegant old-time setting, and hot focaccia sandwiches to go. The *Specialita Verrazzano* is a fine plate of four little *crostini* (like mini *bruschetta*) featuring different local breads, cheeses, and meats (€7). The *Tagliere di Focacce*, a sampler plate of mini–focaccia sandwiches, is also fun. Either of these dishes with a glass of Chianti makes a fine light meal. Paolo describes things to make eating educational. As office workers pop in for a quick bite, it's traditional to share tables at lunchtime (Mon–Sat 12:30–21:00, closed Sun, just off Via Calzaiuoli on a side street across from Orsanmichele Church at Via dei Tavolini 18, tel. 055-268-590).

At **I Fratellini,** a colorful hole-in-a-wall place, the "little brothers" have served peasants rustic sandwiches and cheap glasses of Chianti wine since 1875. Join the local crowd, then sit on a nearby curb or windowsill to munch, placing your glass on the wall rack before you leave (€4 for sandwich and wine, 20 meters in front of Orsanmichele church on Via dei Cimatori).

Ristorante Paoli serves great local cuisine to piles of happy eaters under a richly frescoed Gothic vault. Because of its fame and central location, it's filled mostly with tourists, but for a dressy, traditional splurge meal, this is my choice (Wed–Mon 12:00–14:00 & 19:00–22:00, closed Tue, reserve for dinner, €20 tourist menu, à la carte is pricier, CC, midway between old square and cathedral at Via de Tavolini 12 red, tel. 055-216-215). Salads are flamboyantly cut and mixed from a trolley right at your table.

Trattoria Icche C'è C'è (dialect for "whatever is, is"; pron. ee-kay chay chay) is a small, family-style place where fun-loving Gino serves good traditional meals (moderate, not too touristy, closed Mon, midway between Bargello and river at Via Magalotti 11 red, tel. 055-216-589).

Osteria del Porcellino—a rare place that serves late—is delightful, a bit pricey, packed with a mix of locals and in-the-know tourists, and run with style and enthusiasm by friendly chef Enzo (daily 18:00–01:00, summer lunches, indoor/outdoor, CC, Via Val di Lamona 7 red, half a block behind Mercato Nuovo, reserve for dinner, tel. 055-264-148).

Trattoria Nella serves good, typical Tuscan cuisine at affordable prices, including the best gnocchi in town. Arrive early or be disappointed (Mon–Sat 12:00–14:30 & 19:30–22:00, closed Sun, 3 blocks northwest of Ponte Vecchio, Via delle Terme 19 red, tel. 055-218-925).

Gelato

Gelato is an edible art form. Italy's best ice cream is in Florence— one souvenir that can't break and won't clutter your luggage. But beware of scams at touristy joints on busy streets that turn a simple request for a cone into a €10 "tourist special."

Gelateria Carrozze is very good (daily 11:00–24:00, closes at 21:00 in winter, on riverfront 30 meters from Ponte Vecchio toward the Uffizi, Via del Pesce 3). **Gelateria dei Neri** is another local favorite worth finding (2 blocks east of Palazzo Vecchio at Via Dei Neri 20 red, daily in summer 12:00–23:00, closed Wed in winter).

Vivoli's is the most famous (Tue–Sun 8:00–01:00; closed Mon, the last 3 weeks in Aug, and winter; opposite the Church of Santa Croce, go down Via Torta a block, turn right on Via Stinche). Before ordering, try a free sample of their *riso* flavor—rice.

If you want an excuse to check out the little village-like neighborhood across the river from Santa Croce, enjoy a gelato at the tiny **no-name gelateria** at Via San Miniato 5 red (just before Porta San Miniato).

FLORENCE WITH CHILDREN

Florence with kids: not ideal. But it's certainly good for them!
Here are a few thoughts on family fun in the art capital of Europe.

- Be certain to call ahead to get admission appointments whenever possible. Long museum lines add insult to injury for the preteen being dragged into another old building filled with old paintings.
- The TI's *Florence for the Young* pamphlet lists kid-friendly activities, parks, pools, and sightseeing tips.
- Avoid the midday heat by planning on a cool break such as an air-conditioned, kid-friendly place for lunch.
- Eat dinner early (around 19:00), and you'll miss the romantic crowd. Skip the famous places. Look instead for self-serve cafeterias, bars (kids are welcome), or even fast-food restaurants where kids can move around without bothering others. Picnic lunches and dinners work well. For ready-made picnics, try the *rosticcerie* (delis) and Pizza Rustica shops (cheap take-out pizza; *diavola* is the closest thing on the menu to kid-friendly pepperoni).
- Public WCs are hard to find: Try museums, bars, gelato shops, and fast-food restaurants.
- The smart tour guide/parent incorporates the child's interests into each day's plans. When a child is unhappy, no one has fun.

Sights

The **Science Museum** has cool old telescopes and early chemical and science lab stuff. But the case with Galileo's finger will likely be the highlight here (closed Sun; see Science Museum Tour, page 151).

Climbing the dome of the cathedral is almost like climbing an urban mountain—you'll spiral up in a strange dome-within-a-dome space, see some musty old tools used in the construction, get a bird's-eye peek into the nave from way up, and then pop out with the best city view in town. Arrive by 8:30 to beat the crowds; otherwise it may not be worth the long and slow-moving line (closed Sun; see page 42).

Every kid will want to see Michelangelo's *David* (closed Mon; see Renaissance Walk, page 36). But the most interesting collection of statues—with many bizarre poses—is in the **Bargello** (closed on alternating Sun and Mon; see Bargello Tour, page 74).

The **Museum of Precious Stones** shows 500 different semiprecious stones and then demonstrates the fascinating techniques of inlay and mosaic work (closed Sun, around corner from *David*; see page 25).

The **Uffizi courtyard** is ringed by statues of all the famous Florentines (Amerigo Vespucci, Machiavelli, Leonardo, and so on)—great for putting a face on a sweep through history (see page 49 of Renaissance Walk).

Florence's various **open-air markets** are fun for kids (see Shopping, page 219). Remember to haggle.

The **Boboli Gardens** are a landscaped wonderland. While designed to give adults a break from the city, they are kid-friendly compared to streets and museums (closed first and last Mon of month; see page 33). For a real playground-type park, head west of the old center along the north side of the river to **Parco dello Cascine** (10-min walk, lots of grass, a pool, and rental bikes).

Older kids may enjoy taking a **bike tour** through the countryside around Florence (bike rental at Parco dello Cascine, above) or hiking up to **Piazzale Michelangelo** for the view (see page 34).

Of all the side trips, a jaunt over to see the tower leaning in **Pisa** is probably the most interesting for kids (see Day Trips chapter, page 166).

For fast and kid-friendly **meals** in the old center, there are plenty of hamburger and pizza joints. For a good cafeteria, try Self-Service Ristorante Leonardo (a block from the Duomo; see page 215 of Eating). **Gelaterias** such as Festival del Gelato (Via del Corso 75 red) and Perche No! (Via de Tavolini 19 red) are brash, neon, and provide some of the best high-calorie memories in town.

SHOPPING

Florence is a great shopping town—known for its sense of style since the Medici days. Many people spend entire days shopping. Stores are open from 9:00 to 13:00 and 15:30 to 19:30, usually closed on Sunday, often closed on Monday, and sometimes closed for a couple of weeks around August 15. Many stores have promotional stalls in the market squares.

For shopping ideas, ads, and a list of markets, see the *Florence Concierge Information* magazine (free from TI and many hotels).

Markets

Busy street scenes and markets abound. Prices are soft in the markets—bargain. Perhaps the biggest market fills the streets around the Church of San Lorenzo with countless stalls selling lower-end leather, clothing, T-shirts, handbags, and souvenirs. Beware of fakes (Mon–Sat 9:00–19:00, between the Duomo and train station). The shops behind the street stalls (and along nearby Via Faenza) are great for a workaday peek into Florentine life. The neighboring Mercato Centrale is a giant covered food market (a block north of the Church of San Lorenzo).

Other popular shopping centers are the Santa Croce area (known for leather; check out the "leather school," which is actually inside the Church of Santa Croce—enter to the right of altar); the Ponte Vecchio (traditional for gold and silver); and the old, covered Mercato Nuovo (3 blocks north of Ponte Vecchio, see description on page 33).

For antiques, wander the Oltrarno (south side of river), specifically along Borgo San Jacopo.

A **flea market** litters Piazza dei Ciompi with antiques, odds, and ends Tuesday through Saturday, but is really big only on the first Sunday of each month (near Piazza Santa Croce).

Getting a VAT Refund

Wrapped into the purchase price of your Florentine souvenirs is a Value Added Tax (VAT) that's generally about 17 percent. If you purchase more than €155 worth of goods at a store that participates in the VAT refund scheme, you're entitled to get most of that tax back. Personally I've never felt that VAT refunds are worth the hassle, but if you do, here's the scoop.

If you're lucky, the merchant will subtract the tax when you make your purchase (this is more likely to occur if the store ships the goods to your home). Otherwise, you'll need to:

Get the paperwork. Have the merchant completely fill out the necessary refund document, called a "cheque." You'll have to present your passport.

Get your stamp at the border. Process your cheque(s) at your last stop in the European Union with the customs agent who deals with VAT refunds. It's best to keep your purchases in your carry-on for viewing, but if they're too large or dangerous (such as knives) to carry on, then track down the proper customs agent to inspect them before you check your bag. You're not supposed to use your purchased goods before you leave. If you show up at customs wearing your new shoes, officials might look the other way—or deny you a refund.

Collect your refund. You'll need to return your stamped document to the retailer or its representative. Many merchants work with a service, such as Global Refund or Cashback, which have offices at major airports, ports, or border crossings. These services, which extract a 4 percent fee, can refund your money immediately in your currency of choice or credit your card (within two billing cycles). If you have to deal directly with the retailer, mail the store your stamped documents and then wait. It could take months.

Boutiques and High Fashion

The entire area between the river and the cathedral is busy with inviting boutiques showing off ritzy Italian fashions. The street Via de' Tornabuoni is best for boutique browsing. The main **Ferragamo** store fills a classy 800-year-old building with a fine selection of shoes and boots and an interesting museum upstairs (Via de' Tornabuoni 16, tel. 055-292-123). Also browse the

streets Via della Vigna Nuova (runs west from Via de' Tornabuoni) and Via Strozzi (runs east from Via de' Tornabuoni to
Piazza Repubblica).

Department Stores

Typical chain department stores are **Coin** (Mon–Sat 9:30–20:00,
Sun 11:00–20:00, on Via Calzaiuoli, near Orsanmichele Church);
Standa, a discount clothing/grocery chain (Mon–Sat 9:00–19:55,
closed Sun, at intersection of Via Panzani and Via del Giglio,
near train station); and **la Rinascente** (Piazza della Repubblica,
Mon–Sat 9:00-21:00, Sun 10:30-20:00).

Souvenir Ideas

Shoppers in Florence enjoy art reproductions (posters, calendars,
books, prints, and so on—especially good in and around the Uffizi
and Accademia museums); reproductions of old documents, maps,
and manuscripts; traditional stationery (Il Papiro chain stores);
silk ties and scarves; ceramics; edible goodies (olives, Parmigiano-

Reggiano cheese, and dried
porcini mushrooms); and goofy
knickknacks featuring Renaissance masterpieces (such as
Botticelli mouse pads, Raphael
lipstick-holders, and plaster
*David*s). While I don't fly
with bottles of wine, many
bring home a special bottle of
Chianti Classico or Brunello
di Montalcino. For soaps, skin creams, herbal remedies, and
perfumes, sniff out the antique and palatial perfumery, Farmacia
di Santa Maria Novella (Via della Scala 16, see page 133).

NIGHTLIFE

With so many American and international college students in town, Florence by night can have a frat-party atmosphere. Nighttime is for eating a late meal, catching a concert, strolling through the old-town pedestrian zone and piazzas, or hitting one of the many pubs.

The latest on nightlife is listed in several publications available for free at the TI (such as the monthly *Florence Concierge Information*) or for a small price at newsstands (consider the weekly *Firenze Spettacolo* and the monthly *Florence in Your Pocket*). Also check www.firenze.turismo.toscana.it.

The **Box Office** sells tickets for local events (Mon–Sat 10:00–20:00, closed Sun, on road that runs along west side of train station, Via Alamanni 39, tel. 055-210-804).

American art historians often advertise an **evening talk** (sometimes in a romantic setting, with wine) in TI publications. Consider Florence Art Lectures which offers "Evening Cocktail Hour Art Lectures" and city walking tours at sunset (see also page 22, May–Sept only, Piazza Santa Croce 21, tel. 055-245-354, www.florenceart.org).

On summer Saturdays, several **sights**—the Accademia, Uffizi Gallery, and Palatine Gallery/Royal Apartments (in Pitti Palace)— may stay open until 22:00; confirm at the TI. The Palazzo Vecchio may stay open until 23:00 on summer Mondays and Fridays.

The historic center has a good floodlit ambience, ideal for **strolling.** The entire pedestrian zone from the Uffizi to the Duomo is lively with people. The Piazza della Repubblica is lined with venerable 19th-century cafés and fun people scenes on the square. The Ponte Vecchio is a popular place to enjoy river views (and kiss). Of the great squares, only two feel creepy at night—Piazza Santa Maria Novella and, to a lesser extent,

Piazza Santo Spirito (south of the Arno)—because they're known as rendezvous spots for drug users and pushers.

Piazzale Michelangelo—on a hilltop across the river (bus #12 or #13 from the train station)—is awesome for sunsets and is packed with local Romeos and Juliets on weekend evenings. After dark, it's easier to get there and back by bus or taxi (rather than take a 60-minute round-trip hike). Consider going to **Fiesole** for the sunset (see page 35).

Wine bars *(enotecas)* are fun for sampling local wines and enjoying regional munchies. Consider these *enotecas: Boccadama* (Piazza San Croce 25-26 red), *All' Antico Vinaio* (Via dei Neri 65 red, between Piazza della Signoria and Santa Croce), and *Casa del Vino* (Via dell' Ariento 16 red, near Mercato Centrale). **Irish pubs** continue to be a phenomenon, gathering thirsty locals rather than tourists.

TRANSPORTATION
CONNECTIONS

Florence is the transportation hub for Tuscany, with good connections to virtually anywhere in Italy. The city has a central train station, bus station (next to the train station), and an airport (plus Pisa's airport nearby).

TRAIN STATION

The station soaks up time and generates dazed and sweaty crowds. If you arrive by train, there's no need to linger at the station. Go elsewhere to get onward tickets and train information (at American Express, see page 10). And skip the fake "Tourist Information" office in the station (next to McDonald's) that works for the hotels and books rooms. The real TI is across the square from the station (see page 20).

With your back to the tracks, to your left are most of my recommended hotels, a 24-hour pharmacy (*Farmacia Comunale*, near McDonald's), city buses, and the entrance to the underground mall/passage that goes across the square to the church of Santa Maria Novella (but because the tunnel is frequented by pickpockets, especially the surface point near the church, stay above ground). Baggage check is near track 16.

Types of Trains

You'll encounter several types of trains in Italy. Along with the various local milk-run trains, there are the slow IR (Interregional) and *directo* trains, the medium *expresso*, the fast IC (Intercity), and the bullet-train T.A.V.—*Treno Alta Velocita* (€16 supplement even with train pass). Fast trains, even with supplements, are affordable (including the express supplement, a first-class Florence-to-Venice ticket costs about $40; second-class about $25). Buying supplements on the train comes with a nasty penalty. Buying them at

Italy's Public Transportation

KEY: — RAIL --- BUS ···· SHIP
NOT TO SCALE ● GOOD OVERNIGHT STOPS

the station usually involves a long wait in line. Try to buy them at travel agencies (American Express or CIT) in towns. The cost is the same, the lines and language barrier are smaller, and you'll save time.

Schedules

Newsstands sell up-to-date regional and all-Italy timetables (€3.75, ask for the *orario ferroviario*). There is now a single all-Italy telephone number for train information—848-888-088 (daily 7:00–21:00, automated Italian recording, have an Italian speaker

listen for you). On the Web, check www.trenitalia.it, http://bahn
.hafas.de/bin/query.exe/en, or www.fs-on-line.com.

Strikes are common. Strikes generally last a day, and train
employees will simply say *"Sciopero"* (strike). But, actually, sporadic
trains lumber down the tracks during most strikes.

By train to: Pisa (2/hr, 1 hr 20 min), **La Spezia** (for the
Cinque Terre, 2/day direct, 2 hrs, or change in Pisa), **Milan**
(12/day, 3–5 hrs), **Venice** (7/day, 3 hrs), **Assisi** (3/day, 2 hrs, more
frequent with transfers, direction: Foligno), **Orvieto** (6/day, 2 hrs),
Rome (hrly, 2.5 hrs), **Naples** (10/day, 4 hrs), **Brindisi** (3/day,
11 hrs with change in Bologna), **Frankfurt** (3/day, 12 hrs), **Paris**
(1/day, 12 hrs overnight), **Vienna** (4/day, 9–10 hrs).

BUS STATION

The SITA bus station, a block west of the Florence train station,
is user-friendly. Schedules are posted everywhere, with TV monitors indicating imminent departures. Bus service drops dramatic-
ally on Sunday.

By bus to: San Gimignano (hrly, 1.75 hrs), **Siena** (hrly,
75-min *corse rapide* fast buses are faster than the train, avoid the
2-hr *diretta* slow buses), and the **airport** (hrly, 15 min). Bus info:
tel. 055-214-721 from 9:30 to 12:30; some schedules are in the
Florence Concierge Information magazine.

TAXIS

If you don't want to mess with buses or trains, consider hiring a
taxi to take you to nearby towns. For a small group or people with
more money than time, this can be a good value. For example, for
around €100, you can arrange a ride directly from your Florence
hotel to your Siena hotel. Ask your hotel to call a taxi or go to a
taxi stand (e.g., at the train station).

AIRPORTS

The **Amerigo Vespucci Airport** (www.safnet.it), several kilometers northwest of Florence, has a TI, cash machines, car
rental agencies, and easy connections by airport shuttle bus with
Florence's bus station, a block west of the train station (€4, 2/hr,
30 min, from Florence runs 5:30–23:00, from airport 6:00–23:30).
Airport info: 055-306-1300, flight info: 055-306-1700 (domestic),
055-306-1702 (international). Allow about €16 to €20 for a taxi.

International flights often land at Pisa's **Galileo Galilei
Airport** (also has TI and car rental agencies, www.pisa-airport
.com), an hour from Florence by train (runs hrly; if you're leaving
Florence for this airport, catch the train at Florence's train station
at platform #5). Flight info: 050-500-707.

Driving in Italy

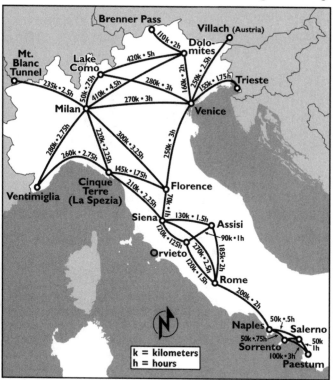

TIPS FOR DRIVERS

If you're taking the autostrada (north or south) to Florence, get off at the Certosa exit and follow signs to *Centro;* at Porta Romana, go to the left of the arch and down Via Francesco Petrarca. After driving and trying to park in Florence, you'll understand why Leonardo never invented the car. Cars flatten the charm of Florence. Don't drive in Florence and don't risk parking illegally (fines up to €150).

The city has plenty of **parking lots.** For a short stay, park underground at the train station (€2/hr). The Fortezza da Basso is clearly marked in the center (€18.50/24 hrs). The least expensive lots are Parcheggio Parterre (Firenze Parcheggi, €10.50/24 hrs, perhaps cheaper with hotel reservation) and Parcheggio Oltrarno (near Porta Romana; pass through gate and on left, €10.50 per day). For parking information, ask at your hotel or call 055-500-1994.

HISTORY

FLORENCE HISTORY—EIGHT CENTURIES IN FOUR PAGES

59 B.C.–A.D. 1200: Roman, Early Christian, Medieval

It's the usual Rome story—military outpost, thriving provincial capital, conversion to Christianity, overrun by barbarians—except Florence really didn't fall. Proud medieval Florentines traced their

roots back to civilized Rome, and the city remained a Tuscan commercial center during the Dark Ages.

Sights:
- Piazza Repubblica (the old Forum)
- Find the ancient Roman military camp on today's street map. The rectangular grid plan—lined up with compass points rather than the river—can still be seen.
- Baptistery (built c. 1050), likely on site of Roman temple
- Roman and Etruscan fragments (Duomo Museum)

1200s: Urban Growth

Woolen cloth manufacture, trade, and banking made urban merchants—organized into guilds—more powerful than rural, feudal nobles. Florence, now a largely independent city-state, allied with nearby cities.

Sights:
- Bargello built (as city hall)
- Santa Croce, Santa Maria Novella, and Badia Fiorentina churches
- Dante's house
- Baptistery interior mosaics

1300s: Prosperity, Plague, Recovery

As part of a budding democracy with civic pride, Florence's guilds and merchants financed major construction projects (some begun in late 1200s). But the population of 90,000 was suddenly decimated by the Black Death (bubonic plague) of 1348. Recovery was slowed by more plagues, bank failures, and political rivalries.

Sights:
- Duomo and Campanile built (original decorations in Duomo Museum)
- Palazzo Vecchio
- Orsanmichele Church
- Giotto's bell-tower design, and paintings in Uffizi, Santa Croce, and Santa Maria Novella

1400s: Renaissance and Medici

While 1500 marks Europe's Renaissance, in Florence— where the whole revival of classical culture got its start—the Renaissance began and ended in the 1400s (the Quattrocento). The Medici (pron. MED-uh-chee), a rich textile-and-banking family whose wealth gave them  political leverage around Europe, ruled the most prosperous city in Italy, appeasing the masses with philanthropy and public art.

Sights:
- Brunelleschi's Duomo dome and Pazzi Chapel
- Donatello's statues in Bargello and Duomo Museum and on Orsanmichele exterior
- Ghiberti's two bronze doors on Baptistery (originals in Duomo Museum)
- Botticelli's paintings in Uffizi
- The Uffizi, tracing painting from medieval to Michelangelo

- The Bargello, tracing sculpture
- Masaccio's frescoes in Santa Maria Novella and Brancacci Chapel
- Fra Angelico paintings (and Savonarola history) in San Marco Museum

1500–1800: Decline, Medici Dukes, Renaissance Goes South

Bankrupt, the anti-democratic Medicis were exiled to Rome, married into royalty, and returned—backed by foreign powers—as even less democratic nobles. The "Renaissance spirit" moved elsewhere, taking Michelangelo, Leonardo, and Raphael with it. In succeeding centuries, the Medici dukes ruled an economically and politically declining city, but still financed art.

Sights:
- Michelangelo's Florentine works—*David*, Medici Chapels, and Laurentian Library
- Pitti Palace and Boboli Gardens (the later Medici palace)
- Later paintings (Uffizi) and statues (Bargello)
- Destruction of the original Duomo facade (Duomo Museum)
- Medici Chapels—pompous tombs of (mostly) later Medicis
- Ponte Vecchio cleaned up for jewelry shops
- Baroque interiors of many older churches
- Galileo's finger, telescopes, and experiments in Science Museum

1800s: Italian Unification

Florence peacefully threw off rule by Austrian nobles, joining the Italian unification movement, even briefly serving as modern Italy's capital (1865–1870). Artistic revival of both medieval (neo-Gothic) and Renaissance (neoclassical) styles.

Sights:
- Duomo's current neo-Gothic facade
- Piazza Repubblica, commemorating unification, fine 19th-century cafés

1900s: Uncontrolled Urbanization, Urban Renewal

Population growth, rapid industri-
alization, WWII destruction, and
the six-meter (20-foot) high flood
of 1966 made Florence a chaotic,
noisy, dirty, traffic-choked city.
In the last 30 years, however, the
tourist zone has been cleaned and
cleared, museums revamped, hours
extended, and the people have

adapted to welcoming foreign visitors. Now if they could just do
something about those Vespas....

FLORENCE TIMELINE

500 B.C.–A.D. 1000— Etruscans, Romans, and "Barbarians"

c. 550 B.C.   Etruscans settle in Fiesole, near Florence.

59 B.C.   Julius Caesar establishes the Roman town of
Florentia (meaning flowering or flourishing) at a
convenient crossing point of the Arno River.

c. A.D. 200   Thriving Roman city, pop. 10,000.

c. 350   In the wake of Constantine's legalization of
Christianity, Bishop (and Saint) Zenobius builds a
church where the Duomo stands today.

450   Rome falls, Ostrogoths, Byzantines (sixth century),
and Lombards sweep through. But Florence survives
as a small trading town.

800   Charlemagne's Franks sweep through; he becomes
the first Holy Roman Emperor. Florence is part of
the Empire for the next 300 years, and is the regional
capital (rather than Fiesole).

1000–1400—Medieval Rise and Political Squabbles

c. 1050   Baptistery built, likely on site of ancient
Roman temple.

1100   Matilda, Countess of Tuscany, allies with
the pope and rises against the German-based
Holy Roman Empire, gaining independence
for Florence.

1200   Florence is the leading city in Tuscany, thriving on wool manufacture, trade, banking, and
moneylending.

Guelphs vs. Ghibellines

Pope	Emperor
Middle-class merchants and craftsmen	Aristocrats of feudal order
Urban (new economy)	Rural (traditional economy)
Independence of city-states under local Italian leaders	Unification of small states under traditional dukes and kings

But really, the fight was about power, not ideology. (It wasn't what you believed, but with whom you were allied.) The names always mean something different depending on the particular place and time.

1215	Political assassination of Buondelmonte epitomizes power struggles between nobles (Ghibellines), rich merchants and craftsmen (Guelphs), and laborers. The different factions seek support from outsiders—Guelphs ally with pope, Ghibellines with emperor. In general, Ghibellines dominate in first half of 1200s.
1222–1235	Florentine armies defeat Pisa, Siena, and Pistoia. Florence is the dominant city-state in Tuscany, heading a rich, commercial marketplace.
1252	Gold florin minted, one of Europe's strongest currencies.
1266	Merchants and craftsmen (Guelphs), organized into guilds, oust nobles and establish the *primo popolo*, the first "rule by the people."
1293	Guelphs solidify rule by the rich middle class, establishing a constitution that forbids nobles and laborers from holding office. The Ghibellines are gone, but bitter political infighting continues, with Florence divided between Black and White Guelphs.
1296	Construction begins on the Duomo. Santa Croce and Santa Maria Novella are also being built.
1302	The poet Dante, a prominent White Guelph, is exiled. Traveling around Europe and Italy, he writes his epic poem *The Divine Comedy*.
1347	Florence's population is 90,000, making it one of Europe's biggest cities.

1348   Population decimated after the horrific bubonic plague. In addition, recent bank failures and ongoing political squabbles make recovery more difficult.

1378   The Ciompi revolt, led by wool-factory workers, is suppressed by rich merchant families. The guilds (workers' unions) lose power as a few wealthy families rise—the Strozzi, Ricci, Alberti, and . . . Medici.

1400s, The "Quattrocento"—A Prosperous Renaissance City under Medici Princes

1401   Baptistery door competition energizes an already civic-minded city.

1406   Florence, by conquering Pisa, gains a port and becomes a sea-trading power.

1421   Giovanni de' Medici, a shrewd businessman, expands the Medici family business from wool manufacture into banking.

1434   Cosimo the Elder (Giovanni's son) returns triumphant from exile to rule Florence. Outwardly, he honors the Florentine constitution, but, in fact, he uses his great wealth to rule as a tyrant, buying popularity with lavish patronage of public art.

1436   Dedication of the Duomo, topped by Brunelleschi's dome.

1440   Battle of Anghiari—Florence defeats Milan.

c. 1440   Donatello's *David*.

1458   Cosimo the Elder creates a rubber-stamp Council of the Hundred.

1464   Cosimo's son, Piero the Gouty, rules stiffly but ably.

1469   Lorenzo the Magnificent, Cosimo's grandson, rules over the most powerful city in Italy. He is a popular politician but a so-so businessman.

1492   Lorenzo dies. Many Medici banks go bankrupt. Lorenzo's son, Piero the Unfortunate, facing an invasion force from France, appears to side with the foreigners.

1494   The Medici family, reviled as bankrupt morally, financially, and politically, is exiled. In the political vacuum, the monk Girolamo Savonarola appears as a voice of moral authority. He re-establishes the Florentine constitution.

1498   Savonarola is hanged and burned on Piazza della Signoria by political enemies and a citizenry tired of his morally strict rule. The constitution-driven republic continues.

1500–1800—The "Later" Medicis Oversee Florence's Decline

1501 Michelangelo begins sculpting *David*.

1512 The Medici family, having established a power base in Rome, returns to take political power as tyrants, backed by the pope and the Spanish army of Emperor Charles V.

1513 Lorenzo the Magnificent's son, Giovanni, becomes Pope Leo X.

1523 Lorenzo's nephew becomes Pope Clement VII.

1527 Imperial troops loot Rome. In the political chaos that follows, Florentines drive the Medicis from Florence, re-establishing a republic.

1530 After a year-long siege, Pope Clement VII and Charles V retake Florence, abolishing the republic and reinstalling Medici rulers.

1533 The Medicis marry off Catherine de' Medici to King Henry II of France.

1537 Cosimo the Younger, a Medici descended from Cosimo the Elder's brother, is made Duke of Florence. He and his wife, Eleanor of Toledo, rule as tyrannical nobles but beautify the city with the Uffizi, a renovated Palazzo Vecchio, and a rebuilt Pitti Palace.

1574 Francesco I becomes duke, soon to be followed by various Ferdinandos and Cosimos. Florence is now a minor player in world affairs, a small duchy with a stagnant economy.

1585–1633 Galileo, backed by the Medici family, works in Florence.

1587 The medieval facade of the Duomo is torn down, remaining bare brick for the next 200 years while they debate different proposals.

1600 Marie de' Medici marries Henry IV, becoming Queen of France.

1737 Gian Gastone, the last of the Medici line, dies. Florence is ruled by Austrian Hapsburg nobles.

1800–2000—Florence Enters the Modern World

1799 Napoleon "liberates" the city, briefly establishing a pseudo-democracy with his sister as duchess.

1814 Napoleon falls and the city returns to Austrian rule, under a distant descendant of the Medici family.

1848 Florentine citizens join an uprising all over Italy against foreign rule. The Risorgimento is on.

1860   Florence joins the kingdom of Victor Emmanuel,
       forming the nucleus of united, democratic,
       modern Italy.

1865   Florence is made Italy's capital (until the liberation
       of Rome in 1870).

1944   Under Nazi occupation as the Allies close in, all
       of the Arno bridges except the Ponte Vecchio
       are blown up.

1966   A disastrous flood, up to six meters (nearly 20 feet)
       high, covers the city's buildings and art treasures in
       mud. The city is a cultural, economic, and touristic
       mess. An international effort slowly brings these
       treasures back into view.

1993   The Mafia tries to strike terror with a bomb that
       destroys a section of the Uffizi, but the museum
       and the city recover. With a thriving university,
       scads of Internet cafés, and sparkling clean museums,
       Florence is a model cultural destination.

2003   You visit Florence, the art capital of Europe.

Renaissance Florence:
Cradle of the Modern World

There was something dynamic about the Florentines. Pope
Boniface VIII said there were five elements: earth, air, fire,
water . . . and Florentines. For 200 years, starting in the early
1300s, their city was a cultural hub.

Florence's contributions to Western culture are immense:
the whole revival of the arts, humanism, and science; the seeds of
democracy; the modern Italian language (which grew out of the
popular Florentine dialect); the art of Botticelli, Leonardo, and
Michelangelo; the writings of Machiavelli, Boccaccio, and Dante;
and the explorations of Amerigo Vespucci, who gave his name to
a newly discovered continent. Florentines considered themselves
descendants of the highly cultured people of the Roman Empire.
But Florence, even in its Golden Age, was always a mixture of
lustiness and refinement. The streets were filled with tough-
talking, hardened, illiterate merchants who strode about singing
verses from Dante's *Divine Comedy*.

Florentine culture came from money, and that money came
from the wool trade, silk factories, and banking. The city had a
large middle class and strong guilds (labor unions for skilled craftsmen). Success was a matter of civic pride, and Florentines showed
that pride in the mountains of money they spent to rebuild and
beautify the city.

Technically, Florence was a republic, ruled by elected citizens rather than a nobility. While there was some opportunity for upward mobility among the middle class, most power was in the hands of a few wealthy banking families. The most powerful was the Medici family. The Medici bank had branches in 10 cities in Europe, including London, Geneva, Bruges (Belgium), and Lyon (France). The pope kept his checking account in the Rome branch. The Florentine florin was the monetary standard of the Continent.

Florence dominated Italy economically and culturally, but not militarily. The independent Italian city-states squabbled and remained scattered until the nationalist movement four centuries later. (When someone suggested to the Renaissance Florentine Niccolo Machiavelli that the Italian city-states might unite against their common enemy, France, he wrote back, "Don't make me laugh.")

Lorenzo de Medici (1449–1492), inheritor of the family's wealth and power and his grandfather Cosimo's love of art, was a central figure of the Golden Age. He was young (20 when he took power), athletic, and intelligent, in addition to being a poet, horseman, musician, and leader. He wrote love songs and humorous dirty songs to be sung loudly and badly at carnival time. His marathon drinking bouts and illicit love affairs were legendary. He learned Greek and Latin and read the classics, yet his great passion was hunting. He was the Renaissance Man—a man of knowledge and action, a patron of the arts, and a scholar and man of the world. He was Lorenzo the Magnificent.

Lorenzo epitomized the Florentine spirit of optimism. Born on New Year's Day and raised in the lap of luxury (Donatello's *David* stood in the family courtyard) by loving parents, he grew up feeling that there was nothing he couldn't do. Florentines saw themselves as part of a "new age," a great undertaking of discovery and progress in man's history. They boasted that within the city walls, there were more "nobly gifted souls than the world has seen in the entire thousand years before." These people invented the term "Dark Ages" for the era that preceded theirs.

Lorenzo surrounded himself with Florence's best and brightest. They formed an informal "Platonic Academy," based on that of ancient Greece, to meet over a glass of wine under the stars at the Medici villa and discuss literature, art, music, and politics— witty conversation was considered an art in itself.

Their "neo-Platonic" philosophy stressed the goodness of man and the created world; they believed in a common truth behind all religion. The Academy was more than just an excuse to go out with the guys: The members were convinced that their discussions were changing the world and improving their souls.

Botticelli was a member of the Platonic Academy. He painted scenes from the classical myths that the group read, weaving contemporary figures and events into the ancient subjects. He gloried in the nude body, which he considered God's greatest creation.

Artists such as Botticelli thrived on the patronage of wealthy individuals, government, the Church, and guilds. Botticelli commanded as much as 100 florins for one work, enough to live for a year in high style, which he did for many years. In Botticelli's art we see the lightness, gaiety, and optimism of Lorenzo's court.

Another of Lorenzo's protégés was the young **Michelangelo.** Impressed with his work, Lorenzo took the poor, unlearned 13-year-old boy into the Medici household and treated him like a son.

Michelangelo's playmates were the Medici children, later to become Popes Leo X and Clement VII, who would give him important commissions. For all the encouragement, education, and contacts Michelangelo received, his most important gift from Lorenzo was simply a place at the dinner table, where Michelangelo could absorb the words of the great men of the time and their love of art for art's sake.

Even with all the art and philosophy of the Renaissance, violence, disease, and warfare were present in medieval proportions. For the lower classes, life was as harsh as it had always been. Many artists and scholars wore swords and daggers as part of everyday dress. This was the time of the ruthless tactics of the Borgias (known for murdering their political enemies) and of other families battling for power. Lorenzo himself barely escaped assassination in the cathedral during Easter Mass; his brother died in the attack.

The center of the Renaissance gradually shifted to Rome, but its artists were mostly Florentine. In the 15th century, the Holy City of Rome was a dirty, decaying, crime-infested place. Then a series of popes, including Lorenzo's son and nephew, launched a building and beautification campaign. They used fat commissions (and outright orders) to lure Michelangelo, Raphael, and others to Rome. The Florentine Renaissance headed south.

APPENDIX

Let's Talk Telephones

Here's a primer on making phone calls. For information specific to Italy, see "Telephones" in the introduction.

Making Calls within a European Country: About half of all European countries use area codes; the other half use a direct-dial system without area codes.

To make calls within a country that uses a direct-dial system (Italy, Belgium, the Czech Republic, Denmark, France, Portugal, Norway, Spain, and Switzerland), you dial the same number whether you're calling across the country or across the street.

In countries that use area codes (such as Austria, Britain, Finland, Germany, Ireland, the Netherlands, and Sweden), you dial only the local number when calling within a city, and you add the area code if calling long-distance within the country.

Making International Calls: You always start with the international access code (011 if you're calling from America or Canada, 00 from Europe), then dial the country code of the country you're calling (see chart below).

What you dial next depends on the phone system of the country you're calling. If the country uses area codes, drop the initial zero of the area code, then dial the rest of the number.

Countries that use direct-dial systems (no area codes) vary in how they're accessed internationally by phone. For instance, if you're making an international call to Italy, the Czech Republic, Denmark, Norway, Portugal, or Spain, simply dial the international access code, country code, and phone number. But if you're calling Belgium, France, or Switzerland, drop the initial zero of the phone number.

International Access Codes

When dialing direct, first dial the international access code (00 if calling from Europe, 011 if calling from the U.S. or Canada). Virtually all European countries—including Italy—use "00" as their international access code; the only exceptions are Finland (990) and Lithuania (810).

Country Codes

After you've dialed the international access code, dial the code of the country you're calling:

Austria—43	Greece—30
Belgium—32	Ireland—353
Britain—44	Italy—39
Canada—1	Morocco—212
Czech Rep.—420	Netherlands—31
Denmark—45	Norway—47
Estonia—372	Portugal—351
Finland—358	Spain—34
France—33	Sweden—46
Germany—49	Switzerland—41
Gibraltar—350	U.S.A.—1

Useful Italian Phone Numbers

Emergency (English-speaking police help): 113
Emergency (military police): 112
Road Service: 116
Directory Assistance (for €0.50, an Italian-speaking robot gives the number twice, very clearly): 12
Telephone help (in English; free directory assistance): 170

Festivals in Florence and National Holidays in 2003

This list includes Florence's major festivals, plus national holidays observed throughout Italy. Many sights close down on national holidays. Note that this isn't a complete list; holidays strike without warning.

For specifics and a more comprehensive listing of festivals, contact the Italian tourist information office in the U.S. (see page 7) and visit www.whatsonwhen.com, www.festivals.com, and www.hostetler.net.

Jan 1 and 6: National holidays.
Mid-Feb: Carnival Celebrations/Mardi Gras in Florence (costumed parades, street water fights, jousting competitions).

European Calling Chart

Just smile and dial, using this key:
AC = Area Code, LN = Local Number.

European Country	Calling long distance within...	Calling from the U.S.A./ Canada to...	Calling from another European country to...
Austria	AC (Area Code) + LN (Local Number)	011 + 43 + AC (without the initial zero) + LN	00 + 43 + AC (without the initial zero) + LN
Belgium	LN	011 + 32 + LN (without initial zero)	00 + 32 + LN (without initial zero)
Britain	AC + LN	011 + 44 + AC (without initial zero) + LN	00 + 44 + AC . (without initial zero) + LN
Czech Republic	LN	011 + 420 + LN	00 + 420 + LN
Denmark	LN	011 + 45 + LN	00 + 45 + LN
Estonia	LN	011 + 372 + LN	00 + 372 + LN
Finland	AC + LN	011 + 358 + AC (without initial zero) + LN	00 + 358 + AC (without initial zero) + LN
France	LN	011 + 33 + LN (without initial zero)	00 + 33 + LN (without initial zero)
Germany	AC + LN	011 + 49 + AC (without initial zero) + LN	00 + 49 + AC (without initial zero) + LN
Gibraltar	LN	011 + 350 + LN	00 + 350 + LN From Spain: 9567 + LN
Greece	LN	011 + 30 + LN	00 + 30 + LN

European Country	Calling long distance within...	Calling from the U.S.A./ Canada to...	Calling from another European country to...
Ireland	AC + LN	011 + 353 + AC (without initial zero) + LN	00 + 353 + AC (without initial zero) + LN
Italy	LN	011 + 39 + LN	00 + 39 + LN
Morocco	LN	011 + 212 + LN (without initial zero)	00 + 212 + LN (without initial zero)
Netherlands	AC + LN	011 + 31 + AC (without initial zero) + LN	00 + 31 + AC (without initial zero) + LN
Norway	LN	011 + 47 + LN	00 + 47 + LN
Portugal	LN	011 + 351 + LN	00 + 351 + LN
Spain	LN	011 + 34 + LN	00 + 34 + LN
Sweden	AC + LN	011 + 46 + AC (without initial zero) + LN	00 + 46 + AC (without initial zero) + LN
Switzerland	LN	011 + 41 + LN (without initial zero)	00 + 41 + LN (without initial zero)
Turkey	AC (if no initial zero is included, add one) + LN	011 + 90 + AC (without initial zero) + LN	00 + 90 + AC (without initial zero) + LN

The instructions above apply whether you're calling a fixed phone or cell phone.

- The international access codes (the first numbers you dial when making an international call) are 011 if you're calling from the U.S.A./Canada, or 00 if you're calling from virtually anywhere in Europe. Finland and Lithuania are the only exceptions. If calling from either of these countries, replace the 00 with 990 in Finland and 810 in Lithuania.
- To call the U.S.A. or Canada from Europe, dial 00 (unless you're calling from Finland or Lithuania), then 1 (the country code for the U.S.A. and Canada), then the area code and number. In short, 00 + 1 + AC + LN = Hi, mom!

2003

JANUARY
S M T W T F S
1 2 3 4
5 6 7 8 9 10 11
12 13 14 15 16 17 18
19 20 21 22 23 24 25
26 27 28 29 30 31

FEBRUARY
S M T W T F S
1
2 3 4 5 6 7 8
9 10 11 12 13 14 15
16 17 18 19 20 21 22
23 24 25 26 27 28

MARCH
S M T W T F S
1
2 3 4 5 6 7 8
9 10 11 12 13 14 15
16 17 18 19 20 21 22
23/30 24/31 25 26 27 28 29

APRIL
S M T W T F S
1 2 3 4 5
6 7 8 9 10 11 12
13 14 15 16 17 18 19
20 21 22 23 24 25 26
27 28 29 30

MAY
S M T W T F S
1 2 3
4 5 6 7 8 9 10
11 12 13 14 15 16 17
18 19 20 21 22 23 24
25 26 27 28 29 30 31

JUNE
S M T W T F S
1 2 3 4 5 6 7
8 9 10 11 12 13 14
15 16 17 18 19 20 21
22 23 24 25 26 27 28
29 30

JULY
S M T W T F S
1 2 3 4 5
6 7 8 9 10 11 12
13 14 15 16 17 18 19
20 21 22 23 24 25 26
27 28 29 30 31

AUGUST
S M T W T F S
1 2
3 4 5 6 7 8 9
10 11 12 13 14 15 16
17 18 19 20 21 22 23
24/31 25 26 27 28 29 30

SEPTEMBER
S M T W T F S
1 2 3 4 5 6
7 8 9 10 11 12 13
14 15 16 17 18 19 20
21 22 23 24 25 26 27
28 29 30

OCTOBER
S M T W T F S
1 2 3 4
5 6 7 8 9 10 11
12 13 14 15 16 17 18
19 20 21 22 23 24 25
26 27 28 29 30 31

NOVEMBER
S M T W T F S
1
2 3 4 5 6 7 8
9 10 11 12 13 14 15
16 17 18 19 20 21 22
23/30 24 25 26 27 28 29

DECEMBER
S M T W T F S
1 2 3 4 5 6
7 8 9 10 11 12 13
14 15 16 17 18 19 20
21 22 23 24 25 26 27
28 29 30 31

April 20 (Easter): Explosion of the Cart in Florence (fireworks, bonfire in wooden cart). Easter is a national holiday.

April 21: Easter Monday, a national holiday.

April 25: Liberation Day, a national holiday.

May 1: Labor Day, a national holiday.

May 9: Ascension Day, a national holiday. Annual Cricket Festival in Florence (music, entertainment, food, crickets sold in cages).

June 1–30: Annual Flower Display in Florence (carpet of flowers on the main square, Piazza della Signoria).

June 11–24: Festival of St. John in Florence (parades, dances, boat races).

June 24:	Calcio Fiorentino (costumed soccer game on Florence's Piazza Santa Croce).
June–August:	Annual Florence Dance Festival (dates not yet set).
Late June–Early Sept:	Florence's Annual Outdoor Cinema Season (contemporary films).
July 2:	Palio horse race in Siena.
Aug 15:	Assumption of Mary, a national holiday.
Aug 16:	Palio horse race in Siena.
Sept—first week:	Festa di Rificolona in Florence (children's procession with lanterns, street performances, parade).
Sept–Oct:	Musica dei Popoli Festival in Florence (ethnic and folk music and dances; dates not yet set).
Nov 1:	All Saints' Day, a national holiday.
Dec 8, 25, and 26:	National holidays.

Florence's Climate Chart

First line, average daily low; second line, average daily high; third line, days of no rain.

J	F	M	A	M	J	J	A	S	O	N	D
32°	35°	43°	49°	57°	63°	67°	66°	61°	52°	43°	35°
40°	46°	56°	65°	74°	80°	84°	82°	75°	63°	51°	43°
25	21	24	22	23	21	25	24	25	23	20	24

Numbers and Stumblers

- Europeans write a few of their numbers differently than we do. 1 = 𝟙 , 4 = 𝟜 , 7 = 𝟟 . Learn the difference or miss your train.
- In Europe, dates appear as day/month/year, so Christmas is 25/12/03.
- Commas are decimal points and decimals commas. A dollar and a half is $1,50, and there are 5.280 feet in a mile.
- When pointing, use your whole hand, palm down.
- When counting with fingers, start with your thumb. If you hold up your first finger to request one item, you'll probably get two.
- What Americans call the second floor of a building is the first floor in Europe.
- Europeans keep the left "lane" open for passing on escalators and moving sidewalks. Keep to the right.

Metric Conversion (approximate)

1 inch = 25 millimeters
1 foot = 0.3 meter
1 yard = 0.9 meter
1 mile = 1.6 kilometers
1 centimeter = 0.4 inch
1 meter = 39.4 inches
1 kilometer = .62 mile

32 degrees F = 0 degrees C
82 degrees F = about 28 degrees C
1 ounce = 28 grams
1 kilogram = 2.2 pounds
1 quart = 0.95 liter
1 square yard = 0.8 square meter
1 acre = 0.4 hectare

Basic Italian Survival Phrases

English	Italian	Pronunciation
Good day.	Buon giorno.	bwohn **jor**-noh
Do you speak English?	Parla inglese?	**par**-lah een-**glay**-zay
Yes. / No.	Sì. / No.	see / noh
I (don't) understand.	(Non) capito.	(nohn) kah-**pee**-toh
Please.	Per favore.	pehr fah-**voh**-ray
Thank you.	Grazie.	**graht**-seeay
I'm sorry.	Mi dispiace.	mee dee-speeah-chay
Excuse me.	Mi scusi.	mee **skoo**-zee
(No) problem.	(Non) c'è un problema.	(nohn) cheh oon proh-**blay**-mah
Good.	Va bene.	vah **behn**-ay
Goodbye.	Arrivederci.	ah-ree-vay-**dehr**-chee
one / two	uno / due	**oo**-noh / **doo**-ay
three / four	tre / quattro	tray / **kwah**-troh
five / six	cinque / sei	**cheeng**-kway / sehee
seven / eight	sette / otto	**seht**-tay / **ot**-toh
nine / ten	nove / dieci	**nov**-ay / **deeay**-chee
How much is it?	Quanto costa?	**kwahn**-toh **kos**-tah
Write it?	Me lo scrive?	may loh **skree**-vay
Is it free?	È gratis?	eh **grah**-tees
Included?	È incluso?	eh een-**kloo**-zoh
Where can I buy / find...?	Dove posso comprare / trovare...?	**doh**-vay **pos**-soh kohm-**prah**-ray / troh-**vah**-ray
I'd like / We'd like...	Vorrei / Vorremo...	vor-**rehe**e / vor-**ray**-moh
...a room.	...una camera.	**oo**-nah **kah**-meh-rah
...the bill.	...il conto.	eel **kohn**-toh
...a ticket to ___.	...un biglietto per___.	oon beel-**yeht**-toh per
Is it possible?	È possibile?	eh poh-**see**-bee-lay
Where is...?	Dov'è...?	**doh**-veh
...the train station	...la stazione	lah staht-seeoh-nay
...the bus station	...la stazione degli autobus	lah staht-seeoh-nay **dayl**-yee ow-toh-boos
...tourist information	...informazioni per turisti	een-for-maht-seeoh-nee pehr too-**ree**-stee
...toilet	...la toilette	lah twah-**leht**-tay
men	uomini, signori	**woh**-mee-nee, seen-**yoh**-ree
women	donne, signore	**don**-nay, seen-**yoh**-ray
left / right	sinistra / destra	see-**nee**-strah / **dehs**-trah
straight	sempre diritto	**sehm**-pray dee-**ree**-toh
When do you open / close?	A che ora aprite / chiudete?	ah kay oh-rah ah-**pree**-tay / keeoo-**day**-tay
At what time?	A che ora?	ah kay **oh**-rah
Just a moment.	Un momento.	oon moh-**mayn**-toh
now / soon / later	adesso / presto / tardi	ah-**dehs**-soh / **prehs**-toh / **tar**-dee
today / tomorrow	oggi / domani	**oh**-jee / doh-**mah**-nee

For more user-friendly Italian phrases, check out *Rick Steves' Italian Phrase Book and Dictionary* or *Rick Steves' French, Italian & German Phrase Book and Dictionary*.

Faxing Your Hotel Reservation

Use this handy form for your fax or find it online at
www.ricksteves.com/reservation. Photocopy and fax away.

One-Page Fax

To: _____ @ _____
                    hotel   fax

From: _____ @ _____
                    name   fax

Today's date: ____ / ____ / ____
                    day   month   year

Dear Hotel _____,

Please make this reservation for me:

Name: _____

Total # of people: _____   # of rooms: _____   # of nights: _____

Arriving: ____ / ____ / ____   My time of arrival (24-hr clock): _____
              day   month   year   (I will telephone if I will be late)

Departing: ____ / ____ / ____
               day   month   year

Room(s): Single___ Double___ Twin___ Triple___ Quad___

With: Toilet___ Shower___ Bath___ Sink only___

Special needs: View___ Quiet___ Cheapest___ Ground Floor___

Credit card: Visa___ MasterCard___ American Express___

Card #: _____

Expiration date: _____

Name on card: _____

You may charge me for the first night as a deposit. Please fax, e-mail, or
mail me confirmation of my reservation, along with the type of room
reserved, the price, and whether the price includes breakfast. Please also
inform me of your cancellation policy. Thank you.

_____
Signature

_____
Name

_____
Address

_____
City   *State*   *Zip Code*   *Country*

_____
E-mail Address

Road Scholar Feedback for FLORENCE 2003

*We're all in the same travelers' school of hard knocks. Your feedback helps us improve this guidebook for future travelers. Please fill this out (or use the online version at www.ricksteves.com/feedback), attach more info or any tips/favorite discoveries if you like, and send it to us. As thanks for your help, we'll send you our quarterly travel newsletter free for one year. Thanks! **Rick***

Of the recommended accommodations/restaurants used, which was:

Best _____

     Why? _____

Worst _____

     Why? _____

Of the sights/experiences/destinations recommended by this book, which was:

Most overrated _____

     Why? _____

Most underrated _____

     Why? _____

Best ways to improve this book:

_____

_____

I'd like a free newsletter subscription:

_____ Yes   _____ No   _____ Already on list

_____
Name

_____
Address

_____
City, State, Zip

_____
E-mail Address

    Please send to: ETBD, Box 2009, Edmonds, WA 98020

INDEX

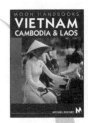

FREE-SPIRITED TOURS FROM

Rick Steves

Great Guides

Big Buses

Small Groups

No Grumps

Best of Europe ▪ Village Europe ▪ Eastern Europe ▪ Turkey ▪ Italy ▪ Village Italy ▪ Britain
Spain/Portugal ▪ Ireland ▪ Heart of France ▪ South of France ▪ Village France ▪ Scandi
Germany/Austria/Switzerland ▪ London ▪ Paris ▪ Rome ▪ Venice ▪ Florence ▪ Prague

Looking for a one, two, or three-week tour that's run in the Rick Steves style? Check out Rick Steves' educational, experiential tours of Europe.

Rick's tours include much more in the "sticker price" than mainstream tours. Here's what you'll get with a Europe or regional Rick Steves tour …

- **Group size:** Your tour group will be no larger than 26.

- **Guides:** You'll have two guides traveling and dining with you on your fully guided Rick Steves tour.

- **Bus:** You'll travel in a full-size bus, with plenty of empty seats for you to spread out and read, snooze, enjoy the passing scenery, get away from your spouse, or whatever.

- **Sightseeing:** Your tour price includes all group sightseeing. There are no hidden extra charges.

- **Hotels:** You'll stay in Rick's favorite small, characteristic, locally-run hotels in the center of each city, within walking distance of the sights you came to see.

- **Price and insurance:** Your tour price is guaranteed for 2003. Single travelers do not pay an extra supplement (we have them room with other singles). ETBD includes prorated tour cancellation/ interruption protection coverage at no extra cost.

- **Tips and kickbacks:** All guide and driver tips are included in your tour price. Because your driver and guides are paid salaries by ETBD, they can focus on giving you the best European travel experience possible.

Interested? Call (425) 771-8303 or visit www.ricksteves.com for a free copy of Rick Steves' 2003 Tours booklet!

Rick Steves' Europe Through the Back Door
130 Fourth Avenue North, PO Box 2009, Edmonds, WA 98020 USA
Phone: (425) 771-8303 ▪ Fax: (425) 771-0833 ▪ www.ricksteves.com

FREE TRAVEL GOODIES FROM

Rick Steves

EUROPEAN TRAVEL NEWSLETTER

My *Europe Through the Back Door* travel company will help you travel better *because* you're on a budget—not in spite of it. To see how, ask for my 64-page *travel newsletter* packed full of savvy travel tips, readers' discoveries, and your best bets for railpasses, guidebooks, videos, travel accessories and free-spirited tours.

2003 GUIDE TO EUROPEAN RAILPASSES

With hundreds of railpasses to choose from in 2003, finding the right pass for your trip has never been more confusing. To cut through the complexity, visit www.ricksteves.com for my online *2003 Guide to European Railpasses.* Once you've narrowed down your choices, we give you unbeatable prices, including important extras with every Eurailpass, free: my 90-minute *Travel Skills Special* video or DVD and your choice of one of my 24 guidebooks.

RICK STEVES' 2003 TOURS

We offer 20 different one, two, and three-week tours (200 departures in 2003) for those who want to experience Europe in Rick Steves' Back Door style, but without the transportation and hotel hassles. If a tour with a small group, modest family-run hotels, lots of exercise, great guides, and no tips or hidden charges sounds like your idea of fun, ask for my 48-page 2003 Tours booklet.

YEAR-ROUND GUIDEBOOK UPDATES

Even though the information in my guidebooks is the freshest around, things do change in Europe between book printings. I've set aside a special section at my website (www.ricksteves.com/update) listing *up-to-the-minute changes* for every Rick Steves guidebook.

Visit www.ricksteves.com to get your...

- ☑ **FREE EUROPEAN TRAVEL NEWSLETTER**
- ☑ **FREE 2003 GUIDE TO EUROPEAN RAILPASSES**
- ☑ **FREE RICK STEVES' 2003 TOURS BOOKLET**

Rick Steves' Europe Through the Back Door

130 Fourth Avenue North, PO Box 2009, Edmonds, WA 98020 USA
Phone: (425) 771-8303 ■ Fax: (425) 771-0833 ■ www.ricksteves.com

Free, fresh travel tips, all year long.

Visit **www.ricksteves.com** to get Rick's free 64-page newsletter… and more!